The Labyrinth of Solitude

The Labyrinth of Solitude
The Other Mexico
Return to the Labyrinth of Solitude
Mexico and the United States
The Philanthropic Ogre

BY OCTAVIO PAZ

TRANSLATED FROM THE SPANISH BY
Lysander Kemp, Yara Milos, and Rachel Phillips Belash

Grove Press, Inc./New York

First Grove Press Edition 1985
First Printing 1985
ISBN: 0-394-52830-1
Library of Congress Catalog Card Number: 82-47999

First Evergreen Edition 1985
First Printing 1985
ISBN: 0-394-17992-7
Library of Congress Catalog Card Number : 82-47999

Library of Congress Cataloging in Publication Data

Paz, Octavio, 1914–
       The labyrinth of solitude, the other Mexico, and other essays.

       1. National characteristics, Mexican—Addresses, essays, lectures.   2. Mexico—Civilization—Addresses, essays, lectures.
I. Title.
F1210.P318   1985   306'.0896872   82-47999
ISBN 9-394-52830-1
ISBN 0-394-17992-7 (pbk.)

Printed in the United States of America

GROVE PRESS, INC., 920 BROADWAY, NEW YORK, N.Y. 10010
     3   5   4

The other *does not exist: this is rational faith, the incurable belief of human reason. Identity* = *reality, as if, in the end, everything must necessarily and absolutely be* one and the same. *But the* other *refuses to disappear; it subsists, it persists; it is the hard bone on which reason breaks its teeth. Abel Martín, with a poetic faith as human as rational faith, believed* in the other, *in "the essential Heterogeneity of being," in what might be called the incurable* otherness *from which* oneness *must always suffer.*

—*Antonio Machado*

Contents

PREFACE

This new edition of *The Labyrinth of Solitude* includes the new texts that complete the book and bring it up to date. First there is, under the title "Critique of the Pyramid," an essay written immediately after the bloody repression, in October 1968, of the student movement, which is at once a postscript and a revision of *The Labyrinth of Solitude*. Likewise included are three important essays: a dialogue with Claude Fell, the French critic, in which Mr. Paz revises, expands and rectifies his ideas on his country's history and culture; some thoughts on the peculiarities of the Mexican political system; and, lastly, an original scrutiny that delves into the principles on which Mexico and the United States were founded and into the relations between the two countries.

The Labyrinth of Solitude

TRANSLATED BY LYSANDER KEMP

CHAPTER ONE

The *Pachuco* and Other Extremes

All of us, at some moment, have had a vision of our existence as something unique, untransferable and very precious. This revelation almost always takes place during adolescence. Self-discovery is above all the realization that we are alone: it is the opening of an impalpable, transparent wall — that of our consciousness — between the world and ourselves. It is true that we sense our aloneness almost as soon as we are born, but children and adults can transcend their solitude and forget themselves in games or work. The adolescent, however, vacillates between infancy and youth, halting for a moment before the infinite richness of the world. He is astonished at the fact of his being, and this astonishment leads to reflection: as he leans over the river of his consciousness, he asks himself if the face that appears there, disfigured by the water, is his own. The singularity of his being, which is pure sensation in children, becomes a problem and a question.

Much the same thing happens to nations and peoples at a certain critical moment in their development. They ask themselves: What are we, and how can we fulfill our obligations to ourselves as we are? The answers we give to these questions are often belied by history, perhaps because what is called the "genius of a people" is only a set of reactions to a given stimulus. The answers differ in different situations, and the national character, which was thought to be immutable, changes with them. Despite the often illusory nature of essays on the psychology of a nation, it seems to me there is something revealing in the insistence with

9

which a people will question itself during certain periods of its growth. To become aware of our history is to become aware of our singularity. It is a moment of reflective repose before we devote ourselves to action again. "When we dream that we are dreaming," Novalis wrote, "the moment of awaking is at hand." It does not matter, then, if the answers we give to our questions must be corrected by time. The adolescent is also ignorant of the future changes that will affect the countenance he sees in the water. The mask of an old man is as indecipherable at first glance as a sacred stone covered with occult symbols: it is the history of various amorphous features that only take shape, slowly and vaguely, after the profoundest contemplation. Eventually these features are seen as a face, and later as a mask, a meaning, a history.

At one time I thought that my preoccupation with the significance of my country's individuality — a preoccupation I share with many others — was pointless and even dangerous. Instead of asking ourselves questions, it would be better, I felt, to create, to work with the realities of our situation. We could not alter those realities by contemplation, only by plunging ourselves into them. We could distinguish ourselves from other peoples by our creations rather than by the dubious originality of our character, which was the result, perhaps, of constantly changing circumstances. I believed that a work of art or a concrete action would do more to define the Mexican — not only to express him but also, in the process, to recreate him — than the most penetrating description. Therefore I considered my questions, like those of others, to be a cowardly excuse for not facing reality; I also felt that all our speculations about the supposed character of the Mexican were nothing but subterfuges of our impotence as creators. I agreed with Samuel Ramos that an inferiority complex influenced our preference for analysis, and that the meagerness of our creative output was due not so much to the growth of our critical faculties at the expense of our creativity as it was to our instinctive doubts about our abilities.

But the adolescent cannot forget himself — when he succeeds in doing so, he is no longer an adolescent — and we cannot escape the necessity of questioning and contemplating ourselves. I am not trying to say that the Mexican is by nature critical, merely that he goes through a reflective stage. It is natural that the Mexican should withdraw into himself after the explosive phase of the Revolution, to spend a few moments in self-contemplation. The questions we all ask ourselves today will probably be incomprehensible fifty years from now. Different circumstances are likely to produce different reactions.

My thoughts are not concerned with the total population of our country, but rather with a specific group made up of those who are conscious of themselves, for one reason or another, as Mexicans. Despite general opinion to the contrary, this group is quite small. Our territory is inhabited by a number of races speaking different languages and living on different historical levels. A few groups still live as they did in prehistoric times. Others, like the Otomíes, who were displaced by successive invasions, exist on the outer margins of history. But it is not necessary to appeal to these extremes: a variety of epochs live side by side in the same areas or a very few miles apart, ignoring or devouring one another. "Catholics of Peter the Hermit and Jacobins of the Third Era," with their different heroes, customs, calendars and moral principles, live under the same sky. Past epochs never vanish completely, and blood still drips from all their wounds, even the most ancient. Sometimes the most remote or hostile beliefs and feelings are found together in one city or one soul, or are superimposed like those pre-Cortesian pyramids that almost always conceal others.[1]

The minority of Mexicans who are aware of their own selves do not make up a closed or unchanging class. They are the only active group, in comparison with the Indian-Spanish inertia of the rest, and every day they are shaping the country more and more into their own image. And they are also increasing. They are conquering Mexico. We can all reach the point of knowing ourselves to be Mexicans. It is enough, for example, simply to cross the border: almost at once we begin to ask ourselves, at least vaguely, the same questions that Samuel Ramos asked in his *Profile of Man and Culture in Mexico*. I should confess that many of the reflections in this essay occurred to me outside of Mexico, during a two-year stay in the United States. I remember that whenever I attempted to examine North American life, anxious to discover its meaning, I encountered my own questioning image. That image, seen against the glittering background of the United States, was the first and perhaps the profoundest answer which that country gave to my questions. Therefore, in attempting to explain to myself some of the traits of the present-day Mexican, I will begin with a group for whom the fact that they are Mexicans is a truly vital problem, a problem of life or death.

When I arrived in the United States I lived for a while in

---

[1] In our recent history there are many examples of this superimposition, as well as of the existence of different historical levels: the neofeudalism of the Porfirio Díaz regime, using positivism (a bourgeois philosophy) to justify itself historically; Antonio Caso and José Vasconcelos, the intellectual initiators of the Revolution, using the ideas of Boutroux and Bergson to combat positivism; socialist education in a country at least incipiently capitalist; revolutionary murals on government walls; etc. These apparent contradictions all demand a new examination of our history and also of our culture, which is a mingling of many currents and epochs.

Los Angeles, a city inhabited by over a million persons of Mexican origin. At first sight, the visitor is surprised not only by the purity of the sky and the ugliness of the dispersed and ostentatious buildings, but also by the city's vaguely Mexican atmosphere, which cannot be captured in words or concepts. This Mexicanism — delight in decorations, carelessness and pomp, negligence, passion and reserve — floats in the air. I say "floats" because it never mixes or unites with the other world, the North American world based on precision and efficiency. It floats, without offering any opposition; it hovers, blown here and there by the wind, sometimes breaking up like a cloud, sometimes standing erect like a rising skyrocket. It creeps, it wrinkles, it expands and contracts; it sleeps or dreams; it is ragged but beautiful. It floats, never quite existing, never quite vanishing.

Something of the same sort characterizes the Mexicans you see in the streets. They have lived in the city for many years, wearing the same clothes and speaking the same language as the other inhabitants, and they feel ashamed of their origin; yet no one would mistake them for authentic North Americans. I refuse to believe that physical features are as important as is commonly thought. What distinguishes them, I think, is their furtive, restless air: they act like persons who are wearing disguises, who are afraid of a stranger's look because it could strip them and leave them stark naked. When you talk with them, you observe that their sensibilities are like a pendulum, but a pendulum that has lost its reason and swings violently and erratically back and forth. This spiritual condition, or lack of a spirit, has given birth to a type known as the *pachuco*. The *pachucos* are youths, for the most part of Mexican origin, who form gangs in Southern cities; they can be identified by their language and behavior as well as by the clothing they affect.

They are instinctive rebels, and North American racism has vented its wrath on them more than once. But the *pachucos* do not attempt to vindicate their race or the nationality of their forebears. Their attitude reveals an obstinate, almost fanatical will-to-be, but this will affirms nothing specific except their determination — it is an ambiguous one, as we will see — not to be like those around them. The *pachuco* does not want to become a Mexican again; at the same time he does not want to blend into the life of North America. His whole being is sheer negative impulse, a tangle of contradictions, an enigma. Even his very name is enigmatic: *pachuco,* a word of uncertain derivation, saying nothing and saying everything. It is a strange word with no definite meaning; or, to be more exact, it is charged like all popular creations with a diversity of meanings. Whether we like it or not, these persons are Mexicans, are one of the extremes at which the Mexican can arrive.

Since the *pachuco* cannot adapt himself to a civilization which, for its part, rejects him, he finds no answer to the hostility surrounding him except this angry affirmation of his personality.[2] Other groups react differently. The Negroes, for example, oppressed by racial intolerance, try to "pass" as whites and thus enter society. They want to be like other people. The Mexicans have suffered a less violent rejection, but instead of attempting a problematical adjustment to society, the *pachuco* actually flaunts his differences. The purpose of his grotesque dandyism and anarchic behavior is not so much to point out

---

[2]Many of the juvenile gangs that have formed in the United States in recent years are reminiscent of the post-war *pachucos*. It could not have been otherwise: North American society is closed to the outside world, and at the same time it is inwardly petrified. Life cannot penetrate it, and being rejected, squanders itself aimlessly on the outside. It is a marginal life, formless but hoping to discover its proper form.

the injustice and incapacity of a society that has failed to assimilate him as it is to demonstrate his personal will to remain different.

It is not important to examine the causes of this conflict, and even less so to ask whether or not it has a solution. There are minorities in many parts of the world who do not enjoy the same opportunities as the rest of the population. The important thing is this stubborn desire to be different, this anguished tension with which the lone Mexican — an orphan lacking both protectors and positive values — displays his differences. The *pachuco* has lost his whole inheritance: language, religion, customs, beliefs. He is left with only a body and a soul with which to confront the elements, defenseless against the stares of everyone. His disguise is a protection, but it also differentiates and isolates him: it both hides him and points him out.

His deliberately aesthetic clothing, whose significance is too obvious to require discussion, should not be mistaken for the outfit of a special group or sect. *Pachuquismo* is an open society, and this in a country full of cults and tribal costumes, all intended to satisfy the middle-class North American's desire to share in something more vital and solid than the abstract morality of the "American Way of Life." The clothing of the *pachuco* is not a uniform or a ritual attire. It is simply a fashion, and like all fashions it is based on novelty — the mother of death, as Leopardi said — and imitation.

Its novelty consists in its exaggeration. The *pachuco* carries fashion to its ultimate consequences and turns it into something aesthetic. One of the principles that rules in North American fashions is that clothing must be comfortable, and the *pachuco*, by changing ordinary apparel into art, makes it "impractical." Hence it negates the very principles of the model that inspired it. Hence its aggresiveness.

This rebelliousness is only an empty gesture, because it is an exaggeration of the models against which he is trying to rebel, rather than a return to the dress of his forebears or the creation of a new style of his own. Eccentrics usually emphasize their decision to break away from society — either to form new and more tightly closed groups or to assert their individuality — through their way of dressing. In the case of the *pachuco* there is an obvious ambiguity: his clothing spotlights and isolates him, but at the same time it pays homage to the society he is attempting to deny.

This duality is also expressed in another, perhaps profounder way: the *pachuco* is an impassive and sinister clown whose purpose is to cause terror instead of laughter. His sadistic attitude is allied with a desire for self-abasement which in my opinion constitutes the very foundation of his character: he knows that it is dangerous to stand out and that his behavior irritates society, but nevertheless he seeks and attracts persecution and scandal. It is the only way he can establish a more vital relationship with the society he is antagonizing. As a victim, he can occupy a place in the world that previously had ignored him; as a delinquent, he can become one of its wicked heroes.

I believe that the North American's irritation results from his seeing the *pachuco* as a mythological figure and therefore, in effect, a danger. His dangerousness lies in his singularity. Everyone agrees in finding something hybrid about him, something disturbing and fascinating. He is surrounded by an aura of ambivalent notions: his singularity seems to be nourished by powers that are alternately evil and beneficent. Some people credit him with unusual erotic prowess; others consider him perverted but still aggressive. He is a symbol of love and joy or of horror and loathing, an embodiment of liberty, of disorder, of the forbidden. He is someone who ought to be destroyed. He is also someone with whom any contact must be made in secret, in the darkness.

The *pachuco* is impassive and contemptuous, allowing all these contradictory impressions to accumulate around him until finally, with a certain painful satisfaction, he sees them explode into a tavern fight or a raid by the police or a riot. And then, in suffering persecution, he becomes his true self, his supremely naked self, as a pariah, a man who belongs nowhere. The circle that began with provocation has completed itself and he is ready now for redemption, for his entrance into the society that rejected him. He has been its sin and its scandal, but now that he is a victim it recognizes him at last for what he really is: its product, its son. At last he has found new parents.

The *pachuco* tries to enter North American society in secret and daring ways, but he impedes his own efforts. Having been cut off from his traditional culture, he asserts himself for a moment as a solitary and challenging figure. He denies both the society from which he originated and that of North America. When he thrusts himself outward, it is not to unite with what surrounds him but rather to defy it. This is a suicidal gesture, because the *pachuco* does not affirm or defend anything except his exasperated will-not-to-be. He is not divulging his most intimate feelings: he is revealing an ulcer, exhibiting a wound. A wound that is also a grotesque, capricious, barbaric adornment. A wound that laughs at itself and decks itself out for the hunt. The *pachuco* is the prey of society, but instead of hiding he adorns himself to attract the hunter's attention. Persecution redeems him and breaks his solitude: his salvation depends on his becoming part of the very society he appears to deny. Solitude and sin, communion and health become synonymous terms.[3]

If this is what happens to persons who have long since left their homeland, who can hardly speak the language of their forebears, and whose secret roots, those that connect a man with his culture, have almost withered away, what is there to say about the rest of us when we visit the United States? Our reaction is not so unhealthy, but after our first dazzled impressions of that country's grandeur, we all instinctively assume a critical attitude. I remember that when I commented to a Mexican friend on the loveliness of Berkeley, she said: "Yes, it's very lovely, but I don't belong here. Even the birds speak English. How can I enjoy a flower if I don't know its right name, its English name, the name that has fused with its colors and petals, the name that's the same thing as the flower? If I say *bugambilia* to you, you think of the bougainvillaea vines you've seen in your own village, with their purple, liturgical flowers, climbing around an ash tree or hanging from a wall in the afternoon sunlight. They're a part of your being, your culture. They're what you remember long after you've seemed to forget them. It's very lovely here, but it isn't mine, because whatever

---

[3]No doubt many aspects of the *pachuco* are lacking in this description. But I am convinced that his hybrid language and behavior reflect a physic oscillation between two irreducible worlds — the North American and the Mexican — which he vainly hopes to reconcile and conquer. He does not want to become either a Mexican or a Yankee. When I arrived in France in 1945, I was amazed to find that the young men and women of certain quarters, especially students and "artists," wore clothing reminiscent of that of the *pachucos* in southern California. Was this a quick, imaginative adaptation of what these young people, after years of isolation, thought was in fashion in North America? I questioned a number of people about it, and almost all of them told me it was a strictly French phenomenon that had come into existence at the end of the Occupation. Some even considered it a manifestation of the Resistance: its Baroque fantasy was a reply to the rigid order of the German. Although I do not exclude the possibility of a more or less indirect imitation, I think the similarity is remarkable and significant.

saying it for me . . . or to me, either."

Yes, we withdraw into ourselves, we deepen and aggravate our awareness of everything that separates or isolates or differentiates us. And we increase our solitude by refusing to seek out our compatriots, perhaps because we fear we will see ourselves in them, perhaps because of a painful, defensive unwillingness to share our intimate feelings. The Mexican succumbs very easily to sentimental effusions, and therefore he shuns them. We live closed up within ourselves, like those taciturn adolescents — I will add in passing that I hardly met any of the sort among North American youths — who are custodians of a secret that they guard behind scowling expressions, but that only waits for the opportune moment in which to reveal itself.

I am not going to expand my description of these feelings or discuss the states of depression or frenzy (or often both) that accompany them. They are all apt to lead to unexpected explosions, which destroy a precarious equilibrium based on the imposition of forms that oppress or mutilate us. Our sense of inferiority — real or imagined — might be explained at least partly by the reserve with which the Mexican faces other people and the unpredictable violence with which his repressed emotions break through his mask of impassivity. But his solitude is vaster and profounder than his sense of inferiority. It is impossible to equate these two attitudes: when you sense that you are alone, it does not mean that you feel inferior, but rather that you feel you are different. Also, a sense of inferiority may sometimes be an illusion, but solitude is a hard fact. We are truly different. And we are truly alone.

This is not the moment to analyze our profound sense of solitude, which alternately affirms and denies itself in melancholy and rejoicing, silence and sheer noise, gratuitous crimes and religious fervor. Man is alone everywhere. But the solitude of the Mexican, under the great stone night of the high plateau that is still inhabited by insatiable gods, is very different from that of the North American, who wanders in an abstract world of machines, fellow citizens and moral precepts. In the Valley of Mexico man feels himself suspended between heaven and earth, and he oscillates between contrary powers and forces, and petrified eyes, and devouring mouths. Reality — that is, the world that surrounds us — exists by itself here, has a life of its own, and was not invented by man as it was in the United States. The Mexican feels himself to have been torn from the womb of this reality, which is both creative and destructive, both Mother and Tomb. He has forgotten the word that ties him to all those forces through which life manifests itself. Therefore he shouts or keeps silent, stabs or prays, or falls asleep for a hundred years.

The history of Mexico is the history of a man seeking his parentage, his origins. He has been influenced at one time or another by France, Spain, the United States and the militant indigenists of his own country, and he crosses history like a jade comet, now and then giving off flashes of lightning. What is he pursuing in his eccentric course? He wants to go back beyond the catastrophe he suffered: he wants to be a sun again, to return to the center of that life from which he was separated one day. (Was that day the Conquest? Independence?) Our solitude has the same roots as religious feelings. It is a form of orphanhood, an obscure awareness that we have been torn from the All, and an ardent search: a flight and a return, an effort to re-establish the bonds that unite us with the universe.

Nothing could be further from this feeling than the solitude of the North American. In the United States man does not feel that he has been torn from the center of creation and suspended between hostile forces. He has built his own world and it is built in his own image: it is his mirror. But now he cannot recognize himself in his inhuman objects, nor in his fellows. His creations, like those of an inept sorcerer, no longer obey him. He is alone among his works, lost — to use the phrase by José Gorostiza — in a "wilderness of mirrors."

Some people claim that the only differences between the North American and ourselves are economic. That is, they are rich and we are poor, and while their legacy is Democracy, Capitalism and the Industrial Revolution, ours is the Counter-reformation, Monopoly and Feudalism. But however influential the systems of production may be in the shaping of a culture, I refuse to believe that as soon as we have heavy industry and are free of all economic imperialism, the differences will vanish. (In fact, I look for the opposite to happen, and I consider this possibility one of the greatest virtues of the Revolution of 1910.) But why search history for an answer that only we ourselves can give? If it is we who feel ourselves to be different, what makes us so, and in what do the differences consist?

I am going to suggest an answer that will perhaps not be wholly satisfactory. I am only trying to clarify the meaning of certain experiences for my own self, and I admit that what I say may be worth no more than a personal answer to a personal question.

When I arrived in the United States I was surprised above all by the self-assurance and confidence of the people, by their apparent happiness and apparent adjustment to the world around them. This satisfaction does not stifle criticism, however, and the criticism is valuable and forthright, of a sort not often heard in the countries to the south, where long periods of dictatorship have made us more cautious about expressing our points of view. But it is a criticism that respects the existing systems and never touches the roots. I thought of Ortega y

Gasset's distinction between uses and abuses, in his definition of the "revolutionary spirit." The revolutionary is always a radical, that is, he is trying to correct the uses themselves rather than the mere abuses of them. Almost all the criticisms I heard from the lips of North Americans were of the reformist variety: they left the social or cultural structures intact and were only intended to limit or improve this or that procedure. It seemed to me then, and it still does, that the United States is a society that wants to realize its ideals, has no wish to exchange them for others, and is confident of surviving, no matter how dark the future may appear. I am not interested in discussing whether this attitude is justified by reason and reality; I simply want to point out that it exists. It is true that this faith in the natural goodness of life, or in its infinite wealth of possibilities, cannot be found in recent North American literature, which prefers to depict a much more somber world; but I found it in the actions, the words and even the faces of almost everyone I met.[4]

On the other hand, I heard a good deal of talk about American realism and also about American ingenuousness, qualities that would seem to be mutually exclusive. To us a realist is always a pessimist. And an ingenuous person would not remain so for very long if he truly contemplated life realistically. Would it not be more accurate to say that the North American wants to use reality rather than to know it? In some matters — death, for example — he not only has no desire to understand it, he obviously avoids the very idea. I met some elderly ladies who still

---

[4]These lines were written before the public was clearly cognizant of the danger of universal annihilation made possible by nuclear weapons. Since then the North Americans have lost their optimism but not their confidence, a confidence based on resignation and obstinacy. The truth is that although many people talk about the danger, secretly no one believes — no one wants to believe — that it is real and immediate.

had illusions and were making plans for the future as if it were inexhaustible. Thus they refuted Nietzsche's statement condemning women to an early onset of skepticism because "men have ideals but women only have illusions." American realism, then, is of a very special kind, and American ingenuousness does not exclude dissimulation and even hypocrisy. When hypocrisy is a character trait it also affects one's thinking, because it consists in the negation of all the aspects of reality that one finds disagreeable, irrational or repugnant.

In contrast, one of the most notable traits of the Mexican's character is his willingness to contemplate horror: he is even familiar and complacent in his dealings with it. The bloody Christs in our village churches, the macabre humor in some of our newspaper headlines, our wakes, the custom of eating skull-shaped cakes and candies on the Day of the Dead, are habits inherited from the Indians and the Spaniards and are now an inseparable part of our being. Our cult of death is also a cult of life, in the same way that love is a hunger for life and a longing for death. Our fondness for self-destruction derives not only from our masochistic tendencies but also from a certain variety of religious emotion.

And our differences do not end there. The North Americans are credulous and we are believers; they love fairy tales and detective stories and we love myths and legends. The Mexican tells lies because he delights in fantasy, or because he is desperate, or because he wants to rise above the sordid facts of his life; the North American does not tell lies, but he substitutes social truth for the real truth, which is always disagreeable. We get drunk in order to confess; they get drunk in order to forget. They are optimists and we are nihilists — except that our nihilism is not intellectual but instinctive, and therefore irrefutable. We are suspicious and they are trusting. We are sorrowful and sarcastic and they are happy and full of jokes. North Americans want to understand and we want to contemplate. They are activists and we are quietists; we enjoy our wounds and they enjoy their inventions. They believe in hygiene, health, work and contentment, but perhaps they have never experienced true joy, which is an intoxication, a whirlwind. In the hubbub of a fiesta night our voices explode into brilliant lights, and life and death mingle together, while their vitality becomes a fixed smile that denies old age and death but that changes life to motionless stone.

What is the origin of such contradictory attitudes? It seems to me that North Americans consider the world to be something that can be perfected, and that we consider it to be something that can be redeemed. Like their Puritan ancestors, we believe that sin and death constitute the ultimate basis of human nature, but with the difference that the Puritan identifies purity with health. Therefore he believes in the purifying effects of asceticism, and the consequences are his cult of work for work's sake, his serious approach to life, and his conviction that the body does not exist or a least cannot lose — or find — itself in another body. Every contact is a contamination. Foreign races, ideas, customs, and bodies carry within themselves the germs of perdition and impurity. Social hygiene complements that of the soul and the body. Mexicans, however, both ancient and modern, believe in communion and fiestas: there is no health without contact. Tlazolteotl, the Aztec goddess of filth and fecundity, of earthly and human moods, was also the goddess of steam baths, sexual love and confession. And we have not changed very much, for Catholicism is also communion.

These two attitudes are irreconcilable, I believe, and, in their present form, insufficient. I would not be telling the truth if I were to say that I had ever seen guilt feelings transformed into anything other than hatred, solitary despair or blind idolatry. The religious feelings of my people are very deep — like their misery and helplessness — but their fervor has done nothing but return again and again to a well that has been empty for centuries. I would also not be telling the truth if I were to say that I can believe in the fertility of a society based on the imposition of certain modern principles. Contemporary history invalidates the belief in man as a creature whose essential being can be modified by social or pedagogical procedures. Man is not simply the result of history and the forces that activate it, as is now claimed; nor is history simply the result of the human will, a belief on which the North American way of life is implicitly predicated. Man, it seems to me, is not *in* history: he *is* history.

The North American system only wants to consider the positive aspects of reality. Men and women are subjected from childhood to an inexorable process of adaptation; certain principles, contained in brief formulas, are endlessly repeated by the press, the radio, the churches and the schools, and by those kindly, sinister beings, the North American mothers and wives. A person imprisoned by these schemes is like a plant in a flowerpot too small for it: he cannot grow or mature. This sort of conspiracy cannot help but provoke violent individual rebellions. Spontaneity avenges itself in a thousand subtle or terrible ways. The mask that replaces the dramatic mobility of the human face is benevolent and courteous but empty of emotion, and its set smile is almost lugubrious: it shows the extent to which intimacy can be devastated by the arid victory of principles over instincts. The sadism underlying almost all types of relationships in contemporary North American life is perhaps nothing more than a way of escaping the petrifaction imposed by that doctrine of aseptic moral purity. The same is true of the new religions and sects, and the liberating drunkenness that opens the doors of "life." It is astonishing what a destructive and almost physiological meaning this word has acquired: to live means to commit excesses, break the rules, go to the limit (of what?), experiment with sensations. The act of love is an "experience" (and therefore unilateral and frustrating). But it is not to my purpose to describe these reactions. It is enough to say that all of them, like their Mexican opposites, seem to me to reveal our mutual inability to reconcile ourselves to the flux of life.

A study of the great myths concerning the origin of man and the meaning of our presence on earth reveals that every culture — in the sense of a complex of values created and shared in common — stems from the conviction that man the intruder has broken or violated the order of the universe. He has inflicted a wound on the compact flesh of the world, and chaos, which is the ancient and, so to speak, *natural* condition of life, can emerge again from this aperture. The return of "ancient Original Disorder" is a menace that has obsessed every consciousness in every period of history. Hölderlin expresses in several different poems his dread of the great empty mouth of chaos with its fatal seduction for man and the universe:

> . . . *if, beyond the straight way,*
> *The captive Elements and the ancient*
> *Laws of the Earth break loose*
> *Like maddened horses. And then a desire to return*
> *To chaos rises incessantly. There is much*
> *To defend, and the faithful are much needed.*[5]

The faithful are much needed because there is *much to defend.* Man collaborates actively in defending universal order, which is always being threatened by chaos. And when it collapses he

---

[5] *Reif sind, in Feuer getaucht . . .*

must create a new one, this time his own. But exile, expiation and penitence should proceed from the reconciliation of man with the universe. Neither the Mexican nor the North American has achieved this reconciliation. What is even more serious, I am afraid we have lost our sense of the very meaning of all human activity, which is to assure the operation of an order in which knowledge and innocence, man and nature are in harmony. If the solitude of the Mexican is like a stagnant pool, that of the North American is like a mirror. We have ceased to be springs of living water.

It is possible that what we call "sin" is only a mythical expression of our self-consciousness, our solitude. I remember that in Spain during the civil war I had a revelation of "the other man" and of another kind of solitude: not closed, not mechanical, but open to the transcendent. No doubt the nearness of death and the brotherhood of men-at-arms, at whatever time and in whatever country, always produce an atmosphere favorable to the extraordinary, to all that rises above the human condition and breaks the circle of solitude that surrounds each one of us. But in those faces — obtuse and obstinate, gross and brutal, like those the great Spanish painters, without the least touch of complacency and with an almost flesh-and-blood realism, have left us — there was something like a desperate hopefulness, something very concrete and at the same time universal. Since then I have never seen the same expression on any face.

My testimony can be dismissed as an illusion, but I consider it futile to attempt any answer to this objection: the evidence is now a part of my being. I believed and still believe that "the other man" dawned in those men. The Spanish dream was broken and defiled later, not because it was Spanish but because it was universal and, at the same time, concrete, an embodied dream with wide, astonished eyes. The faces I saw have become as they were before they were transformed by that elated sureness (of what: of life or of death?); they are the faces of coarse and humble people. But the memory will never leave me. Anyone who has looked Hope in the face will never forget it. He will search for it everywhere he goes, among all kinds of men. And he will dream of finding it again someday, somewhere, perhaps among those closest to him. In every man there is the possibility of his being — or, to be more exact, of his becoming once again — another man.

CHAPTER TWO

Mexican Masks

Impassioned heart,
disguise your sorrow . . .
—Popular song

The Mexican, whether young or old, *criollo* or *mestizo*,[1] general or laborer or lawyer, seems to me to be a person who shuts himself away to protect himself: his face is a mask and so is his smile. In his harsh solitude, which is both barbed and courteous, everything serves him as a defense: silence and words, politeness and disdain, irony and resignation. He is jealous of his own privacy and that of others, and he is afraid even to glance at his neighbor, because a mere glance can trigger the rage of these electrically charged spirits. He passes through life like a man who has been flayed; everything can hurt him, including words and the very suspicion of words. His language is full of reticences, of metaphors and allusions, of unfinished phrases, while his silence is full of tints, folds, thunderheads, sudden rainbows, indecipherable threats. Even in a quarrel he prefers veiled expressions to outright insults: "A word to the wise is sufficient." He builds a wall of indifference and remoteness between reality and himself, a wall that is no less impenetrable for being invisible. The Mexican is always remote, from the world and from other people. And also from himself.

The speech of our people reflects the extent to which we protect ourselves from the outside world: the ideal of manliness

---

[1] *Criollo:* a person of pure Spanish blood living in the Americas. — *Tr.*
Mestizo: a person of mixed Spanish and Indian blood. — *Tr.*

29

is never to "crack," never to back down. Those who "open themselves up" are cowards. Unlike other people, we believe that opening oneself up is a weakness or a betrayal. The Mexican can bend, can bow humbly, can even stoop, but he cannot back down, that is, he cannot allow the outside world to penetrate his privacy. The man who backs down is not to be trusted, is a traitor or a person of doubtful loyalty; he babbles secrets and is incapable of confronting a dangerous situation. Women are inferior beings because, in submitting, they open themselves up. Their inferiority is constitutional and resides in their sex, their submissiveness, which is a wound that never heals.

Hermeticism is one of the several recourses of our suspicion and distrust. It shows that we instinctively regard the world around us to be dangerous. This reaction is justifiable if one considers what our history has been and the kind of society we have created. The harshness and hostility of our environment, and the hidden, indefinable threat that is always afloat in the air, oblige us to close ourselves in, like those plants that survive by storing up liquid within their spiny exteriors. But this attitude, legitimate enough in its origins, has become a mechanism that functions automatically. Our response to sympathy and tenderness is reserve, since we cannot tell whether those feelings are genuine or simulated. In addition, our masculine integrity is as much endangered by kindness as it is by hostility. Any opening in our defenses is a lessening of our manliness.

Our relationships with other men are always tinged with suspicion. Every time a Mexican confides in a friend or acquaintance, every time he opens himself up, it is an abdication. He dreads that the person in whom he has confided will scorn him. Therefore confidences result in dishonor, and they are as dangerous for the person to whom they are made as they are for the person who makes them. We do not drown ourselves, like

Narcissus, in the pool that reflects us; we try to stop it up instead. Our anger is prompted not only by the fear of being used by our confidants — that fear is common to everyone — but also by the shame of having renounced our solitude. To confide in others is to dispossess oneself; when we have confided in someone who is not worthy of it, we say, "I sold myself to So-and-so." That is, we have "cracked," have let someone into our fortress. The distance between one man and another, which creates mutual respect and mutual security, has disappeared. We are at the mercy of the intruder. What is worse, we have actually abdicated.

All these expressions reveal that the Mexican views life as combat. This attitude does not make him any different from anyone else in the modern world. For other people, however, the manly ideal consists in an open and aggressive fondness for combat, whereas we emphasize defensiveness, the readiness to repel any attack. The Mexican *macho* — the male — is a hermetic being, closed up in himself, capable of guarding both himself and whatever has been confided to him. Manliness is judged according to one's invulnerability to enemy arms or the impacts of the outside world. Stoicism is the most exalted of our military and political attributes. Our history is full of expressions and incidents that demonstrate the indifference of our heroes toward suffering or danger. We are taught from childhood to accept defeat with dignity, a conception that is certainly not ignoble. And if we are not all good stoics like Juárez and Cuauhtémoc, at least we can be resigned and patient and long-suffering. Resignation is one of our most popular virtues. We admire fortitude in the face of adversity more than the most brilliant triumph.

This predominance of the closed over the open manifests itself not only as impassivity and distrust, irony and suspicion, but also as love for Form. Form surrounds and sets bounds to our privacy, limiting its excesses, curbing its explosions, isolating and preserving it. Both our Spanish and Indian heritages have influenced our fondness for ceremony, formulas, and order. A superficial examination of our history might suggest otherwise, but actually the Mexican aspires to create an orderly world regulated by clearly stated principles. The turbulence and rancor of our political struggles prove that juridical ideas play an important role in our public life. The Mexican also strives to be formal in his daily life, and his formalities are very apt to become formulas. This is not difficult to understand. Order — juridical, social, religious or artistic — brings security and stability, and a person has only to adjust to the models and principles that regulate life; he can express himself without resorting to the perpetual inventiveness demanded by a free society. Perhaps our traditionalism, which is one of the constants of our national character, giving coherence to our people and our history, results from our professed love for Form.

The ritual complications of our courtesy, the persistence of classical Humanism, our fondness for closed poetic forms (the sonnet and the *décima,* for example), our love for geometry in the decorative arts and for design and composition in painting, the poverty of our Romantic art compared with the excellence of our Baroque art, the formalism of our political institutions, and, finally, our dangerous inclination toward formalism, whether social, moral or bureaucratic, are further expressions of that tendency in our character. The Mexican not only does not open himself up to the outside world, he also refuses to emerge from himself, to "let himself go."

Sometimes Form chokes us. During the past century the liberals tried vainly to force the realities of the country into the strait jacket of the Constitution of 1857. The results were the dictatorship of Porfirio Díaz and the Revolution of 1910. In a certain sense the history of Mexico, like that of every Mexican, is a struggle between the forms and formulas that have been imposed on us and the explosions with which our individuality avenges itself. Form has rarely been an original creation, an equilibrium arrived at through our instincts and desires rather than at their expense. On the contrary, our moral and juridical forms often conflict with our nature, preventing us from expressing ourselves and frustrating our true wishes.

Our devotion to Form, even when empty, can be seen throughout the history of Mexican art from pre-Conquest times to the present. Antonio Castro Leal, in his excellent study of Juan Ruiz de Alarcón, shows how our reserved attitude toward Romanticism — which by definition is expansive and open — revealed itself as early as the seventeenth century, that is, before we were even aware of ourselves as a nation. Alarcón's contemporaries were right in accusing him of being an interloper, although they were referring more to his physical characteristics than to the singularity of his work. In effect, the most typical portions of his plays deny the values expressed by his Spanish contemporaries. And his negation contains in brief what Mexico has always opposed to Spain. His plays were an answer to Spanish vitality, which was affirmative and splendid in that epoch, expressing itself in a great Yes! to history and the passions. Lope de Vega exalted love, heroism, the superhuman, the incredible; Alarcón favored other virtues, more subtle and bourgeois: dignity, courtesy, a melancholy stoicism, a smiling modesty. Lope was very little interested in moral problems: he loved action, like all his contemporaries. Later, Calderón showed the same contempt for psychology. Moral conflicts and the hesitations and changes of the human soul were only metaphors in a theological drama whose two personae were Original

Sin and Divine Grace. In Alarcón's most representative plays, on the other hand, Heaven counts for little, as little as the passionate wind that sweeps away Lope's characters. The Mexican tells us that human beings are a mixture, that good and evil are subtly blended in their souls. He uses analysis rather than synthesis: the hero becomes a problem. In several of his comedies he takes up the question of lying. To what extent does a liar really lie? Is he really trying to deceive others? Is he not the first victim of his deceit, and the first to be deceived? The liar lies to himself, because he is afraid of himself. By discussing the problem of authenticity, Alarcón anticipated one of the constant themes of Mexican thinking, later taken up by Rodolfo Usigli in his play *The Gesticulator*.

Neither passion nor Grace triumph in Alarcón's world. Everything is subordinated to reason, or to reasonableness, and his archetypes are those of a morality that smiles and forgives. When he replaces the vital, Romantic values of Lope with the abstract values of a universal and reasonable morality, is he not evading us, tricking us? His negation, like that of his homeland, does not affirm our individuality vis-à-vis that of the Spaniards. The values that Alarcón postulates belong to all men and are a Greco-Roman inheritance as well as a prophecy of the bourgeois code. They do not express our nature or resolve our conflicts: they are Forms we have neither created nor suffered, are mere masks. Only in our own day have we been able to answer the Spanish Yes with a Mexican Yes rather than with an intellectual affirmation containing nothing of our individual selves. The Revolution, by discovering popular art, originated modern Mexican painting, and by discovering the Mexican language it created a new poetry.

While the Mexican tries to create closed worlds in his politics and in the arts, he wants modesty, prudence, and a ceremonious reserve to rule over his everyday life. Modesty results from shame at one's own or another's nakedness, and with us it is an almost physical reflex. Nothing could be further from this attitude than that fear of the body which is characteristic of North American life. We are not afraid or ashamed of our bodies; we accept them as completely natural and we live physically with considerable gusto. It is the opposite of Puritanism. The body exists, and gives weight and shape to our existence. It causes us pain and it gives us pleasure; it is not a suit of clothes we are in the habit of wearing, not something apart from us: we *are* our bodies. But we are frightened by other people's glances, because the body reveals rather than hides our private selves. Therefore our modesty is a defense, like our courtesy's Great Wall of China or like the fences of organ-pipe cactus that separate the huts of our country people. This explains why prudence is the virtue we most admire in women, just as reserve is in men. Women too should defend their privacy.

No doubt an element of masculine vanity, the vanity of the "señor," of the lord or chieftain (it is an inheritance from both our Indian and Spanish ancestors), enters into our conception of feminine modesty. Like almost all other people, the Mexican considers woman to be an instrument, sometimes of masculine desires, sometimes of the ends assigned to her by morality, society and the law. It must be admitted that she has never been asked to consent to these ends and that she participates in their realization only passively, as a "repository" for certain values. Whether as prostitute, goddess, *grande dame* or mistress, woman transmits or preserves — but does not believe in — the values and energies entrusted to her by nature or society. In a world made in man's image, woman is only a reflection of masculine will and desire. When passive, she becomes a goddess, a beloved one, a being who embodies the ancient, stable elements of the universe: the earth, motherhood, virginity. When active, she is always function and means, a receptacle and a channel. Womanhood, unlike manhood, is never an end in itself.

In other countries these functions are realized in public, often with something of a flair. There are countries that revere prostitutes or virgins, and countries that worship mothers; the *grande dame* is praised and respected almost everywhere. In contrast, we prefer these graces and virtues to be hidden. Woman should be secretive. She should confront the world with an impassive smile. She should be "decent" in the face of erotic excitements and "long-suffering" in the face of adversity. In either event her response is neither instinctive nor personal: it conforms to a general model, and it is the defensive and passive aspects of this model, as in the case of the *macho,* that are emphasized, in a gamut ranging from modesty and "decency" to stoicism, resignation and impassivity.

Our Spanish-Arabic inheritance is only a partial explanation of this conduct. The Spanish attitude toward women is very simple. It is expressed quite brutally and concisely in these two sayings: "A woman's place is in the home, with a broken leg" and "Between a female saint and a male saint, a wall of mortared stone." Woman is a domesticated wild animal, lecherous and sinful from birth, who must be subdued with a stick and guided by the "reins of religion." Therefore Spaniards consider other women — especially those of a race or religion different from their own — to be easy game. The Mexican considers woman to be a dark, secret and passive being. He does not attribute evil instincts to her; he even pretends that she does not have any. Or, to put it more exactly, her instincts are not her own but those of the species, because she is an incarnation of the life force, which is essentially impersonal. Thus it is impossible for her to have a personal, private life, for if she were to be herself

— if she were to be mistress of her own wishes, passions or whims — she would be unfaithful to herself. The Mexican, heir to the great pre-Columbian religions based on nature, is a good deal more pagan than the Spaniard, and does not condemn the natural world. Sexual love is not tinged with grief and horror in Mexico as it is in Spain. Instincts themselves are not dangerous; the danger lies in any personal, individual expression of them. And this brings us back to the idea of passivity: woman is never herself, whether lying stretched out or standing up straight, whether naked or fully clothed. She is an undifferentiated manifestation of life, a channel for the universal appetite. In this sense she has no desires of her own.

North Americans also claim that instincts and desires do not exist, but the basis of their pretense is different from ours, even the opposite of it. The North American hides or denies certain parts of his body and, more often, of his psyche: they are immoral, ergo they do not exist. By denying them he inhibits his spontaneity. The Mexican woman quite simply has no will of her own. Her body is asleep and only comes really alive when someone awakens her. She is an answer rather than a question, a vibrant and easily worked material that is shaped by the imagination and sensuality of the male. In other countries women are active, attempting to attract men through the agility of their minds or the seductivity of their bodies, but the Mexican woman has a sort of hieratic calm, a tranquillity made up of both hope and contempt. The man circles around her, courts her, sings to her, sets his horse (or his imagination) to performing caracoles for her pleasure. Meanwhile she remains behind the veil of her modesty and immobility. She is an idol, and like all idols she is mistress of magnetic forces whose efficacy increases as their source of transmission becomes more and more passive and secretive. There is a cosmic analogy here: woman does not seek, she attracts, and the center of attraction is her hidden, passive sexuality. It is a secret and immobile sun.

The falsity of this conception is obvious enough when one considers the Mexican woman's sensitivity and restlessness, but at least it does not turn her into an object, a mere thing. She is a symbol, like all women, of the stability and continuity of the race. In addition to her cosmic significance she has an important social role, which is to see to it that law and order, piety and tenderness are predominant in everyday life. We will not allow anyone to be disrespectful to women, and although this is doubtless a universal notion, the Mexican carries it to its ultimate consequences. Thanks to woman, many of the asperities of "man-to-man" relationships are softened. Of course we should ask the Mexican woman for her own opinion, because this "respect" is often a hypocritical way of subjecting her and preventing her from expressing herself. Perhaps she would usually prefer to be treated with less "respect" (which anyway is granted to her only in public) and with greater freedom and truthfulness; that is, to be treated as a human being rather than as a symbol or function. But how can we agree to let her express herself when our whole way of life is a mask designed to hide our intimate feelings?

Despite her modesty and the vigilance of society, woman is always vulnerable. Her social situation — as the repository of honor, in the Spanish sense — and the misfortune of her "open" anatomy expose her to all kinds of dangers, against which neither personal morality nor masculine protection is sufficient. She is submissive and open by nature. But, through a compensation-mechanism that is easily explained, her natural frailty is made a virtue and the myth of the "long-suffering Mexican woman" is created. The idol — always vulnerable, always in process of transforming itself into a human being — becomes a victim, but a victim hardened and insensible to suffering, bearing her tribulations in silence. (A "long-suffering" person is less sensitive to pain than a person whom adversity has hardly touched.) Through suffering, our women become like our men: invulnerable, impassive, and stoic.

It might be said that by turning what ought to be a cause for shame into a virtue, we are only trying to relieve our guilt feelings and cover up a cruel reality. This is true, but it is also true that in attributing to her the same invulnerability that we strive to achieve ourselves, we provide her with a moral immunity to shield her unfortunate anatomical openness. Thanks to suffering and her ability to endure it without protest, she transcends her condition and acquires the same attributes as men.

It is interesting to note that the image of the *mala mujer* — the "bad woman" — is almost always accompanied by the idea of aggressive activity. She is not passive like the "self-denying mother," the "waiting sweetheart," the hermetic idol: she comes and goes, she looks for men and then leaves them. Her extreme mobility, through a mechanism similar to that described above, renders her invulnerable. Activity and immodesty unite to petrify her soul. The *mala* is hard and impious and independent like the *macho*. In her own way she also transcends her physiological weakness and closes herself off from the world.

It is likewise significant that masculine homosexuality is regarded with a certain indulgence insofar as the active agent is concerned. The passive agent is an abject, degraded being. This ambiguous conception is made very clear in the word games or battles -- full of obscene allusions and double meanings — that are so popular in Mexico City. Each of the speakers tries to humiliate his adversary with verbal traps and ingenious linguistic combinations, and the loser is the person who cannot think of a comeback, who has to swallow his opponent's jibes.

These jibes are full of aggressive sexual allusions; the loser is possessed, is violated, by the winner, and the spectators laugh and sneer at him. Masculine homosexuality is tolerated, then, on condition that it consists in violating a passive agent. As with heterosexual relationships, the important thing is not to open oneself up and at the same time to break open one's opponent.

It seems to me that all of these attitudes, however different their sources, testify to the "closed" nature of our reactions to the world around us or to our fellows. But our mechanisms of defense and self-preservation are not enough, and therefore we make use of dissimulation, which is almost habitual with us. It does not increase our passivity; on the contrary, it demands an active inventiveness and must reshape itself from one moment to another. We tell lies for the mere pleasure of it, like all imaginative peoples, but we also tell lies to hide ourselves and to protect ourselves from intruders. Lying plays a decisive role in our daily lives, our politics, our love-affairs and our friendships, and since we attempt to deceive ourselves as well as others, our lies are brilliant and fertile, not like the gross inventions of other peoples. Lying is a tragic game in which we risk a part of our very selves. Hence it is pointless to denounce it.

The dissembler pretends to be someone he is not. His role requires constant improvisation, a steady forward progress across shifting sands. Every moment he must remake, re-create, modify the personage he is playing, until at last the moment arrives when reality and appearance, the lie and the truth, are one. At first the pretense is only a fabric of inventions intended to baffle our neighbors, but eventually it becomes a superior — because more artistic — form of reality. Our lies reflect both what we lack and what we desire, both what we are not and what we would like to be. Through dissimulation we come closer to our model, and sometimes the gesticulator, as Usigli saw so profoundly, becomes one with his gestures and thus makes them authentic. The death of Professor Rubio changed him into what he wanted to be: General Rubio, a sincere revolutionary and a man capable of giving the stagnating Revolution a fresh impetus and purity. In the Usigli play Professor Rubio invents a new self and becomes a general, and his lie is so truthlike that the corrupt Navarro has no other course than to murder him, as if he were murdering his old commander, General Rubio, all over again. By killing him he kills the truth of the Revolution.

If we can arrive at authenticity by means of lies, an excess of sincerity can bring us to refined forms of lying. When we fall in love we open ourselves up and reveal our intimate feelings, because an ancient tradition requires that the man suffering from love display his wounds to the loved one. But in displaying them the lover transforms himself into an image, an object he presents for the loved one's — and his own — contemplation. He asks her to regard him with the same worshipful eyes with which he regards himself. And now the looks of others do not strip him naked; instead, they clothe him in piety. He has offered himself as a spectacle, asking the spectators to see him as he sees himself, and in so doing he has escaped from the game of love, has saved his true self by replacing it with an image.

Human relationships run the risk, in all lands and ages, of becoming equivocal. This is especially true of love. Narcissism and masochism are not exclusively Mexican traits, but it is notable how often our popular songs and sayings and our everyday behavior treat love as falsehood and betrayal. We almost always evade the perils of a naked relationship by exaggerating our feelings. At the same time, the combative nature of our eroticism is emphasized and aggravated. Love is an attempt to penetrate another being, but it can only be realized if the surrender is mutual. It is always difficult to give oneself up; few persons anywhere ever succed in doing so, and even fewer transcend the possessive stage to know love for what it actually is: a perpetual discovery, an immersion in the waters of reality, and an unending re-creation. The Mexican conceives of love as combat and conquest. It is not so much an attempt to penetrate reality by means of the body as it is to violate it. Therefore the image of the fortunate lover — derived, perhaps, from the Spanish Don Juan — is confused with that of the man who deliberately makes use of his feelings, real or invented, to win possession of a woman.

Dissimulation is an activity very much like that of actors in the theater, but the true actor surrenders himself to the role he is playing and embodies it fully, even though he sloughs it off again, like a snake its skin, when the final curtain comes down. The dissembler never surrenders or forgets himself, because he would no longer be dissembling if he became one with his image. But this fiction becomes an inseparable — and ·spurious — part of his nature. He is condemned to play his role throughout life, since the pact between himself and his impersonation cannot be broken except by death or sacrifice. The lie takes command of him and becomes the very foundation of his personality.

To simulate is to invent, or rather to counterfeit, and thus to evade our condition. Dissimulation requires greater subtlety: the person who dissimulates is not counterfeiting but attempting to become invisible, to pass unnoticed without renouncing his individuality. The Mexican excels at the dissimulation of his passions and himself. He is afraid of others' looks and therefore he withdraws, contracts, becomes a shadow, a phantasm, an echo. Instead of walking, he glides; instead of stating, he hints; instead of replying, he mumbles; instead of complaining, he smiles. Even when he sings he does so — unless he explodes, ripping open his breast — between clenched teeth and in a lowered voice, dissimulating his song:

> *And so great is the tyranny*
> *of this dissimulation*
> *that although my heart swells*
> *with profoundest longing,*
> *there is challenge in my eyes*
> *and resignation in my voice.*

Perhaps our habit of dissimulating originated in colonial times. The Indians and *mestizos* had to sing in a low voice, as in the poem by Alfonso Reyes, because "words of rebellion cannot be heard well from between clenched teeth." The colonial world has disappeared, but not the fear, the mistrust, the suspicion. And now we disguise not only our anger but also our tenderness. When our country people beg one's pardon, they say: "Pretend it never happened, señor." And we pretend. We dissimulate so eagerly that we almost cease to exist.

In its most radical forms dissimulation becomes mimicry. The Indian blends into the landscape until he is an indistinguishable part of the white wall against which he leans at twilight, of the dark earth on which he stretches out to rest at midday, of the silence that surrounds him. He disguises his human singularity to such an extent that he finally annihilates it and turns into a stone, a tree, a wall, silence, and space. I am not saying that he communes with the All like a pantheist, or that he sees an individual tree as an archetype of all trees, what I am saying is that he actually blends into specific objects in a concrete and particular way.

Roger Caillois has pointed out that mimicry is not always an attempt to foil the enemies that swarm in the outside world. Insects will sometimes "play dead" or imitate various kinds of decomposed material, out of a fascination for death, for the inertia of space. This fascination — I would call it life's gravitational force — is common to all living things, and the fact that it expresses itself in mimicry shows that we must consider it as something more than an instinctive device for escaping from danger or death.

Mimicry is a change of appearance rather than of, nature, and it is significant that the chosen representation is either of death or of inert space. The act of spreading oneself out, of blending with space, of becoming space, is a way of rejecting appearances, but it is also a way of being nothing except Appearance. The Mexican is horrified by appearances, although his leaders profess to love them, and therefore he disguises himself to the point of blending into the objects that surround him. That is, he becomes mere Appearance because of his fear of appearances. He seems to be something other than what he is, and he even prefers to appear dead or nonexistent rather than to change, to open up his privacy. Dissimulation as mimicry, then, is one of the numerous manifestations of our hermeticism. The gesticulator resorts to a mask, and the rest of us wish to pass unnoticed. In either case we hide our true selves, and sometimes deny them. I remember the afternoon I heard a noise in the room next to mine, and asked loudly: "Who is in there?" I was answered by the voice of a servant who had recently come to us from her village: "No one, señor. I am."

We dissimulate in order to deceive ourselves, and turn transparent and phantasmal. But that is not the end of it: we also pretend that our fellow-man does not exist. This is not to say that we deliberately ignore or discount him. Our dissimulation here is a great deal more radical: we change him from somebody into nobody, into nothingness. And this nothingness takes on its own individuality, with a recognizable face and figure, and suddenly becomes Nobody.

Don No One, who is Nobody's Spanish father, is able, well fed, well respected; he has a bank account, and speaks in a loud, self-assured voice. Don No One fills the world with his empty, garrulous presence. He is everywhere, and has friends everywhere. He is a banker, an ambassador, a businessman. He can be seen in all the salons, and is honored in Jamaica and Stockholm and London. He either holds office or wields influence, and his manner of not-being is aggressive and conceited. On the other hand, Nobody is quiet, timid, and resigned. He is also intelligent and sensitive. He always smiles. He always waits. When he wants to say something, he meets a wall of silence; when he greets someone, he meets a cold shoulder; when he pleads or weeps or cries out, his gestures and cries are lost in the emptiness created by Don No One's interminable chatter. Nobody is afraid not to exist: he vacillates, attempting now and then to become Somebody. Finally, in the midst of his useless gestures, he disappears into the limbo from which he emerged.

It would be a mistake to believe that others prevent him from existing. They simply dissimulate his existence and behave as if he did not exist. They nullify him, cancel him out, turn him to nothingness. It is futile for Nobody to talk, to publish books, to paint pictures, to stand on his head. Nobody is the blankness in our looks, the pauses in our conversations, the reserve in our silences. He is the name we always and inevitably forget, the eternal absentee, the guest we never invite, the emptiness we can never fill. He is an omission, and yet he is forever present. He is our secret, our crime, and our remorse. Thus the person who creates Nobody, by denying Somebody's existence, is also changed into Nobody. And if we are all Nobody, then none of us exists. The circle is closed and the shadow of Nobody spreads out over our land, choking the Gesticulator and covering everything. Silence — the prehistoric silence, stronger than all the pyramids and sacrifices, all the churches and uprisings and popular songs — comes back to rule over Mexico.

CHAPTER THREE

The Day of the Dead

The solitary Mexican loves fiestas and public gatherings. Any occasion for getting together will serve, any pretext to stop the flow of time and commemorate men and events with festivals and ceremonies. We are a ritual people, and this characteristic enriches both our imaginations and our sensibilities, which are equally sharp and alert. The art of the fiesta has been debased almost everywhere else, but not in Mexico. There are few places in the world where it is possible to take part in a spectacle like our great religious fiestas with their violent primary colors, their bizarre costumes and dances, their fireworks and ceremonies, and their inexhaustible welter of surprises: the fruit, candy, toys and other objects sold on these days in the plazas and open-air markets.

Our calendar is crowded with fiestas. There are certain days when the whole country, from the most remote villages to the largest cities, prays, shouts, feasts, gets drunk and kills, in honor of the Virgin of Guadalupe or Benito Juárez. Each year on the fifteenth of September, at eleven o'clock at night, we celebrate the fiesta of the *Grito*[1] in all the plazas of the Republic, and the excited crowds actually shout for a whole hour . . . the better, perhaps, to remain silent for the rest of the year. During the days before and after the twelfth of December,[2] time comes to a full stop, and instead of pushing us toward a deceptive tomor-

---

[1] Padre Hidalgo's call-to-arms against Spain, 1810. — *Tr.*
[2] Fiesta of the Virgin of Guadalupe. — *Tr.*

row that is always beyond our reach, offers us a complete and perfect today of dancing and revelry, of communion with the most ancient and secret Mexico. Time is no longer succession, and becomes what it originally was and is: the present, in which past and future are reconciled.

But the fiestas which the Church and State provide for the country as a whole are not enough. The life of every city and village is ruled by a patron saint whose blessing is celebrated with devout regularity. Neighborhoods and trades also have their annual fiestas, their ceremonies and fairs. And each one of us — atheist, Catholic, or merely indifferent — has his own saint's day, which he observes every year. It is impossible to calculate how many fiestas we have and how much time and money we spend on them. I remember asking the mayor of a village near Mitla, several years ago, "What is the income of the village government?" "About 3,000 pesos a year. We are very poor. But the Governor and the Federal Government always help us to meet our expenses." "And how are the 3,000 pesos spent?" "Mostly on fiestas, señor. We are a small village, but we have two patron saints."

This reply is not surprising. Our poverty can be measured by the frequency and luxuriousness of our holidays. Wealthy countries have very few: there is neither the time nor the desire for them, and they are not necessary. The people have other things to do, and when they amuse themselves they do so in small groups. The modern masses are agglomerations of solitary individuals. On great occasions in Paris or New York, when the populace gathers in the squares or stadiums, the absence of people, in the sense of *a* people, is remarkable: there are couples and small groups, but they never form a living community in which the individual is at once dissolved and redeemed. But how could a poor Mexican live without the two or three annual fiestas that make up for his poverty and misery? Fiestas are our only luxury. They replace, and are perhaps better than, the theater and vacations, Anglo-Saxon weekends and cocktail parties, the bourgeois reception, the Mediterranean café.

In all of these ceremonies — national or local, trade or family — the Mexican opens out. They all give him a chance to reveal himself and to converse with God, country, friends or relations. During these days the silent Mexican whistles, shouts, sings, shoots off fireworks, discharges his pistol into the air. He discharges his soul. And his shout, like the rockets we love so much, ascends to the heavens, explodes into green, red, blue, and white lights, and falls dizzily to earth with a trail of golden sparks. This is the night when friends who have not exchanged more than the prescribed courtesies for months get drunk together, trade confidences, weep over the same troubles, discover that they are brothers, and sometimes, to prove it, kill each other. The night is full of songs and loud cries. The lover wakes up his sweetheart with an orchestra. There are jokes and conversations from balcony to balcony, sidewalk to sidewalk. Nobody talks quietly. Hats fly in the air. Laughter and curses ring like silver pesos. Guitars are brought out. Now and then, it is true, the happiness ends badly, in quarrels, insults, pistol shots, stabbings. But these too are part of the fiesta, for the Mexican does not seek amusement: he seeks to escape from himself, to leap over the wall of solitude that confines him during the rest of the year. All are possessed by violence and frenzy. Their souls explode like the colors and voices and emotions. Do they forget themselves and show their true faces? Nobody knows. The important thing is to go out, open a way, get drunk on noise, people, colors. Mexico is celebrating a fiesta. And this fiesta, shot through with lightning and delirium, is the brilliant reverse to our silence and apathy, our reticence and gloom.

According to the interpretation of French sociologists, the fiesta is an excess, an expense. By means of this squandering the community protects itself against the envy of the gods or of men. Sacrifices and offerings placate or buy off the gods and the patron saints. Wasting money and expending energy affirms the community's wealth in both. This luxury is a proof of health, a show of abundance and power. Or a magic trap. For squandering is an effort to attract abundance by contagion. Money calls to money. When life is thrown away it increases; the orgy, which is sexual expenditure, is also a ceremony of regeneration; waste gives strength. New Year celebrations, in every culture, signify something beyond the mere observance of a date on the calendar. The day is a pause: time is stopped, is actually annihilated. The rites that celebrate its death are intended to provoke its rebirth, because they mark not only the end of an old year but also the beginning of a new. Everything attracts its opposite. The fiesta's function, then, is more utilitarian than we think: waste attracts or promotes wealth, and is an investment like any other, except that the returns on it cannot be measured or counted. What is sought is potency, life, health. In this sense the fiesta, like the gift and the offering, is one of the most ancient of economic forms.

This interpretation has always seemed to me to be incomplete. The fiesta is by nature sacred, literally or figuratively, and above all it is the advent of the unusual. It is governed by its own special rules, that set it apart from other days, and it has a logic, an ethic and even an economy that are often in conflict with everyday norms. It all occurs in an enchanted world: time is transformed to a mythical past or a total present; space, the scene of the fiesta, is turned into a gaily decorated world of its own; and the persons taking part cast off all human or social rank and become, for the moment, living images. And everything takes place as if it were not so, as if it were a dream. But whatever happens, our actions have a greater lightness, a different gravity. They take on other meanings and with them we contract new obligations. We throw down our burdens of time and reason.

In certain fiestas the very notion of order disappears. Chaos comes back and license rules. Anything is permitted: the customary hierarchies vanish, along with all social, sex, caste, and trade distinctions. Men disguise themselves as women, gentlemen as slaves, the poor as the rich. The army, the clergy, and the law are ridiculed. Obligatory sacrilege, ritual profanation is committed. Love becomes promiscuity. Sometimes the fiesta becomes a Black Mass. Regulations, habits and customs are violated. Respectable people put away the dignified expressions and conservative clothes that isolate them, dress up in gaudy colors, hide behind a mask, and escape from themselves.

Therefore the fiesta is not only an excess, a ritual squandering of the goods painfully accumulated during the rest of the year; it is also a revolt, a sudden immersion in the formless, in pure being. By means of the fiesta society frees itself from the norms it has established. It ridicules its gods, its principles, and its laws: it denies its own self.

The fiesta is a revolution in the most literal sense of the word. In the confusion that it generates, society is dissolved, is drowned, insofar as it is an organism ruled according to certain laws and principles. But it drowns in itself, in its own original chaos or liberty. Everything is united: good and evil, day and night, the sacred and the profane. Everything merges, loses shape and individuality and returns to the primordial mass. The fiesta is a cosmic experiment, an experiment in disorder, reuniting contradictory elements and principles in order to bring about a renascence of life. Ritual death promotes a rebirth;

vomiting increases the appetite; the orgy, sterile in itself, renews the fertility of the mother or of the earth. The fiesta is a return to a remote and undifferentiated state, prenatal or presocial. It is a return that is also a beginning, in accordance with the dialectic that is inherent in social processes.

The group emerges purified and strengthened from this plunge into chaos. It has immersed itself in its own origins, in the womb from which it came. To express it in another way, the fiesta denies society as an organic system of differentiated forms and principles, but affirms it as a source of creative energy. It is a true "re-creation," the opposite of the "recreation" characterizing modern vacations, which do not entail any rites or ceremonies whatever and are as individualistic and sterile as the world that invented them.

Society communes with itself during the fiesta. Its members return to original chaos and freedom. Social structures break down and new relationships, unexpected rules, capricious hierarchies are created. In the general disorder everybody forgets himself and enters into otherwise forbidden situations and places. The bounds between audience and actors, officials and servants, are erased. Everybody takes part in the fiesta, everybody is caught up in its whirlwind. Whatever its mood, its character, its meaning, the fiesta is participation, and this trait distinguishes it from all other ceremonies and social phenomena. Lay or religious, orgy or saturnalia, the fiesta is a social act based on the full participation of all its celebrants.

Thanks to the fiesta the Mexican opens out, participates, communes with his fellows and with the values that give meaning to his religious or political existence. And it is significant that a country as sorrowful as ours should have so many and such joyous fiestas. Their frequency, their brilliance and excitement, the enthusiasm with which we take part, all suggest that without them we would explode. They free us, if only momentarily, from the thwarted impulses, the inflammable desires that we carry within us. But the Mexican fiesta is not merely a return to an original state of formless and normless liberty: the Mexican is not seeking to return, but to escape from himself, to exceed himself. Our fiestas are explosions. Life and death, joy and sorrow, music and mere noise are united, not to re-create or recognize themselves, but to swallow each other up. There is nothing so joyous as a Mexican fiesta, but there is also nothing so sorrowful. Fiesta night is also a night of mourning.

If we hide within ourselves in our daily lives, we discharge ourselves in the whirlwind of the fiesta. It is more than an opening out: we rend ourselves open. Everything — music, love, friendship — ends in tumult and violence. The frenzy of our festivals shows the extent to which our solitude closes us off from communication with the world. We are familiar with delirium, with songs and shouts, with the monologue . . . but not with the dialogue. Our fiestas, like our confidences, our loves, our attempts to reorder our society, are violent breaks with the old or the established. Each time we try to express ourselves we have to break with ourselves. And the fiesta is only one example, perhaps the most typical, of this violent break. It is not difficult to name others, equally revealing: our games, which are always a going to extremes, often mortal; our profligate spending, the reverse of our timid investments and business enterprises; our confessions. The somber Mexican, closed up in himself, suddenly explodes, tears open his breast and reveals himself, though not without a certain complacency, and not without a stopping place in the shameful or terrible mazes of his intimacy. We are not frank, but our sincerity can reach extremes that horrify a European. The explosive, dramatic, sometimes even suicidal manner in which we strip ourselves, surrender ourselves, is evidence that something inhibits and suffocates us. Something impedes us from being. And since we cannot or dare not confront our own selves, we resort to the fiesta. It fires us into the void; it is a drunken rapture that burns itself out, a pistol shot in the air, a skyrocket.

Death is a mirror which reflects the vain gesticulations of the living. The whole motley confusion of acts, omissions, regrets and hopes which is the life of each one of us finds in death, not meaning or explanation, but an end. Death defines life; a death depicts a life in immutable forms; we do not change except to disappear. Our deaths illuminate our lives. If our deaths lack meaning, our lives also lacked it. Therefore we are apt to say, when somebody has died a violent death, "He got what he was looking for." Each of us dies the death he is looking for, the death he has made for himself. A Christian death or a dog's death are ways of dying that reflect ways of living. If death betrays us and we die badly, everyone laments the fact, because we should die as we have lived. Death, like life, is not transferable. If we do not die as we lived, it is because the life we lived was not really ours: it did not belong to us, just as the bad death that kills us does not belong to us. Tell me how you die and I will tell you who you are.

The opposition between life and death was not so absolute to the ancient Mexicans as it is to us. Life extended into death, and vice versa. Death was not the natural end of life but one phase of an infinite cycle. Life, death and resurrection were stages of a cosmic process which repeated itself continuously. Life had no higher function than to flow into death, its opposite and complement; and death, in turn, was not an end in itself: man fed the insatiable hunger of life with his death. Sacrifices had a double purpose: on the one hand man participated in the creative process, at the same time paying back to the gods the debt contracted by his species; on the other hand he nourished cosmic life and also social life, which was nurtured by the former.

Perhaps the most characteristic aspect of this conception is the impersonal nature of the sacrifice. Since their lives did not belong to them, their deaths lacked any personal meaning. The dead — including warriors killed in battle and women dying in childbirth, companions of Huitzilopochtli the sun god — disappeared at the end of a certain period, to return to the undifferentiated country of the shadows, to be melted into the air, the earth, the fire, the animating substance of the universe. Our indigenous ancestors did not believe that their deaths belonged to them, just as they never thought that their lives were really theirs in the Christian sense. Everything was examined to determine, from birth, the life and death of each man: his social class, the year, the place, the day, the hour. The Aztec was as little responsible for his actions as for his death.

Space and time were bound together and formed an inseparable whole. There was a particular "time" for each place, each of the cardinal points and the center in which they were immobilized. And this complex of space-time possessed its own virtues and powers, which profoundly influenced and determined human life. To be born on a certain day was to pertain to a place, a time, a color and a destiny. All was traced out in advance. Where we dissociate space and time, mere stage sets for the actions of our lives, there were as many "space-times" for the Aztecs as there were combinations in the priestly calendar, each one endowed with a particular qualitative significance, superior to human will.

Religion and destiny ruled their lives, as morality and freedom rule ours. We live under the sign of liberty, and everything

— even Greek fatality and the grace of the theologians — is election and struggle, but for the Aztecs the problem reduced itself to investigating the never-clear will of the gods. Only the gods were free, and only they had the power to choose — and therefore, in a profound sense, to sin. The Aztec religion is full of great sinful gods — Quetzalcóatl is the major example — who grow weak and abandon their believers, in the same way that Christians sometimes deny God. The conquest of Mexico would be inexplicable without the treachery of the gods, who denied their own people.

The advent of Catholicism radically modified this situation. Sacrifice and the idea of salvation, formerly collective, became personal. Freedom was humanized, embodied in man. To the ancient Aztecs the essential thing was to assure the continuity of creation; sacrifice did not bring about salvation in another world, but cosmic health; the universe, and not the individual, was given life by the blood and death of human beings. For Christians it is the individual who counts. The world — history, society — is condemned beforehand. The death of Christ saved each man in particular. Each one of us is Man, and represents the hopes and possibilities of the species. Redemption is a personal task.

Both attitudes, opposed as they may seem, have a common note: life, collective or individual, looks forward to a death that in its way is a new life. Life only justifies and transcends itself when it is realized in death, and death is also a transcendence, in that it is a new life. To Christians death is a transition, a somersault between two lives, the temporal and the otherworldly; to the Aztecs it was the profoundest way of participating in the continuous regeneration of the creative forces, which were always in danger of being extinguished if they were not provided with blood, the sacred food. In both systems life and death lack autonomy, are the two sides of a single reality. They are references to the invisible realities.

Modern death does not have any significance that transcends it or that refers to other values. It is rarely anything more than the inevitable conclusion of a natural process. In a world of facts, death is merely one more fact. But since it is such a disagreeable fact, contrary to all our concepts and to the very meaning of our lives, the philosophy of progress ("Progress toward what, and from what?" Scheler asked) pretends to make it disappear, like a magician palming a coin. Everything in the modern world functions as if death did not exist. Nobody takes it into account, it is suppressed everywhere: in political pronouncements, commercial advertising, public morality and popular customs; in the promise of cut-rate health and happiness offered to all of us by hospitals, drugstores and playing fields. But death enters into everything we undertake, and it is no longer a transition but a great gaping mouth that nothing can satisfy. The century of health, hygiene and contraceptives, miracle drugs and synthetic foods, is also the century of the concentration camp and the police state, Hiroshima and the murder story. Nobody thinks about death, about his own death, as Rilke asked us to do, because nobody lives a personal life. Collective slaughter is the fruit of a collectivized way of life.

Death also lacks meaning for the modern Mexican. It is no longer a transition, an access to another life more alive than our own. But although we do not view death as a transcendence, we have not eliminated it from our daily lives. The word death is not pronounced in New York, in Paris, in London, because it burns the lips. The Mexican, in contrast, is familiar with death, jokes about it, caresses it, sleeps with it, celebrates it; it is one of his favorite toys and his most steadfast love. True, there is perhaps as much fear in his attitude as in that of others, but at least death is not hidden away: he looks at it face to face, with impatience, disdain or irony. "If they are going to kill me tomorrow, let them kill me right away."[3]

The Mexican's indifference toward death is fostered by his indifference toward life. He views not only death but also life as nontranscendent. Our songs, proverbs, fiestas and popular beliefs show very clearly that the reason death cannot frighten us is that "life has cured us of fear." It is natural, even desirable, to die, and the sooner the better. We kill because life — our own or another's — is of no value. Life and death are inseparable, and when the former lacks meaning, the latter becomes equally meaningless. Mexican death is the mirror of Mexican life. And the Mexican shuts himself away and ignores both of them.

Our contempt for death is not at odds with the cult we have made of it. Death is present in our fiestas, our games, our loves and our thoughts. To die and to kill are ideas that rarely leave us. We are seduced by death. The fascination it exerts over us is the result, perhaps, of our hermit-like solitude and of the fury with which we break out of it. The pressure of our vitality, which can only express itself in forms that betray it, explains the deadly nature, aggressive or suicidal, of our explosions. When we explode we touch against the highest point of that tension, we graze the very zenith of life. And there, at the height of our frenzy, suddenly we feel dizzy: it is then that death attracts us.

Another factor is that death revenges us against life, strips it of all its vanities and pretensions and converts it into what it really is: a few neat bones and a dreadful grimace. In a closed world where everything is death, only death has value. But our affirmation is negative. Sugar-candy skulls, and tissue-paper skulls and skeletons strung with fireworks . . . our popular

---

[3]From the popular folk song *La Valentina.* — *Tr.*

images always poke fun at life, affirming the nothingness and insignificance of human existence. We decorate our houses with death's heads, we eat bread in the shape of bones on the Day of the Dead, we love the songs and stories in which death laughs and cracks jokes, but all this boastful familiarity does not rid us of the question we all ask: What is death? We have not thought up a new answer. And each time we ask, we shrug our shoulders: Why should I care about death if I have never cared about life?

Does the Mexican open out in the presence of death? He praises it, celebrates it, cultivates it, embraces it, but he never surrenders himself to it. Everything is remote and strange to him, and nothing more so than death. He does not surrender himself to it because surrender entails a sacrifice. And a sacrifice, in turn, demands that someone must give and someone receive. That is, someone must open out and face a reality that transcends him. In a closed, nontranscendent world, death neither gives nor receives: it consumes itself and is self-gratifying. Therefore our relations with death are intimate — more intimate, perhaps, than those of any other people — but empty of meaning and devoid of erotic emotion. Death in Mexico is sterile, not fecund like that of the Aztecs and the Christians.

Nothing is more opposed to this attitude than that of the Europeans and North Americans. Their laws, customs and public and private ethics all tend to preserve human life. This protection does not prevent the number of ingenious and refined murders, of perfect crimes and crime-waves, from increasing. The professional criminals who plot their murders with a precision impossible to a Mexican, the delight they take in describing their experiences and methods, the fascination with which the press and public follow their confessions, and the recognized inefficiency of the systems of prevention, show that the respect for life of which Western civilization is so proud is either incomplete or hypocritical.

The cult of life, if it is truly profound and total, is also the cult of death, because the two are inseparable. A civilization that denies death ends by denying life. The perfection of modern crime is not merely a consequence of modern technical progress and the vogue of the murder story: it derives from the contempt for life which is inevitably implicit in any attempt to hide death away and pretend it does not exist. It might be added that modern technical skills and the popularity of crime stories are, like concentration camps and collective extermination, the results of an optimistic and unilateral conception of existence. It is useless to exclude death from our images, our words, our ideas, because death will obliterate all of us, beginning with those who ignore it or pretend to ignore it.

When the Mexican kills — for revenge, pleasure or caprice — he kills a person, a human being. Modern criminals and statesmen do not kill: they abolish. They experiment with beings who have lost their human qualities. Prisoners in the concentration camps are first degraded, changed into mere objects; then they are exterminated en masse. The typical criminal in the large cities — beyond the specific motives for his crimes — realizes on a small scale what the modern leader realizes on a grand scale. He too experiments, in his own way: he poisons, destroys corpses with acids, dismembers them, converts them into objects. The ancient relationship between victim and murderer, which is the only thing that humanizes murder, that makes it even thinkable, has disappeared. As in the novels of Sade, there is no longer anything except torturers and objects, instruments of pleasure and destruction. And the nonexistence of the victim makes the infinite solitude of the murderer even more intolerable. Murder is still a relationship in Mexico, and in this sense it has the same liberating significance as the fiesta or the confession. Hence its drama, its poetry and — why not say it? — its grandeur. Through murder we achieve a momentary transcendence.

At the beginning of his eighth Duino Elegy, Rilke says that the "creature," in his condition of animal innocence, "beholds the open" ... unlike ourselves, who never look forward, toward the absolute. Fear makes us turn our backs on death, and by refusing to contemplate it we shut ourselves off from life, which is a totality that includes it. The "open" is where contraries are reconciled, where light and shadow are fused. This conception restores death's original meaning: death and life are opposites that complement each other. Both are halves of a sphere that we, subjects of time and space, can only glimpse. In the pre-natal world, life and death are merged; in ours, opposed; in the world beyond, reunited again, not in the animal innocence that precedes sin and the knowledge of sin, but as in innocence regained. Man can transcend the temporal opposition separating them (and residing not in them but in his own consciousness) and perceive them as a superior whole. This recognition can take place only through detachment: he must renounce his temporal life and his nostalgia for limbo, for the animal world. He must open himself out to death if he wishes to open himself out to life. Then he will be "like the angels."

Thus there are two attitudes toward death: one, pointing forward, that conceives of it as creation; the other, pointing backward, that expresses itself as a fascination with nothingness or as a nostalgia for limbo. No Mexican or Spanish-American poet, with the possible exception of César Vallejo, approaches the first of these two concepts. The absence of a mystic — and only a mystic is capable of offering insights like those of Rilke

— indicates the extent to which modern Mexican culture is insensible to religion. But two Mexican poets, José Gorostiza and Xavier Villaurrutia, represent the second of these two attitudes. For Gorostiza life is a "death without end," a perpetual falling into nothingness; for Villaurrutia it is no more than a "nostalgia for death."

The phrase that Villaurrutia chose for his book, *Nostalgia de la Muerte,* is not merely a lucky hit. The author has used it in order to tell us the ultimate meaning of his poetry. Death as nostalgia, rather than as the fruition or end of life, is death as origin. The ancient, original source is a bone, not a womb. This statement runs the risk of seeming either an empty paradox or an old commonplace: "For thou art dust, and unto dust shalt thou return." I believe that the poet hopes to find in death (which is, in effect, our origin) a revelation that his temporal life has denied him: the true meaning of life. When we die,

> *The second hand*
> *will race around its dial,*
> *all will be contained in an instant . . .*
> *and perhaps it will be possible*
> *to live, even after death.*

A return to original death would be a return to the life before life, the life before death: to limbo, to the maternal source.

Muerte sin Fin, the poem by José Gorostiza, is perhaps the best evidence we have in Latin America of a truly modern consciousness, one that is turned in upon itself, imprisoned in its own blinding clarity. The poet, in a sort of lucid fury, wants to rip the mask off existence in order to see it as it is. The dialogue between man and the world, which is as old as poetry and love, is transformed into a dialogue between the water and the glass that contains it, between the thought and the form into which it is poured and which it eventually corrodes. The poet warns us from his prison of appearances — trees and thoughts, stones and emotions, days and nights and twilights are all simply metaphors, mere colored ribbons — that the breath which informs matter, shaping it and giving it form, is the same breath that corrodes and withers and defeats it. It is a drama without personae, since all are merely reflections, the various disguises of a suicide who talks to himself in a language of mirrors and echoes, and the mind also is nothing more than a reflection of death, of death in love with itself. Everything is immersed in its own clarity and brilliance, everything is directed toward this transparent death: life is only a metaphor, an invention with which death — death too! — wants to deceive itself. The poem is a variation on the old theme of Narcissus, although there is no allusion to it in the text. And it is not only the consciousness that contemplates itself in its empty, transparent water (both mirror and eye at the same time, as in the Valéry poem): nothingness, which imitates form and life, which feigns corruption and death, strips itself naked and turns in upon itself, loves itself, falls into itself: a tireless death without end.

If we open out during fiestas, then, or when we are drunk or exchanging confidences, we do it so violently that we wound ourselves. And we shrug our shoulders at death, as at life, confronting it in silence or with a contemptuous smile. The fiesta, the crime of passion and the gratuitous crime reveal that the equilibrium of which we are so proud is only a mask, always in danger of being ripped off by a sudden explosion of our intimacy.

All of these attitudes indicate that the Mexican senses the presence of a stigma both on himself and on the flesh of his country. It is diffused but none the less living, original, and ineradicable. Our gestures and expressions all attempt to hide this wound, which is always open, always ready to catch fire and burn under the rays of a stranger's glance.

Now, every separation causes a wound. Without stopping to investigate how and when the separation is brought about, I want to point out that any break (with ourselves or those around us, with the past or the present) creates a feeling of solitude. In extreme cases — separation from one's parents, matrix or native land, the death of the gods or a painful self-consciousness — solitude is identified with orphanhood. And both of them generally manifest themselves as a sense of sin. The penalties and guilty feelings inflicted by a state of separation can be considered, thanks to the ideas of expiation and redemption, as necessary sacrifices, as pledges or promises of a future communion that will put an end to the long exile. The guilt can vanish, the wound heal over, the separation resolve itself in communion. Solitude thus assumes a purgative, purifying character. The solitary or isolated individual transcends his solitude, accepting it as a proof or promise of communion.

The Mexican does not transcend his solitude. On the contrary, he locks himself up in it. We live in our solitude like Philoctetes on his island, fearing rather than hoping to return to the world. We cannot bear the presence of our companions. We hide within ourselves — except when we rend ourselves open in our frenzy — and the solitude in which we suffer has no reference either to a redeemer or a creator. We oscillate between intimacy and withdrawal, between a shout and a silence, between a fiesta and a wake, without ever truly surrendering ourselves. Our indifference hides life behind a death mask; our wild shout rips off this mask and shoots into the sky, where it swells, explodes, and falls back in silence and defeat. Either way, the Mexican shuts himself off from the world: from life and from death.

CHAPTER FOUR

The Sons of La Malinche

Our hermeticism is baffling or even offensive to strangers, and it has created the legend of the Mexican as an inscrutable being. Our suspicions keep us at a distance. Our courtesy may be attractive but our reserve is chilling, and the stranger is always disconcerted by the unforeseen violence that lacerates us, by the solemn or convulsive splendor of our fiestas, by our cult of death. The impression we create is much like that created by Orientals. They too — the Chinese, the Hindus, the Arabs — are hermetic and indecipherable. They too carry about with them, in rags, a still-living past. There is a Mexican mystery just as there is a yellow mystery or a black. The details of the image formed of us often vary with the spectator, but it is always an ambiguous if not contradictory image: we are insecure, and our responses, like our silences, are unexpected and unpredictable. Treachery, loyalty, crime and love hide out in the depths of our glance. We attract and repel.

It is not difficult to understand the origins of this attitude toward us. The European considers Mexico to be a country on the margin of universal history, and everything that is distant from the center of his society strikes him as strange and impenetrable. The peasant — remote, conservative, somewhat archaic in his ways of dressing and speaking, fond of expressing himself in traditional modes and formulas — has always had a certain fascination for the urban man. In every country he represents the most ancient and secret element of society. For everyone but himself he embodies the occult, the hidden, that which surrenders itself only with great difficulty: a buried treasure, a seed that sprouts in the bowels of the earth, an ancient wisdom hiding among the folds of the land.

Woman is another being who lives apart and is therefore an enigmatic figure. It would be better to say that she is the Enigma. She attracts and repels like men of an alien race or nationality. She is an image of both fecundity and death. In almost every culture the goddesses of creation are also goddesses of destruction. Woman is a living symbol of the strangeness of the universe and its radical heterogeneity. As such, does she hide life within herself, or death? What does she think? Or does she think? Does she truly have feelings? Is she the same as we are? Sadism begins as a revenge against feminine hermeticism or as a desperate attempt to obtain a response from a body we fear is insensible. As Luis Cernuda has said, "Desire is a question that has no answer." Despite woman's full, rounded nakedness, there is always something on guard in her:

> *Eve and Aphrodite concentrate the mystery*
> *of the world's heart.*

Rubén Darío, like all the other great poets, considered woman to be not only an instrument of knowledge but also knowledge itself. It is a knowledge we will never possess, the sum of our definitive ignorance: the supreme mystery.

It is noteworthy that our images of the working class are not colored with similar feelings, even though the worker also lives apart from the center of society, physically as well as otherwise, in districts and special communities. When a contemporary novelist introduces a character who symbolizes health or destruction, fertility or death, he rarely chooses a worker, despite the fact that the worker represents the death of an old society and the birth of a new. D. H. Lawrence, one of the profoundest and most violent critics of the modern world, repeatedly describes the virtues that would transform the fragmentary man of our time into a true man with a total vision of the world, In order to embody these virtues he creates characters who belong to ancient or non-European races, or he invents the figure of Mellors the gamekeeper, a son of the earth. It is possible that Lawrence's childhood among the coal mines of England explains this deliberate omission: we know that he detested workers as much as he did the bourgeoisie. But how can we explain the fact that in the great revolutionary novels the proletariat again does not provide the heroes, merely the background? In all of them the hero is an adventurer, an intellectual, or a professional revolutionary: an isolated individual who has renounced his class, his origins or his homeland. It is no doubt a legacy from Romanticism that makes the hero an antisocial being. Also, the worker is too recent, and he resembles his boss because they are both sons of the machine.

The modern worker lacks individuality. The class is stronger than the individual and his personality dissolves in the generic. That is the first and gravest mutilation a man suffers when he transforms himself into an industrial wage earner. Capitalism deprives him of his human nature (this does not happen to the servant) by reducing him to an element in the work process, *i.e.*, to an object. And like any object in the business world, he can be bought and sold. Because of his social condition he quickly loses any concrete and human relationship to the world. The machines he operates are not his and neither are the things he produces. Actually he is not a worker at all, because he does not create individual works or is so occupied with one aspect of production that he is not conscious of those he does create. He is a laborer, which is an abstract noun designating a mere function rather than a specific job. Therefore his efforts, unlike those of a doctor, an engineer or a carpenter, cannot be distinguished from those of other men. The abstraction that characterizes him — work measured by time — does not separate him from other abstractions. On the contrary, it binds him to them. This is the reason he is lacking in mystery, in strangeness. It is the cause of his transparency, which is no different from that of any other instrument.

The complexity of contemporary society and the specialization required by its work extend the abstract condition of the worker to other social groups. It is said that we live in a world of techniques. Despite the differences in salary and way of life, the situation of the technician is essentially like that of the worker: he too is salaried and lacks a true awareness of what he creates. A government of technicians — the ideal of contemporary society — would thus be a government of instruments. Functions would be substituted for ends, and means for creators. Society would progress with great efficiency but without aim, and the repetition of the same gesture, a distinction of the machine, would bring about an unknown form of immobility, that of a mechanism advancing from nowhere toward nowhere.

The totalitarian regimes have done nothing but extend this condition and make it general, by means of force or propaganda. Everyone under their rule suffers from it. In a certain sense it is a transposition of the capitalist system to the social and political sphere. Mass production is characterized by the fabricating of separate units which are then put together in special workshops. Propaganda and totalitarian politics, such as terrorism and repression, employ the same system. Propaganda spreads incomplete truths, in series and as separate units. Later these fragments are organized and converted into political theories, which become absolute truths for the masses. Terrorism obeys the same rules. It begins with the persecution of isolated groups

— races, classes, dissenters, suspects — until gradually it touches everyone. At the outset, a part of society regards the extermination of other groups with indifference, or even contributes to their persecution, because it is corrupted by internal hatreds. Everyone becomes an accomplice and the guilt feelings spread through the whole society. Terrorism becomes generalized, until there are no longer either persecutors or persecuted. The persecutor is soon transformed into the persecuted. One turn of the political mechanism is enough. And no one can escape from this fierce dialectic, not even the leaders themselves.

The world of terrorism, like that of mass production, is a world of things, of utensils. (Hence the vanity of the dispute over the historical validity of modern terrorism.) Utensils are never mysterious or enigmatic, since mystery comes from the indetermination of the being or object that contains it. A mysterious ring separates itself immediately from the generic ring; it acquires a life of its own and ceases to be an object. Surprise lurks in its form, hidden, ready to leap out. Mystery is an occult force or efficacy that does not obey us, and we never know how or when it will manifest itself. But utensils do not hide anything; they never question us and they never answer our questions. They are unequivocal and transparent, mere prolongations of our hands, with only as much life as our will lends them. When they are old and worn out, we throw them away without a thought, into the wastebasket, the automobile graveyard, the concentration camp. Or we exchange them with our allies or enemies for other objects.

All our faculties, and all our defects as well, are opposed to this conception of work as an impersonal action repeated in equal and empty portions of time. The Mexican works slowly and carefully; he loves the completed work and each of the details that make it up; and his innate good taste is an ancient heritage. If we do not mass produce products, we vie with one another in the difficult, exquisite and useless art of dressing fleas. This does not mean that the Mexican is incapable of being converted into what is called a "good worker." It is only a question of time. Nothing except a historical change, daily more remote and unlikely, can prevent the Mexican — who is still a problem, an enigmatic figure — from becoming one more abstraction.

When this moment arrives, it will resolve all our contradictions by annihilating them, but meanwhile I want to point out that the most extraordinary fact of our situation is that we are enigmatic not only to strangers but also to ourselves. The Mexican is always a problem, both for other Mexicans and for himself. There is nothing simpler, therefore, than to reduce the whole complex group of attitudes that characterize us — especially the problem that we constitute for our own selves — to what may be called the "servant mentality," in opposition to the "psychology of the master" and also to that of modern man, whether proletarian or bourgeois.

Suspicion, dissimulation, irony, the courtesy that shuts us away from the stranger, all of the psychic oscillations with which, in eluding a strange glance, we elude ourselves, are traits of a subjected people who tremble and disguise themselves in the presence of the master. It is revealing that our intimacy never flowers in a natural way, only when incited by fiestas, alcohol or death. Slaves, servants and submerged races always wear a mask, whether smiling or sullen. Only when they are alone, during the great moments of life, do they dare to show themselves as they really are. All their relationships are poisoned by fear and suspicion: fear of the master and suspicion of their equals. Each keeps watch over the other because every companion could also be a traitor. To escape from himself the servant must leap walls, get drunk, forget his condition. He must live alone, without witnesses. He dares to be himself only in solitude.

The unquestionable analogy that can be observed between certain of our attitudes and those of groups subservient to the power of a lord, a caste or a foreign state could be resolved in this statement: the character of the Mexican is a product of the social circumstances that prevail in our country, and the history of Mexico, which is the history of these circumstances, contains the answer to every question. The situation that prevailed during the colonial period would thus be the source of our closed, unstable attitude. Our history as an independent nation would contribute to perpetuating and strengthening this servant psychology, for we have not succeeded in overcoming the misery of the common people and our exasperating social differences, despite a century and a half of struggle and constitutional experience. The use of violence as a dialectical resource, the abuse of authority by the powerful (a vice that has not disappeared) and, finally, the scepticism and resignation of the people — all of these more visible today than ever before, due to our successive post-revolution disillusionments — would complete the historical explication.

The fault of interpretations like the one I have just sketched out is their simplicity. Our attitude toward life is not conditioned by historical events, at least not in the rigorous manner in which the velocity or trajectory of a missile is determined by a set of known factors. Our living attitude — a factor we can never know completely, since change and indetermination are the only constants of our existence — is history also. This is to say that historical events are something more than events because they are colored by humanity, which is always problematical. And they are not merely the result of other events, but rather of a single will that is capable, within certain limits, of ruling their outcome. History is not a mechanism, and the influences among diverse components of an historical event are reciprocal, as has been said so often. What distinguishes one historical event from another is its historical character: in itself and by itself it is an irreducible unity. Irreducible and inseparable. A historical event is not the sum of its component factors but an indissoluble reality. Historical circumstances explain our character to the extent that our character explains those circumstances. Both are the same. Thus any purely historical explanation is insufficient... which is not the same as saying it is false.

One observation will be enough to reduce the analogy between the psychology of the servant and our own to its true proportions: the habitual reactions of the Mexican are not limited to a single class, race or isolated group in an inferior position. The wealthy classes also shut themselves away from the exterior world, and lacerate themselves whenever they open out. It is an attitude that goes beyond historical circumstances, although it makes use of them to manifest itself and is modified by contact with them. The Mexican, like all men, converts these circumstances into plastic material. As he molds them he also molds himself.

If it is not possible to identify our character with that of submerged groups, it is also impossible to deny a close relationship. In both situations the individual and the group struggle simultaneously and contradictorily to hide and to reveal themselves. But a difference separates us. Servants, slaves or races victimized by an outside power (the North American Negro, for example) struggle against a concrete reality. We, however, struggle with imaginary entities, with vestiges of the past or self-engendered phantasms. These vestiges and phantasms are real, at least to us. Their reality is of a subtle and cruel order, because it is a phantasmagoric reality. They are impalpable and invincible because they are not outside us but within us. In the struggle which our will-to-be carries on against them, they are supported by a secret and powerful ally, our fear of being. Everything that makes up the present-day Mexican, as we have seen, can be reduced to this: the Mexican does not want or does not dare to be himself.

In many instances these phantasms are vestiges of past realities. Their origins are in the Conquest, the Colonial period, the Independence period or the wars fought against the United States and France. Others reflect our current problems, but in an indirect manner, concealing or distorting their true nature. Is it not extraordinary that the effects persist after the causes have disappeared? And that the effects hide the causes? In this sphere it is impossible to distinguish between causes and effects. Actually there *are* no causes and effects, merely a complex of interpenetrating reactions and tendencies. The persistence of certain attitudes, and the freedom and independence they assume in relation to the causes that created them, induce us to study them in the living flesh of the present rather than in history books.

History, then, can clarify the origins of many of our phantasms, but it cannot dissipate them. We must confront them ourselves. Or to put it another way: history helps us to understand certain traits of our character, provided we are capable of isolating and defining them beforehand. We are the only persons who can answer the questions asked us by reality and our own being.

In our daily language there is a group of words that are prohibited, secret, without clear meanings. We confide the expression of our most brutal or subtle emotions and reactions to their magical ambiguities. They are evil words, and we utter them in a loud voice only when we are not in control of ourselves. In a confused way they reflect our intimacy: the explosions of our vitality light them up and the depressions of our spirit darken them. They constitute a sacred language like those of children, poetry and sects. Each letter and syllable has a double life, at once luminous and obscure, that reveals and hides us. They are words that say nothing and say everything. Adolescents, when they want to appear like men, speak them in a hoarse voice. Women also repeat them, sometimes to demonstrate their freedom of spirit, sometimes to prove the truth of their feelings. But these words are definitive and categorical, despite their ambiguities and the ease with which their meanings change. They are the bad words, the only living language in a world of anemic vocables. They are poetry within the reach of everyone.

Each country has its own. In ours, with their brief, aggressive, electric syllables, resembling the flash given off by a knife when it strikes a hard opaque body, we condense all our appetites, all our hatreds and enthusiasms, all the longings that rage unexpressed in the depths of our being. The word is our sign and seal. By means of it we recognize each other among strangers, and we use it every time the real conditions of our being rise to our lips. To know it, to use it, to throw it in the air like a toy or to make it quiver like a sharp weapon, is a way of affirming that we are Mexican.

All of our anxious tensions express themselves in a phrase we use when anger, joy or enthusiasm cause us to exalt our condition as Mexicans: "*¡Viva México, hijos de la chingada!*" This phrase is a true battle cry, charged with a peculiar electricity; it is a challenge and an affirmation, a shot fired against an imaginary enemy, and an explosion in the air. Once again, with a certain pathetic and plastic fatality, we are presented with the image of a skyrocket that climbs into the sky, bursts in a shower of sparks and then falls in darkness. Or with the image of that howl that ends all our songs and possesses the same ambiguous resonance: an angry joy, a destructive affirmation ripping open the breast and consuming itself.

When we shout this cry on the fifteenth of September, the anniversary of our independence, we affirm ourselves in front of, against and in spite of the "others." Who are the "others"? They are the *hijos de la chingada*: strangers, bad Mexicans, our enemies, our rivals. In any case, the "others," that is, all those who are not as we are. And these "others" are not defined except as the sons of a mother as vague and indeterminate as themselves.

Who is the *Chingada*? Above all, she is the Mother. Not a Mother of flesh and blood but a mythical figure. The *Chingada* is one of the Mexican representations of Maternity, like *La Llorona* or the "long-suffering Mexican mother" we celebrate on the tenth of May.[1] The *Chingada* is the mother who has suffered — metaphorically or actually — the corrosive and defaming action implicit in the verb that gives her her name. It would be worth while to examine that verb.

Darío Rubio, in his *Anarquía del lenguaje en la América Española*, examines the origins of *chingar* and enumerates the meanings given it by almost all Spanish-American people. It probably comes from the Aztecs: *chingaste* (lees, residue, sediment) is *xinachtli* (garden seed) or *xinaxtli* (fermented maguey juice). The word and its derivatives are used in most of America

---

[1] The "Weeping Woman," who wanders through the streets late at night, weeping and crying out. This belief, still current in some parts of Mexico, derives from pre-Conquest times, when "La Llorona" was the earth-goddess Cihuacóatl. The 10th of May is Mother's Day. — *Tr.*

and parts of Spain in association with drinks, alcoholic or otherwise. In Guatemala and El Salvador *chingaste* means the residue or dregs that remain in a glass. In Oaxaca coffee lees are called *chingaditos*. Throughout Mexico alcohol is called *chínguere* — or, significantly, *piquete*.[2] In Chile, Peru and Ecuador a *chingana* is a tavern. In Spain *chingar* means to drink a great deal, to get drunk. In Cuba a *chinguirito* is a shot of alcohol.

Chingar also implies the idea of failure. In Chile and Argentina a petard *se chinga* when it fails to explode, and businesses that fail, fiestas that are rained out, actions that are not completed, also *se chingan*. In Colombia *chingarse* means to be disappointed. In Argentina a torn dress is a *vestido chingado*. Almost everywhere *chingarse* means to be made a fool of, to be involved in a fiasco. In some parts of South America *chingar* means to molest, to censure, to ridicule. It is always an aggressive verb, as can be seen in these further meanings: to dock an animal, to incite or prod a fighting-cock, to make merry, to crack a whip, to endanger, to neglect, to frustrate.

In Mexico the word has innumerable meanings. It is a magical word: a change of tone, a change of inflection, is enough to change its meaning. It has as many shadings as it has intonations, as many meanings as it has emotions. One may be a *chingón*, a *gran chingón* (in business, in politics, in crime or with women), or a *chingaquedito* (silent, deceptive, fashioning plots in the shadows, advancing cautiously and then striking with a club), or a *chingoncito*. But in this plurality of meanings the ultimate meaning always contains the idea of aggression, whether it is the simple act of molesting, pricking or censuring, or the violent act of wounding or killing. The verb denotes violence, an emergence from oneself to penetrate another by force. It also means to injure, to lacerate, to violate — bodies,

---

[2] Literally, a bite, prick or sting; a picket or stake. — *Tr.*

souls, objects — and to destroy. When something breaks, we say: *"Se chingó."* When someone behaves rashly, in defiance of the rules, we say: *"Hizo una chingadera."*

The idea of breaking, of ripping open, appears in a great many of these expressions. The word has sexual connotations but it is not a synonym for the sexual act: one may *chingar* a woman without actually possessing her. And when it does allude to the sexual act, violation or deception gives it a particular shading. The man who commits it never does so with the consent of the *chingada. Chingar,* then, is to do violence to another. The verb is masculine, active, cruel: it stings, wounds, gashes, stains. And it provokes a bitter, resentful satisfaction.

The person who suffers this action is passive, inert and open, in contrast to the active, aggressive and closed person who inflicts it. The *chingón* is the *macho,* the male; he rips open the *chingada,* the female, who is pure passivity, defenseless against the exterior world. The relationship between them is violent, and it is determined by the cynical power of the first and the impotence of the second. The idea of violence rules darkly over all the meanings of the word, and the dialectic of the "closed" and the "open" thus fulfills itself with an almost ferocious precision.

The magic power of the word is intensified by the fact that it is prohibited. No one uses it casually in public. Only an excess of anger or a delirious enthusiasm justifies its use. It is a word that can only be heard among men or during the big fiestas. When we shout it out, we break a veil of silence, modesty or hypocrisy. We reveal ourselves as we really are. The forbidden words boil up in us, just as our emotions boil up. When they finally burst out, they do so harshly, brutally, in the form of a shout, a challenge, an offense. They are projectiles or knives. They cause wounds.

The Spaniards also abuse their strongest expressions; indeed, the Mexican is singularly nice in comparison. But while the Spaniards enjoy using blasphemy and scatology, we specialize in cruelty and sadism. The Spaniard is simple: he insults God because he believes in Him. Blasphemy, as Machado wrote, is a prayer in reverse. The pleasure that many Spaniards, including some of their greatest poets, derive from allusions to body wastes, and from mixing excrement with sacred matters, is reminiscent of children playing with mud. In addition to resentment, there is that delight in contrasts which produced the Baroque style and the drama of great Spanish painting. Only a Spaniard can speak with authority about Onan and Don Juan. In Mexican expressions, on the contrary, we cannot find the Spanish duality that is symbolized by the opposition of the real and the ideal, the mystics and the picaresque heroes, the funereal Quevedo and the scatalogical Quevedo. What we find is the dichotomy between the closed and the open. The verb *chingar* signifies the triumph of the closed, the male, the powerful, over the open.

If we take into account all of its various meanings, the word defines a great part of our life and qualifies our relationships with our friends and compatriots. To the Mexican there are only two possibilities in life: either he inflicts the actions implied by *chingar* on others, or else he suffers them himself at the hands of others. This conception of social life as combat fatally divides society into the strong and the weak. The strong — the hard, unscrupulous *chingones* — surround themselves with eager followers. This servility toward the strong, especially among the *políticos* (that is, the professionals of public business), is one of the more deplorable consequences of the situation. Another, no less degrading, is the devotion to personalities rather than to principles. Our politicians frequently mix public business with private. It does not matter. Their wealth or their influence in government allows them to maintain a flock of supporters whom the people call, most appositely, *lambiscones* (from the word *lamer:* "to lick").

The verb *chingar* — malign and agile and playful, like a caged animal — creates many expressions that turn our world into a jungle: there are tigers in business, eagles in the schools and the army, lions among our friends. A bribe is called a "bite." The bureaucrats gnaw their "bones" (public employment). And in a world of *chingones,* of difficult relationships, ruled by violence and suspicion — a world in which no one opens out or surrenders himself — ideas and accomplishments count for little. The only thing of value is manliness, personal strength, a capacity for imposing oneself on others.

The word also has another, more restricted meaning. When we say, "*Vete a la chingada,*"[3] we send a person to a distant place. Distant, vague and indeterminate. To the country of broken and worn-out things. A gray country, immense and empty, that is not located anywhere. It is not only because of simple phonetic association that we compare it with China, for China is also immense and remote. The *chingada,* because of constant usage, contradictory meanings and the friction of angry or enthusiastic lips, wastes away, loses its contents and disappears. It is a hollow word. It says nothing. It is Nothingness itself.

After this digression, it is possible to answer the question, "What is the *Chingada?*" The *Chingada* is the Mother forcibly opened, violated or deceived. The *hijo de la Chingada* is the offspring of violation, abduction or deceit. If we compare this expression with the Spanish *hijo de puta* (son of a whore), the

---

[3] Somewhat stronger than "Go to Hell." — *Tr.*

difference is immediately obvious. To the Spaniard, dishonor consists in being the son of a woman who voluntarily surrenders herself: a prostitute. To the Mexican it consists in being the fruit of a violation.

Manuel Cabrera points out that the Spanish attitude reflects a moral and historical conception of original sin, while that of the Mexican, deeper and more genuine, transcends both ethics and anecdotes. In effect, every woman — even when she gives herself willingly — is torn open by the man, is the *Chingada*. In a certain sense all of us, by the simple fact of being born of woman, are *hijos de la Chingada*, sons of Eve. But the singularity of the Mexican resides, I believe, in his violent, sarcastic humiliation of the Mother and his no less violent affirmation of the Father. A woman friend of mine (women are more aware of the strangeness of this situation) has made me see that this admiration for the Father — who is a symbol of the closed, the aggressive — expresses itself very clearly in a saying we use when we want to demonstrate our superiority: "I am your father." The question of origins, then, is the central secret of our anxiety and anguish. It is worth studying the significance of this fact.

We are alone. Solitude, the source of anxiety, begins on the day we are deprived of maternal protection and fall into a strange and hostile world. We have fallen, and this fall — this knowledge that we have fallen — makes us guilty. Of what? Of a nameless wrong: that of having been born. These feelings are common to all men and there is nothing specifically Mexican in them. Therefore it is not necessary to repeat a description that has been given many times before. What *is* necessary is to isolate certain traits and emotions that cast a particular light on the universal condition of man.

In all civilizations, God the Father becomes an ambivalent

figure once he has dethroned the feminine deities. On the one hand, the Father embodies the generative power, the origin of life, whether he be Jehovah, God the Creator, or Zeus, king of creation, ruler of the cosmos. On the other hand, he is the first principle, the One, from whom all is born and to whom all must return. But he is also the lord of the lightning bolt and the whip; he is the tyrant, the ogre who devours life. This aspect — angry Jehovah, God of wrath, or Saturn, or Zeus the violator of women — is the one that appears almost exclusively in Mexican representations of manly power. The *macho* represents the masculine pole of life. The phrase "I am your father" has no paternal flavor and is not said in order to protect or to guide another, but rather to impose one's superiority, that is, to humiliate. Its real meaning is no different from that of the verb *chingar* and its derivatives. The *macho* is the *gran chingón*. One word sums up the aggressiveness, insensitivity, invulnerability and other attributes of the *macho*: power. It is force without the discipline of any notion of order: arbitrary power, the will without reins and without a set course.

Unpredictability adds another element to the character of the *macho*. He is a humorist. His jokes are huge and individual, and they always end in absurdity. The anecdote about the man who "cured" the headache of a drinking companion by emptying his pistol into his head is well known. True or not, the incident reveals the inexorable rigor with which the logic of the absurd is introduced into life. The *macho* commits *chingaderas,* that is, unforseen acts that produce confusion, horror and destruction. He opens the world; in doing so, he rips and tears it, and this violence provokes a great, sinister laugh. And in its own way, it is just: it re-establishes the equilibrium and puts things in their places, by reducing them to dust, to misery, to nothingness. The humor of the *macho* is an act of revenge.

A psychologist would say that resentment is the basis of his character. It would not be difficult to perceive certain homosexual inclinations also, such as the use and abuse of the pistol, a phallic symbol which discharges death rather than life, and the fondness for exclusively masculine guilds. But whatever may be the origin of these attitudes, the fact is that the essential attribute of the *macho* — power — almost always reveals itself as a capacity for wounding, humiliating, annihilating. Nothing is more natural, therefore, than his indifference toward the off-spring he engenders. He is not the founder of a people; he is not a patriarch who exercises *patria potestas;* he is not a king or a judge or the chieftain of a clan. He is power isolated in its own potency, without relationship or compromise with the outside world. He is pure incommunication, a solitude that devours itself and everything it touches. He does not pertain to our world; he is not from our city; he does not live in our neighborhood. He comes from far away: he is always far away. He is the Stranger. It is impossible not to notice the resemblance between the figure of the *macho* and that of the Spanish conquistador. This is the model — more mythical than real — that determines the images the Mexican people form of men in power: caciques, feudal lords, hacienda owners, politicians, generals, captains of industry. They are all *machos, chingones.*

The *macho* has no heroic or divine counterpart. Hidalgo, the "father of the fatherland" as it is customary to call him in the ritual gibberish of the Republic, is a defenseless old man, more an incarnation of the people's helplessness against force than an image of the wrath and power of an awe-inspiring father. Among the numerous patron saints of the Mexicans there is none who resembles the great masculine divinities. Finally, there is no especial veneration for God the Father in the Trinity. He is a dim figure at best. On the other hand, there is profound devotion to Christ as the Son of God, as the youthful God, above all as the victimized Redeemer. The village churches have a great many images of Jesus — on the cross, or covered with thorns and wounds — in which the insolent realism of the Spaniards is mingled with the tragic symbolism of the Indians. On the one hand, the wounds are flowers, pledges of resurrection; on the other, they are a reiteration that life is the sorrowful mask of death.

The fervor of the cult of God the Son would seem to be explained, at first glance, as an inheritance from the pre-Hispanic religions. When the Spaniards arrived, almost all of the great masculine divinities — with the exception of the rain-god Tláloc, a child and an old man at the same time, and a deity of greater antiquity — were sons of gods, like Xipe, god of the young corn, and Huitzilopochtli, the "Warrior of the South." Perhaps it is not idle to recall that the birth of Huitzilopochtli offers more than one analogy with that of Christ: he too was conceived without carnal contact; the divine messenger was likewise a bird (that dropped a feather into the lap of the earth-goddess Coatlicue); and finally, the infant Huitzilopochtli also had to escape the persecution of a mythical Herod. Nevertheless, it would be a mistake to use these analogies to explain that devotion to Christ, just as it would be to attribute that devotion to a mere survival of the cult of the sons of gods. The Mexican venerates a bleeding and humiliated Christ, a Christ who has been beaten by the soldiers and condemned by the judges, because he sees in him a transfigured image of his own identity. And this brings to mind Cuauhtémoc, the young Aztec emperor who was dethroned, tortured and murdered by Cortés.

Cuauhtémoc means "Falling Eagle." The Mexican chieftain rose to power at the beginning of the siege of México-Tenochtitlán, when the Aztecs had been abandoned by their gods, their vassals and their allies. Even his relationship with a woman fits the archetype of the young hero, at one and the same time the lover and the son of the goddess. Thus López Velarde wrote that Cuauhtémoc went out to meet Cortés — that is, to the final sacrifice — "separated from the curved breast of the Empress." He is a warrior but he is also a child. The exception is that the heroic cycle does not end with his death: the fallen hero awaits resurrection. It is not surprising that for the majority of Mexicans Cuauhtémoc should be the "young grandfather," the origin of Mexico: the hero's tomb is the cradle of the people. This is the dialectic of myth, and Cuauhtémoc is more a myth than a historical figure. Another element enters here, an analogy that makes this history a true poem in search of fulfillment: the location of Cuauhtémoc's tomb is not known. The mystery of his burial place is one of our obsessions. To discover it would mean nothing less than to return to our origins, to reunite ourselves with our ancestry, to break out of our solitude. It would be a resurrection.

If we ask about the third figure of the triad, the Mother, we hear a double answer. It is no secret to anyone that Mexican Catholicism is centered about the cult of the Virgin of Guadalupe. In the first place, she is an Indian Virgin; in the second place, the scene of her appearance to the Indian Juan Diego was a hill that formerly contained a sanctuary dedicated to Tonantzin, "Our Mother," the Aztec goddess of fertility. We know that the Conquest coincided with the apogee of the cult of two masculine divinities: Quetzalcóatl, the self-sacrificing god, and Huitzilopochtli, the young warrior-god. The defeat of these gods — which is what the Conquest meant to the Indian world, because it was the end of a cosmic cycle and the inauguration of a new divine kingdom — caused the faithful to return to the ancient feminine deities. This phenomenon of a return to the maternal womb, so well known to the psychologist, is without doubt one of the determining causes of the swift popularity of the cult of the Virgin. The Indian goddesses were goddesses of fecundity, linked to the cosmic rhythms, the vegetative processes and agrarian rites. The Catholic Virgin is also the Mother (some Indian pilgrims still call her Guadalupe-Tonantzin), but her principal attribute is not to watch over the fertility of the earth but to provide refuge for the unfortunate. The situation has changed: the worshipers do not try to make sure of their harvests but to find a mother's lap. The Virgin is the consolation of the poor, the shield of the weak, the help of the oppressed. In sum, she is the Mother of orphans. All men are born disinherited and their true condition is orphanhood, but this is particularly true among the Indians and the poor in Mexico. The cult of the Virgin reflects not only the general condition of man but also a concrete historical situation, in both the spiritual and material realms. In addition, the Virgin — the universal Mother — is also the intermediary, the messenger, between disinherited man and the unknown, inscrutable power: the Strange.

In contrast to Guadalupe, who is the Virgin Mother, the *Chingada* is the violated Mother. Neither in her nor in the Virgin do we find traces of the darker attributes of the great goddesses: the lasciviousness of Amaterasu and Aphrodite, the cruelty of Artemis and Astarte, the sinister magic of Circe or the bloodlust of Kali. Both of them are passive figures. Guadalupe is pure receptivity, and the benefits she bestows are of the same order: she consoles, quiets, dries tears, calms passions. The *Chingada* is even more passive. Her passivity is abject: she does not resist violence, but is an inert heap of bones, blood and dust. Her taint is constitutional and resides, as we said earlier, in her sex. This passivity, open to the outside world, causes her to lose her identity: she is the *Chingada*. She loses her name; she is no one; she disappears into nothingness; she *is* Nothingness. And yet she is the cruel incarnation of the feminine condition.

If the *Chingada* is a representation of the violated Mother, it is appropriate to associate her with the Conquest, which was also a violation, not only in the historical sense but also in the very flesh of Indian women. The symbol of this violation is doña Malinche, the mistress of Cortés. It is true that she gave herself voluntarily to the conquistador, but he forgot her as soon as her usefulness was over. Doña Marina⁴ becomes a figure representing the Indian women who were fascinated, violated or seduced by the Spaniards. And as a small boy will not forgive his mother if she abandons him to search for his father, the Mexican people have not forgiven La Malinche for her betrayal. She embodies the open, the *chingado,* to our closed, stoic, impassive Indians. Cuauhtémoc and Doña Marina are thus two antagonistic and complementary figures. There is nothing surprising about our cult of the young emperor — "the only hero at the summit of art," an image of the sacrificed son — and there is also nothing surprising about the curse that weighs against La Malinche. This explains the success of the contemptuous adjective *malinchista* recently put into circulation by the newspapers to denounce all those who have been corrupted by foreign influences. The *malinchistas* are those who want Mexico to open itself to the outside world: the true sons of La Malinche, who is the *Chingada* in person. Once again we see the opposition of the closed and the open.

When we shout "*¡Viva México, hijos de la chingada!*" we express our desire to live closed off from the outside world and, above all, from the past. In this shout we condemn our origins

---

⁴ The name given to La Malinche by the Spaniards. — *Tr.*

and deny our hybridism. The strange permanence of Cortés and La Malinche in the Mexican's imagination and sensibilities reveals that they are something more than historical figures: they are symbols of a secret conflict that we have still not resolved. When he repudiates La Malinche — the Mexican Eve, as she was represented by José Clemente Orozco in his mural in the National Preparatory School — the Mexican breaks his ties with the past, renounces his origins, and lives in isolation and solitude.

The Mexican condemns all his traditions at once, the whole set of gestures, attitudes and tendencies in which it is now difficult to distinguish the Spanish from the Indian. For that reason the Hispanic thesis, which would have us descend from Cortés to the exclusion of La Malinche, is the patrimony of a few extremists who are not even pure whites. The same can be said of indigenist propaganda, which is also supported by fanatical *criollos* and *mestizos*, while the Indians have never paid it the slightest attention. The Mexican does not want to be either an Indian or a Spaniard. Nor does he want to be descended from them. He denies them. And he does not affirm himself as a mixture, but rather as an abstraction: he is a man. He becomes the son of Nothingness. His beginnings are in his own self.

This attitude is revealed not only in our daily life but also in the course of our history, which at certain moments has been the embodiment of a will to eradicate all that has gone before. It is astonishing that a country with such a vivid past — a country so profoundly traditional, so close to its roots, so rich in ancient legends even if poor in modern history — should conceive of itself only as a negation of its origins.

Our shout strips us naked and discloses the wound that we alternately flaunt and conceal, but it does not show us the causes of this separation from, and negation of, the Mother, not even when we recognize that such a rupture has occurred. In lieu of a closer examination of the problem, we will suggest that the liberal Reform movement of the middle of the last century seems to be the moment when the Mexican decided to break with his traditions, which is a form of breaking with oneself. If our Independence movement cut the ties that bound us to Spain, the Reform movement denied that the Mexican nation as a historical project should perpetuate the colonial tradition. Juárez and his generation founded a state whose ideals are distinct from those that animated New Spain or the pre-Cortesian cultures. The Mexican state proclaimed an abstract and universal conception of man: the Republic is not composed of *criollos,* Indians and *mestizos* (as the Laws of the Indies, with a great love for distinctions and a great respect for the heterogeneous nature of the colonial world, had specified) but simply of men alone. All alone.

The Reform movement is the great rupture with the Mother. This separation was a necessary and inevitable act, because every life that is truly autonomous begins as a break with its family and its past. But the separation still hurts. We still suffer from that wound. That is why the feeling of orphanhood is the constant background of our political endeavors and our personal conflicts. Mexico is all alone, like each one of her sons.

The Mexican and his Mexicanism must be defined as separation and negation. And, at the same time, as a search, a desire to transcend this state of exile. In sum, as a vivid awareness of solitude, both historical and personal. History, which could not tell us anything about the nature of our feelings and conflicts, can now show us how that break came about and how we have attempted to transcend our solitude.

CHAPTER FIVE

The Conquest and Colonialism

Any contact with the Mexican people, however brief, reveals that the ancient beliefs and customs are still in existence beneath Western forms. These still-living remains testify to the vitality of the pre-Cortesian cultures. And after the discoveries of archaeologists and historians it is no longer possible to refer to those societies as savage or primitive tribes. Over and above the fascination or horror they inspire in us, we must admit that when the Spaniards arrived in Mexico they found complete and refined civilizations.

Mesoamerica — that is, the nucleus of what was later to be New Spain — was a territory that included the central and southern parts of present-day Mexico and a portion of Central America. To the north, the Chichimecas wandered among the deserts and uncultivated plains. (Chichimeca is a generic term, without national distinctions, that was applied to the barbarians by the inhabitants of the Central Plateau.) The frontiers between were unstable, like those of ancient Rome, and the last centuries of Mesoamerican history can be summed up as the history of repeated encounters between waves of northern hunters — almost all of them belonging to the Náhuatl family — and the settled populations. The Aztecs were the last to enter the Valley of Mexico. The previous work of erosion by their predecessors, and the wasting away of the intimate springs of the ancient local cultures, made it possible for them to accomplish the extraordinary task of founding what Arnold Toynbee calls a Universal Empire, based on the remains of older societies.

According to Toynbee, the Spaniards did nothing except act as substitutes, resolving through political synthesis the tendency toward dispersal that threatened the Mesoamerican world.

When we consider what Mexico was like at the arrival of Cortés, we are surprised at the large number of cities and cultures, in contrast to the relative homogeneity of their most characteristic traits. The diversity of the indigenous nuclei and the rivalries that lacerated them indicate that Mesoamerica was made up of a complex of autonomous peoples, nations and cultures, each with its own traditions, exactly as in the Mediterranean and other cultural areas. Mesoamerica was a historical world in itself.

In addition, the cultural homogeneity of these centers shows that the primitive individuality of each culture had been replaced, perhaps within a fairly recent period, by uniform religious and political structures. The mother cultures in the central and southern areas had in fact been extinguished several centuries before. Their successors had combined and re-created all that variety of local expression, and the work of synthesis had culminated in the erection of a model which, with slight differences, was the same for all.

Although historical analogies deserved the discredit they have suffered, it is almost impossible not to compare the Mesoamerican world at the beginning of the sixteenth century with the Hellenic world at the moment when Rome began its career of universal domination. The existence of several great states, and the survival of a great number of independent cities, especially in continental Greece and the islands, underscores rather than negates the prevailing cultural uniformity. The Seleucids, the Ptolemies, the Macedonians and many small and ephemeral states were not distinctive because of the diversity and originality of their respective societies, but rather because of the quarrels that fatally divided them. The same can be said of the Mesoamerican societies. In both worlds, differing traditions and cultural heritages mixed together and at last became one. This cultural heterogeneity contrasts strongly with the perpetual quarrels that divided them.

In the Hellenic world this uniformity was achieved by the predominance of Greek culture, which absorbed the Oriental cultures. It is difficult to determine the element that unified our indigenous societies. One hypothesis, valuable mainly as a theme for reflection, suggests that the role played by Greek culture in the ancient world was fulfilled in Mesoamerica by the great culture that flourished in Tula and Teotihuacán and that has inaccurately been called "Toltec." The influence of the cultures of the Central Plateau on those of the south, especially in the area occupied by the so-called Second Mayan Empire, justifies this idea. It is noteworthy that no Mayan influence has been found in the remains of Teotihuacán, whereas Chichén-Itzá was a "Toltec" city. Everything seems to indicate that at a certain time the cultural forms of central Mexico spread out and became predominant.

Mesoamerica has been described very generally as a uniform historical area characterized by the constant presence of certain elements common to all its cultures: an agriculture based on maize, a ritual calendar, a ritual ball-game, human sacrifices, solar and vegetation myths, etc. It is said that all of these elements originated in the south and were assimilated at various times by the immigrants from the north. If this were true, Mesoamerican culture would be the result of various southern creations that were adopted, developed and systematized by nomadic groups. But this scheme neglects the originality of each local culture. The resemblances among the religious, political and mythical conceptions of the Indo-European peoples, for instance, do not deny the originality of each one of them. But, apart from the particular originality of each culture, it is evident that all of them, because of decadence or debilitation, were on the point of being absorbed into the Aztec Empire, which was heir to the civilizations of the Central Plateau.

Those societies were impregnated with religion. The Aztec state was both military and theocratic. Therefore, political unification was preceded or completed by religious unification, or corresponded to it in one way or another. Each pre-Cortesian city worshiped gods who steadily became more alike: their names were different but the ceremonies honoring them were similar. The agrarian deities — the gods of the earth, of vegetation and fertility, like Tláloc — and the Nordic gods — celestial warriors like Tezcatlipoca, Huitzilopochtli and Mixcóatl — belonged to a single cult. The most outstanding characteristic of Aztec religion at the time of the Conquest was the incessant theological speculation that reformed, systematized and unified diverse beliefs, both its own and others. This synthesis was not the result of a popular religious movement like the proletarian religions that existed in the ancient world at the beginning of Christianity. It was the work of a caste located at the apex of the social pyramid. The systematizations, adaptations and reforms undertaken by the priestly caste show that the process was one of superimposition, which was also characteristic of religious architecture. Just as an Aztec pyramid often covers an older structure, so this theological unification affected only the surface of the Aztec consciousness, leaving the primitive beliefs intact. The situation prefigured the introduction of Catholicism, which is also a religion superimposed upon an original and still-living religious base. Everything was prepared for Spanish domination.

The conquest of Mexico would be inexplicable without these

antecedents. The arrival of the Spaniards seemed a liberation to the people under Aztec rule. The various city-states allied themselves with the conquistadors or watched with indifference — if not with pleasure — the fall of each of their rivals, especially that of the most powerful, Tenochtitlán. But the political genius of Cortés, the superior techniques of the Spaniards (lacking in such decisive actions as the battle of Otumba), and the defection of vassals and allies, could not have brought about the ruin of the Aztec Empire if it had not suddenly felt a sense of weakness, an intimate doubt that caused it to vacillate and surrender. When Moctezuma opened the gates of Tenochtitlán to the Spaniards and welcomed Cortés with gifts, the Aztecs lost the encounter. Their final struggle was a form of suicide, as we can gather from all the existing accounts of that grandiose and astounding event.

Why did Moctezuma give up? Why was he so fascinated by the Spaniards that he experienced a vertigo which it is no exaggeration to call sacred — the lucid vertigo of the suicide on the brink of the abyss? The gods had abandoned him. The great betrayal with which the history of Mexico begins was not committed by the Tlaxcaltecas or by Moctezuma and his group: it was committed by the gods. No other people have ever felt so completely helpless as the Aztec nation felt at the appearance of the omens, prophecies and warnings that announced its fall. We are unlikely to understand the meaning of these signs and predictions for the Indians if we forget their cyclical conception of time. As with many other peoples and civilizations, time was not an empty, abstract measurement to the Aztecs, but rather something concrete, a force or substance or fluid perpetually being used up. Hence the necessity of rites and sacrifices to reinvigorate the year or the century. But time — or, more precisely, each period of time — was not only something living that

was born, grew up, decayed and was reborn. It was also a succession that returned: one period of time ended and another
came back. The arrival of the Spaniards was interpreted by
Moctezuma, at least at the beginning, not so much as a threat
from outside than as the internal conclusion of one cosmic period
and the commencement of another. The gods departed because
their period of time was at an end, but another period returned
and with it, other gods and another era.

This divine desertion becomes even more pathetic when we
consider the youth and vigor of the nascent Aztec state. All of
the ancient empires, such as Rome and Byzantium, felt the
seduction of death at the close of their long histories. The people
merely shrugged their shoulders when the final blow was struck.
There is such a thing as imperial fatigue, and servitude seems
a light burden after the exhausting weight of power. But the
Aztecs experienced the chill of death in their youth, while they
were still approaching maturity. The Conquest of Mexico is a
historical event made up of many very different circumstances,
but what seems to me the most significant — the suicide of the
Aztec people — is often forgotten. We should remember that
fascination with death is not so much a trait of maturity or old
age as it is of youth. Noon and midnight are the hours of ritual
suicide. At noonday everything stops for a moment, vacillating;
life, like the sun, asks itself whether it is worth the effort to go
on. At this moment of immobility, which is also the moment of
vertigo, the Aztec people raise their eyes toward the heavens:
the celestial omens are adverse, and the people feel the attraction of death.

> *Je pense, sur le bord doré de l'univers*
> *A ce goût de périr qui prend la Pythanise*
> *En qui mugit l'espoir que le monde finisse.*

One part of the Aztec people lost heart and sought out the invader. The other, betrayed on all sides and without hope of salvation, chose death. The mere presence of the Spaniards caused a split in Aztec society, a split corresponding to the dualism of their gods, their religious system and their higher castes.

Aztec religion, like that of all conquering people, was a solar religion. The Aztecs concentrated all their aspirations and warlike aims in the sun, the god who is the source of life, the bird-god who breaks through the mists and establishes himself in the center of the sky like a conquering army in the center of a battlefield. But the gods were not mere representations of nature. They also embodied the will and desire of society, which made itself divine in them. Jacques Soustelle has written that Huitzilopochtli, the warrior of the south, "is the tribal god of war and sacrifice . . . and his career begins with a massacre. Quetzalcóatl-Nanauatzin is the sun-god of the priests, who consider voluntary self-sacrifice the highest expression of their doctrine of life and the world: Quetzalcóatl is a priest-king who respects ritual and the decrees of destiny, refusing to fight and dying in order to be reborn. Huitzilopochtli, on the contrary, is the sun-hero of the warriors, defending himself and triumphing in battle: he is the *invictus sol* who destroys his enemies with the flames of his *xiucóatl*.[1] Each of these divine personalities corresponds to the ideal of some important segment of the ruling class."[2]

The duality of Aztec religion, reflected in its theocratic-military division and its social system, corresponds to the contradic-

---

[1] The war-god and sun-god Huitzilopochtli was also a fire-god; in this latter role he wore the mask of the ancient fire-god Xiuhtecuhtli. The mask was called "xiucóatl" or "xiuhcóatl" ("fire-serpent"). — *Tr.*

[2] Jacques Soustelle: *La pensée cosmologique des anciens mexicains* (Paris: 1940).

tory impulses that motivate all human beings and groups. The death-wish and the will-to-live conflict in each one of us. These profound tendencies impregnate the activities of all classes, castes and individuals, and in critical moments they reveal themselves in complete nakedness. The victory of the death-wish shows that the Aztecs suddenly lost sight of their destiny. Cuauhtémoc fought in the knowledge that he would be defeated. The tragic nature of his struggle lies in this bold and intimate acceptance of defeat. The drama of a consciousness that sees everything around it destroyed — even the gods — appears to preside over our whole history. Cuauhtémoc and his people died alone, abandoned by their friends, their allies, their vassals and their gods. They died as orphans.

The fall of Aztec society precipitated that of the rest of the Indian world. All the nations that composed it were overwhelmed by the same horror, which almost always expressed itself as a fascinated acceptance of death. Few documents are as impressive as the remaining handful that describe this catastrophe. Here is an expression of the suffering of the Mayas, as recorded in the *Chilam Balam de Chumayel:* "II Ahan Katun: the blond-bearded strangers arrived, the sons of the sun, the pale-colored men. Ah, how sad we were when they arrived! . . . The white man's stick will fall, will descend from on high, will strike everywhere. . . . The words of Hunab-Ku, our one god, will be words of sorrow when the words of the God of Heaven spread out over the earth. . . ." And later: "The hangings will begin, and lightning will flash from the white man's hands. . . . The hardships of battle will fall upon the Brothers, and tribute will be demanded after the grand entrance of Christianity, and the Seven Sacraments will be established, and travail and misery will rule this land."

The character of the Conquest is equally complex from the point of view expressed in the various accounts by the Spaniards. Everything is contradictory. Like the reconquest of Spain, it was both a private undertaking and a national accomplishment. Cortés and the Cid fought on their own responsibility and against the will of their superiors, but in the name of — and on behalf of — the king. They were vassals, rebels and crusaders. Opposing concepts fought within their own minds and those of their soldiers: the interests of the Monarchy and of individuals, the interests of the Faith and of personal greed for gold. Each conquistador and missionary and bureaucrat was a field of battle. Considered separately, each one represented the great powers that struggled for the control of society — feudalism, the Church and absolute Monarchy — but other tendencies struggled within them. These were the same tendencies that distinguished Spain from the rest of Europe and made her, in the literal sense of the word, an eccentric nation.

Spain was the defender of the Faith and her soldiers were soldiers of Christ. This circumstance did not prevent the Emperor and his successors from carrying on such heated disputes with the Papacy that the Council of Trent could not completely settle them. Spain was still a medieval nation, and many of the institutions she brought to the New World, like many of the men who established them, were also medieval. At the same time, the discovery and conquest of America was a Renaissance undertaking. Therefore Spain also participated in the Renaissance, although it is sometimes thought that her overseas conquests — the result of Renaissance science and technology, even Renaissance dreams and utopias — did not form a part of that historical movement.

On the other hand, the conquistadors were not merely repetitions of the medieval warriors who fought the Moors and infidels. They were adventurers, that is, men who opened up new lands and risked the unknown. This was another Renaissance characteristic. The medieval knight, on the contrary, lived in a closed world. His great undertaking was the Crusades, a historical episode very different from the conquest of America. The former was a winning back; the latter, a discovery and a founding. Also, many of the conquistadors — Cortés, for example, or Jiménez de Quesada — are unimaginable in the Middle Ages. Their literary tastes as well as their political realism, their awareness of the work they were doing as well as what Ortega y Gasset would call their "style of life," have small resemblance to the medieval sensibility.

If Spain renounced the future and closed herself off from the West at the moment of the Counter Reformation, she did not do so without first adopting almost all the artistic forms of the Renaissance: poetry, the novel, painting and architecture. These forms, along with certain philosophical and political ideas, all permeated with Spanish traditions of a medieval nature, were transplanted to our continent. It is significant that the most vital part of the Spanish heritage in America is made up of those universal elements that Spain assimilated during a period when her history was likewise universal. The absence of castes, traditionalism and Hispanism (in the medieval sense that has been given to the word: crust and husk of the Castilian caste[3]) is a permanent trait of Spanish-American culture, which is always open to the outside world and has a longing for universality. Juan Ruiz de Alarcón, Sor Juana Inés de la Cruz, Darío and Bello were none of them traditional, pure-bred spirits. The Spanish tradition that we Spanish-Americans inherited is one that in Spain itself has been looked on with suspicion or con-

---

[3]"Costra y cáscara de la casta Castilla."

tempt: that of heterodoxy, open to French or Italian influences. Our culture, like a certain portion of Spanish culture, is a free election by a few free spirits. Therefore, as Jorge Cuesta pointed out, it is a form of liberty contrasting with the passive traditionalism of our people. It is sometimes superimposed on or indifferent to the reality that sustains it. Its greatness results from this characteristic, but so does its occasional vacuity or impotence. The flowering of our lyricism — which is by nature a dialogue between the poet and the world — and the relative poverty of our epic and dramatic forms, reside perhaps in this alien, unreal aspect of our tradition.

The disparity of elements that can be observed in the Conquest does not obscure its clear historical unity. They all reflect the nature of the Spanish state, whose most notable characteristic was the fact that it was an artificial creation, a political construction in the strictest sense of the word. The Spanish monarchy was born from violence, the violence which the Catholic kings inflicted on the diversity of peoples and nations under their rule. Spanish unity was and still is the result of the political will of the state, which ignored the will of the elements that made it up. (Spanish Catholicism has always expressed the same will; hence, perhaps, its belligerent, authoritarian, inquisitorial tone.) The speed with which the Spanish state assimilated and organized the conquests made by many individuals demonstrates that a single will, pursued with a certain coherent inflexibility, animated both the European and overseas undertakings. In a brief time the Spanish colonies achieved a complexity and perfection that contrast sharply with the slow development of those founded by other countries. The previous existence of mature and stable societies undoubtedly facilitated the task of the Spaniards, but the Spanish will to create a world in its own image was also evident. In 1604, less than a century after the fall of Tenochtitlán, Balbuena told the world of the *Grandeza Mexicana.*

The Conquest, then, whether considered from the native or the Spanish point of view, must be judged as an expression of a will to unity. Despite the contradictions that make it up, it was a historical act intended to create unity out of the cultural and political plurality of the pre-Cortesian world. The Spaniards postulated a single language, a single faith and a single lord against the variety of races, languages, tendencies and states of the pre-Hispanic world. If Mexico was born in the sixteenth century, we must agree that it was the child of a double violence, imperial and unifying: that of the Aztecs and that of the Spaniards.

The empire that Cortés founded on the remains of the old aboriginal cultures was a subsidiary organism, a satellite of the Spanish sun. The fate of the Indians could have been that of so many peoples who have seen their national culture humiliated but have not seen the new order — a mere tyrannous superimposition — open its doors to the participation of the conquered. The state founded by the Spaniards was an open order, however, and deserves a sustained examination, as do the modes of participation by the conquered in the central activity of the new society, that is, in religion. The history of Mexico, and even that of each Mexican, derives precisely from this situation. Therefore a study of the colonial order is indispensable. By determining the salient features of colonial religion, whether in its popular manifestations or in those of its most representative spirits, we can discover the meaning of our culture and the origins of many of our later conflicts.

The rapidity with which the Spanish state recreated its new possessions in the image and likeness of the metropolis — despite the ambitions of its military commanders, the infidelities of its judges, and rivalries of every kind — is as amazing as the solidity of the social edifice it constructed. Colonial society was an order built to endure. That is, it was a society designed in conformance with judicial, economic and religious principles that were fully coherent among themselves and that established a vital and harmonious relationship between the parts and the whole. It was a self-sufficient world, closed to the exterior but open to the other world.

It is very easy to laugh at the religious pretensions of colonial society. It is still easier to denounce them as empty forms intended to cover up the abuses of the conquistadors or to justify them to themselves and their victims. To a certain extent this accusation is true, but it is no less true that these other-worldly aspirations were more than a simple addition: they were part of a living faith which, like the roots of a tree, sustained other cultural and economic forms. Catholicism was the center of colonial society because it was the true fountain of life, nourishing the activities, the passions, the virtues and even the sins of both lords and servants, functionaries and priests, merchants and soldiers. Thanks to religion the colonial order was not a mere superimposition of new historical forms but a living organism. The Church used the key of baptism to open the doors of society, converting it into a universal order open to everyone. And when I speak of the Catholic Church I am not referring only to the apostolic labors of the missionaries but to the Church as a whole, with its saints, its rapacious prelates, its pedantic ecclesiastics, its impassioned jurists, its works of charity and its accumulation of riches.

It is quite clear that the reason the Spaniards did not exterminate the Indians was that they needed their labor for the cultivation of the vast haciendas and the exploitation of the mines. The Indians were goods that should not be wasted. It is difficult to realize that along with this consideration there were others of a humanitarian nature. Anyone who knows the treatment of the Indians by the military will laugh at this hypothesis, but the fate of the Indians would have been very different if it had not been for the Church. I am not thinking only of its struggle to improve their living conditions and to organize them in a more just and Christian manner, but also of the opportunity that baptism offered them to form a part of one social order and one religion. This possibility of belonging to a living order, even if it was at the bottom of the social pyramid, was cruelly denied to the Indians by the Protestants of New England. It is often forgotten that to belong to the Catholic faith meant that one found a place in the cosmos. The flight of their gods and the death of their leaders had left the natives in a solitude so complete that it is difficult for a modern man to imagine it. Catholicism re-established their ties with the world and the other world. It gave them back a sense of their place on earth; it nurtured their hopes and justified their lives and deaths.

It is unnecessary to add that the religion of the Indians was a mixture of new and ancient beliefs. It could not have been otherwise, because Catholicism was an imposed religion. From another point of view, this circumstance was of the very highest importance, but it lacked any immediate interest for the new believers. The important thing was that their social, human and religious relationships with the surrounding world and with the divine had been re-established. Their personal existence became part of a greater order. It was not out of simple devotion or servility that the Indians called the missionaries *tatas* (dads) and the Virgin of Guadalupe *madre* (mother).

The difference between colonial Mexico and the English colonies was immense. New Spain committed many horrors, but at least it did not commit the gravest of all: that of denying a place, even at the foot of the social scale, to the people who composed it. There were classes, castes and slaves, but there were no pariahs, no persons lacking a fixed social condition and a legal, moral and religious status. Its difference from the world of modern totalitarian societies was equally decisive.

It is true that New Spain, as a satellite society, did not create any original forms of art, thought, myth or government. (The only truly original creations of America — and of course I do not exclude the United States — were pre-Columbian.) It is also true that the technical superiority of the colonial world, and the introduction of richer and more complex cultural forms than those of the Mesoamericans, are not enough to justify an epoch. But the creation of a universal order, which was the most extraordinary accomplishment of colonialism, does justify that society and redeems it from its limitations. Colonial poetry, Baroque art, the Laws of the Indies, the chroniclers, historians and philosophers, and, above all, neo-Hispanic architecture — in which all things, even fantastic fruits and profane dreams, were harmonized within an order as rigorous as it was ample — are reflections of the equilibrium of a society in which all men and all races found a place, a justification and a meaning. That society was shaped by a Christian order no different from that which we can see in temples and in poems.

I am not attempting to justify colonial society. In the strictest sense, no society can be justified while one or another form of oppression subsists in it. I want to understand it as a living and therefore contradictory whole. In the same way, I refuse to regard the human sacrifices of the Aztecs as an isolated expression of cruelty without relation to the rest of that civilization. Their tearing-out of hearts and their monumental pyramids, their sculpture and their ritual cannibalism, their poetry and their "war of flowers," their theocracy and their great myths, are all an indissoluble one. To deny this would be as infantile as to deny Gothic art or Provençal poetry in the name of the medieval serfs, or to deny Aeschylus because there were slaves in Athens. History has the cruel reality of a nightmare, and the grandeur of man consists in his making beautiful and lasting works out of the real substance of that nightmare. Or, to put it another way, it consists in transforming the nightmare into vision; in freeing ourselves from the shapeless horror of reality — if only for an instant — by means of creation.

Over the centuries Spain digested and perfected the ideas that existence had given her. Intellectual activity did not cease to be creative, but only in the realm of art and within known limits. Criticism, which in those centuries and in other regions was the highest form of creation, hardly existed in this closed and satisfied world. True, there were satire, theological disputes, and a constant effort to extend, strengthen and perfect the edifice that lodged so many and such different peoples. But the principles that ruled society were immutable and untouchable. Spain no longer invented or discovered: she extended her rule, defended herself, enjoyed herself. She did not want to change; what she wanted was to endure. The same thing took place in her overseas possessions. After the first epoch of storms and disturbances, the Spanish colonies still suffered periodic crises like that which troubled Sigüenza y Góngora and Sor Juana, but none of them touched the roots of the regime or brought into judgment the principles on which it was founded.

The colonial world was a projection of a society that had already grown mature and stable in Europe. It showed almost no originality whatever. New Spain did not seek or invent: it applied and adapted. All its creations, including its own self, were reflections of Spain. And the ease with which the Hispanic forms gradually admitted the modifications demanded by neo-Hispanic realities does not negate the conservative character of the colonial world. Traditional societies, as Ortega y Gasset has said, are realistic; they distrust sudden leaps and change slowly, accepting the suggestions of reality. The "grandeur of Mexico" was that of an immobile sun, a premature noonday that no longer had anything to conquer except its own decay.

Religious speculation had ended centuries before. Doctrine had been established and an attempt was made to live up to it. The Church in Europe became stationary and defensive. Scholasticism, its main defense, was as ineffective as the ponderous Spanish ships that were defeated by the lighter vessels of England and the Netherlands. The decadence of European Catholicism coincided with its apogee in Spanish America: it spread out over new lands at the very moment it had ceased to be creative. It offered a set philosophy and a petrified faith, so that the originality of the new believers found no way of expressing itself. Their adherence to it was passive. The fervor and profundity of Mexican religious feeling contrasts with the relative poverty of its creations. We do not have a great religious poetry, just as we do not have an original philosophy nor a single important mystic or reformer.

This paradoxical but real situation explains a good-part of our history and is the origin of many of our psychic conflicts. Catholicism offered a refuge to the descendants of those who had seen the extermination of their ruling classes, the destruction of their temples and manuscripts, and the suppression of the superior forms of their culture; but for the same reason that it was decadent in Europe, it denied them any chance of expressing their singularity. It reduced the participation of the faithful to the most elementary and passive religious attitudes.

Very few could gain a larger understanding of their new beliefs, and the immobility of these beliefs, like that of the rust-clogged scholastic machinery, made any creative participation still more difficult. Thus they were a people with an impoverished cultural tradition (the repositories of religious and magical knowledge — the priests and warriors — had been exterminated or Hispanicized). Religious creativity was forbidden to the believers as a consequence of the circumstances that determined their participation. Hence the comparative sterility of colonial Catholicism, especially if we remember its fertility among the barbarians and Romans, who were Christianized at a moment when religion was the only living force in the ancient world. It is not difficult to understand, therefore, that our antitraditional attitude and the ambiguity of our position relative to Catholicism derive from this fact. Religion and tradition have always been offered to us as dead and useless forms that mutilate or stifle our individuality.

Under these conditions, the persistence of the pre-Cortesian background is not surprising. The Mexican is a religious being and his experience of the divine is completely genuine. But who is his god? The ancient earth-gods or Christ? This question is answered very clearly by an invocation of the Chamulas (from *Juan Pérez Jolote* by Ricardo Pozas A.). It is a true prayer despite the presence of certain magical elements.

Holy Earth, holy Heaven; Lord God, God the Son, Holy Earth, holy Heaven, holy Glory, take charge of me and represent me; see my work, see my struggles, see my sufferings. Great Man, great Lord, great father, great spirit of woman, help me. I place the tribute in your hands; here is the resting-place of his *chulel*.[*] In

---

[*]The Chamulas believe that each human being has two souls; one, the *chulel*, dwells within an animal (the name "Jolote" is a version of the word *guajolote*, which means "turkey"), while the other dwells within the body. — *Tr.*

return for my incense and my candles, spirit of the Moon, virgin mother of Heaven, virgin mother of the Earth; Holy Rose, for your first son, for your first glory, see your child oppressed in his spirit, in his *chulel.*

In many instances Catholicism only covers over the ancient cosmogonic beliefs. Here is the same Juan Pérez Jolote — our contemporary according to the Civil Registry, but our ancestor if we consider his beliefs — describing the image of Christ in a church in his village and explaining what it means to him and his people:

> This is Señor San Manuel here in this coffin; he is also called Señor San Salvador or Señor San Mateo; he watches over the people and the animals. We pray to him to watch over us at home, on the road, in the fields. This other figure on the cross is also Señor San Mateo; he is showing us how he died on the cross, to teach us respect. . . . Before San Manuel was born, the sun was as cold as the moon, and the *pukujes*,[5] who ate people, lived on the earth. The sun began to grow warm after the birth of the Child-God, Señor San Salvador, who is the son of the Virgin.

In this account we can see both the superimposed religion and the ineradicable presence of the indigenous myths. Before the birth of Christ, the sun — the eye of God — did not give warmth. The sun is an attribute of divinity. Therefore the Chamula says that thanks to the presence of God, nature becomes active. Is this not a badly deformed version of the beautiful myth of creation? In Teotihuacán the gods also confronted the problem of the sun as the source of life. Only the sacrifice of Quetzalcóatl could set the sun in motion and save the world from the divine conflagration. The persistence of the pre-Cortesian myth underlines the difference between the Christian

------

[5] A *pukuj* is the *chulel* of a warlock. — *Tr.*

and indigenous conceptions. Christ saved the world because He redeemed us and washed away the stain of Original Sin, but Quetzalcóatl was not so much a redeemer as a re-creator. Among the Indians the idea of sin is still bound to the idea of health and sickness, personal, social and cosmic. The Christian attempts to save the individual soul, disconnected from the group and the body. Christianity condemns the world, while the Indian conceives of personal salvation only as a part of the salvation of society and the cosmos.

Nothing has been able to destroy the filial relationship of our people with the divine. It is a constant force that gives permanence to our nation and depth to the affective life of the dispossessed. But at the same time, nothing has succeeded in making this relationship more active and fecund, not even the Mexicanization of Catholicism, not even the Virgin of Guadalupe herself. Consequently the greater spirits have not hesitated to detach themselves from the body of the Church and to go out into the storm. There, in the solitude and nakedness of spiritual combat, they have breathed a little of that "religious fresh air" which Jorge Cuesta demanded.

The epoch of Charles II (1665-1700) was one of the saddest and emptiest in the history of Spain. All of its spiritual reserves had been devoured by the flames of a dynamic life and art full of antitheses and extremes. The decadence of Spanish culture on the Peninsula coincided with its noonday in America. Baroque art reached the moment of its fulfillment in this period. The great spirits did more than write poetry. They were interested in astronomy, physics or American antiquities. They were awakened intellects in a society that had been immobilized by the letter of the law. They were forerunners of other epochs and other preoccupations, while at the same time they carried the aesthetic tendencies of the period to their ultimate consequences. In all of them we can trace a certain opposition between their religious concepts and the exigencies of their intellectual curiosity and precision. Some of them attempted an impossible synthesis. Sor Juana, for example, undertook the composition of her poem "First Dream," in an attempt to reconcile science and poetry, illuminism and the Baroque.

It would be inaccurate to identify the drama of this generation with that which troubled their European contemporaries and which was made patent by the eighteenth century. The conflict within them — and it ended by reducing them to silence — was not so much that of faith against reason as of the petrifaction of certain beliefs which had lost all their freshness and fertility and were therefore incapable of satisfying the appetites of the spirit. Edmundo O'Gorman describes the terms of the conflict thus: "An intermediate state in which reason lays waste to tranquillity and in which the consolations of religion are no longer enough."[6] But the consolations of the faith were not enough because it was a dry and immobile faith. The critique of reason would come later in America. O'Gorman defines the nature of the break as follows: "To have faith in God and reason at the same time is to live with one's being rooted (or, if you prefer, uprooted) in possibility, in a real, unique, extreme and contradictory possibility made up of two impossible possibles of human existence." This penetrating description is valid if we diminish the poles of these impossible possibilities. We cannot deny the authenticity of the religious sentiments of that generation, but at the same time we cannot overlook its immobility and exhaustion. In so far as the other pole of the break

---

[6] Edmundo O'Gorman: *Crisis y porvenir de la ciencia histórica* (Mexico, 1947).

is concerned, the rationalism of Sigüenza or Sor Juana should not be exaggerated, because they never had a clear awareness of the problem that was beginning to divide their spirits. It seems to me that the struggle was between their intellectual vitality — especially their desire to explore little-known worlds — and the inefficacy of the instruments provided them by theology and neo-Hispanic culture. This conflict reveals the conflict of colonial society, which also did not doubt but which could not express itself in petrified forms. The colonial order was imposed from above and its social, economic, judicial and religious forms were immutable. It was a society ruled by divine right and an absolute monarchy, having been created in all its aspects as an immense, complicated artifact designed to endure but not to change. In the epoch of Sor Juana the better minds began to show — however vaguely and timidly — an intellectual liveliness and curiosity in obvious contrast to the benighted Spain of Charles II (whose nickname, significantly, was "The Bewitched"). Sigüenza y Góngora took an interest in the ancient Indian civilizations and, with Sor Juana and others, in the philosophy of Descartes, experimental physics and astronomy. The Church looked with suspicion on all these interests, while the state, for its part, increased the political, economic and spiritual isolation of the colonies until it converted them into closed precincts. There were disturbances in rural areas and in the cities but they were implacably suppressed. In this closed world the generation of Sor Juana asked certain questions — they were more suggested than formulated, more sensed than thought out — to which its spiritual tradition made no reply. (The answers had already been given elsewhere, in the free air of European culture.) This explains, perhaps, why none of them, despite their daring, undertook to criticize the principles on which colonial society was founded, nor to propose others. When the crisis became apparent, that generation abdicated. Its ambitious struggle ceased and its renunciation, which had nothing to do with a religious conversion, took place in silence. It did not surrender itself to God: it simply denied itself. Its negation was that of the colonial world, which closed itself within itself. There was no exit except by a forcible break-out.

No one embodied the duality of that world like Sor Juana, even though the surface of her work, like that of her life, does not reveal any fissures. All of her being responded to what the times could ask of a woman. At one and the same time — and with no profound contradictions — she was a poet and a nun, a friend of the Countess de Paredes and a dramatist. Her amorous ecstasies (if they were real and not merely inflamed rhetorical inventions), her love of conversation and music, her literary efforts, and even the sexual tendencies that some have attributed to her, were not in conflict as they sought their exemplary ends. Sor Juana affirmed her times, and her times affirmed themselves in her. But two of her works, the "Reply to Sor Filotea" and the "First Dream," cast a strange light on her figure and her epoch, and they make her an example in a sense very different from that which her Catholic panegyrists imagine.

The "First Dream" has been compared to the "Solitudes" of Góngora. In effect, the poem by Sor Juana is an imitation of that by Don Luis de Góngora, but the differences are greater than the resemblances. Menéndez y Pelayo reproached Góngora for his emptiness. If we substitute the word "superficiality" we are closer to Góngora's poetic conception, for he was simply attempting to construct — or, as Bernardo de Balbuena said, to "counterfeit" — a world of appearances. The plot of the "Solitudes" counts for little, and the philosophical content, if it exists, counts for even less. Everything is a pretext for descriptions and digressions, and each dissolves in turn into images, antitheses and rhetorical figures. If anything moves in the poem, it is not the castaway or his thoughts but the imagination of the poet. As he said himself in the prologue, his verses are the "wandering steps of a pilgrim." And this pilgrim's song, this singing pilgrim, halts at a word or color, fondles it and prolongs it, and makes of each period an image, of each image a world. The poetic discourse flows slowly along, divides into "leafy parentheses" that are like beautiful islands, and continues to meander among landscapes, shadows, lights and realities, all of which it redeems and immobilizes. The poem is pure pleasure, an artificial re-creation of an idealized Nature, as Dámaso Alonso has pointed out. Hence there is no conflict between substance and form because Góngora turns everything into form, into a crystalline or tremulous, polished or undulating surface.

Sor Juana utilized Góngora's procedures, but she undertook a philosophical poem. She wanted to penetrate reality, not to transmute it into a delightful surface. Her poem is doubly obscure: in its syntax and mythologies and in its concepts. Alfonso Reyes has said that the poem is an attempt to create "a poetry of pure intellectual emotion." The vision offered us in "First Dream" is that of a dream of universal night in which the world and mankind dream and are dreamt of, a cosmos that dreams until it dreams it is awake. Nothing could be further from the physical and spiritual night of the mystics than this intellectual night. Sor Juana's poem has no antecedents in the poetry of the Spanish language; as Vossler suggests, it prefigures the poetic movement in Germany called "Illustration." But "First Dream" is an attempt rather than an attainment, in contrast to the "Solitudes" (even though their author never finished them). It could not have been otherwise, for there was a neutral zone, an empty place, both in her poem and in her life. It produced the clash of opposing tendencies that she could not reconcile and that eventually consumed her.

Sor Juana has left us a revealing prose text, at once a declaration of faith in the intelligence and a renunciation of its exercise: the "Reply to Sor Filotea."[7] It is a defense of the intellectual and of women, but it is also the history of a calling. If we can place confidence in her confessions, there was hardly a science that she did not study. Her curiosity was not that of a man of science but rather of a cultivated man who aspires to integrate all the particulars of knowledge in one coherent vision. She sensed an occult link among all truths. Referring to the diversity of her studies, she said that their contradictions were more apparent than real, "at least in the realm of the formal and the speclative." The arts and sciences, however contrary they may be, not only do not hinder a general comprehension of Nature but actually assist it, "shedding light and opening avenues from one to the other, through variations and occult ties . . . in such a manner that they seem to correspond and to be united in a wonderful coalescence and concert. . . ."

If she was not a scientist, she was also not a philosopher, because she lacked the power of abstraction. Her thirst for knowledge was not at variance with her sense of irony and her versatility, and in other times she would have written essays and criticism. She did not live for an idea, nor create new ones: she lived ideas, which were her natural climate and sustenance. She was an intellectual, a consciousness. It is impossible to question the sincerity of her religious sentiments, but where a devout spirit would have discovered proofs for the presence of God or His power, Sor Juana found occasion to formulate hypotheses and questions. Although she often repeated that everything

---

[7]In response to a letter from the Bishop of Puebla, who, using the pseudonym Sor Filotea, bade her give up her secular learning and devote herself to religion. — *Tr.*

comes from God, she always sought a rational explanation: "Two little girls were playing with a top in my presence, and I had hardly seen the movement and figure when I began to consider, with this insanity of mine, the easy *motu* of spherical forms. . . ."

These declarations contrast with those of the Spanish writers of the period — and also with those of later generations. The physical world was no problem for any of them: they either accepted reality as it was or else they condemned it. Spanish literature of the Golden Age seems to say to us that outside of action there is nothing but contemplation. The historical life of Spain moves between adventure and renunciation. Neither Gracián nor Quevedo — not to mention the religious writers — showed any interest in knowledge as such. They were contemptuous of intellectual curiosity and all their attention was devoted to conduct, morality or salvation. As has been said, Stoics and Christians ignore pure intellectual activity, and Faust is unthinkable in this tradition. The intelligence gives them no pleasure: it is a dangerous weapon that can serve to defeat our enemies but can also cause us to lose our souls. The lonely figure of Sor Juana became more and more isolated in that world of affirmations and negations, a world that denied the value of doubt and inquiry.

The "Reply" is not only a self-portrait but also the self-defense of a spirit that was always adolescent and eager, always ironic and impassioned and reticent. Her double solitude, as a woman and as an intellectual, revealed a conflict that was also double: that of her society and that of her femininity. The "Reply to Sor Filotea" is a defense of women. The fact that she wrote this defense and dared to proclaim her fondness for disinterested thought makes her a modern figure. If it is accurate to see her affirmation of the value of experience as an instinctive reaction against traditional Spanish thought, then there is an implicit defense of the intellectual conscience and consciousness in her conception of knowledge (which should not be confused with erudition, nor identified with religion). Everything caused her to conceive of the world more as a problem or enigma than as a place of salvation or perdition. This gives her thought an originality that deserved something more than the eulogies of her contemporaries or the reproaches of her confessor, and in our own day it demands a deeper judgment and a more daring examination.

Vossler asked: "How was it possible that sounds so pregnant with the future should suddenly issue from a convent of Mexican nuns?" His answer was: "Her interest in ancient mythology and modern physics, in Aristotle and Harvey, in the ideas of Plato and the magic lantern of Kircher . . . would not have prospered in the pedantic and timorously dogmatic universities of Old Spain." It did not prosper in Mexico, either, for very long. After the uprisings of 1692, intellectual life was quickly muffled. Sigüenza y Góngora abruptly gave up his historical and archaeological pursuits. Sor Juana renounced her books and died shortly after. As Vossler noted, the social crisis coincided with that of the spirit.

Despite the brilliance of her career, the pathos of her death, and the admirable geometry that shapes her best poetic creations, there is something unrealized and fragmentary in the life and work of Sor Juana. We can sense the melancholy of a spirit who never succeeded in forgiving herself for her boldness and her condition as a woman. Her epoch did not provide her with the intellectual nourishment her appetite required, and she herself could not — and who can? — create a world of ideas in which to live alone. An awareness of her singularity was always very alive in her: "What can women know except the philosophy of the kitchen?" she asked with a smile. But the wound hurt her: "Who would not believe, hearing such general applause, that I have voyaged full-sail on the handclaps of popular acclamation?" Sor Juana was a solitary figure. Indecisive and smiling, she lived an ambiguous life; she was conscious of the duality of her condition and the impossibility of her task. We often hear reproaches against men who have not fulfilled their destinies. Should we not grieve, however, for the ill fortune of a woman who was superior both to her society and her culture?

Her image is that of a melancholy recluse who smiles and keeps silent. Silence, she herself said, is peopled with voices. And what does her silence say to us? If colonial society expresses and affirms itself in Sor Juana's work, the same society is condemned by her silence. The experience of Sor Juana, ending in silence and abdication, thus completes our examination of the colonial order. It was a world open to participation, was even a living cultural order, but it was implacably closed to all personal expression and all adventure: it was a world closed to the future. To be ourselves, we had to break with this exitless order, even at the risk of becoming orphans. The nineteenth century was the century of this break, and also of our attempt to create new ties with another tradition, more remote but no less universal than that offered us by the Catholic church: European rationalism.

CHAPTER SIX

From Independence
to the Revolution

The reforms undertaken by the Bourbon dynasty, especially by Charles III (1759-1788), improved the economy and made business operations more efficient, but they accentuated the centralization of administrative functions and changed New Spain into a true colony, that is, into a territory subject to systematic exploitation and strictly controlled by the center of power. The absolutism of the Austrian house was of a different nature: the colonies were kingdoms possessing a certain autonomy, and the Empire resembled a solar system. New Spain, at least at the beginning, revolved around the Crown like a minor planet, but it shone with its own light, as did the other possessions and kingdoms. The Bourbons transformed New Spain from a vassal kingdom to a mere overseas territory. The creation of the Intendencias, the impulse given to scientific investigation, the development of humanism, the construction of monumental public works, even the good government of various Viceroys, were not enough to reanimate colonial society. The colony, like the metropolis itself, was now only a form, an empty body. From the end of the seventeenth century the ties that united Madrid with her possessions had ceased to be the harmonious ties that bind together a living organism. The Empire survived due to the perfection and complexity of its structure, its physical grandeur and its inertia. Due, also, to the quarrels that divided its rivals. The reforms of Charles III show to what extent mere political action is insufficient if it is not preceded by a transformation of the very structure of society and by an examination of the assumptions on which it is based.

The eighteenth century prepared the way for the Independence movement. In fact, the science and philosophy of the epoch (in the scholastic reforms of men like Francisco Javier Clavijero or in the thought and action of others like Benito Díaz de Gamarra and Antonio Alzate) were the necessary intellectual antecedents of the *Grito de Dolores*. But it is forgotten that Independence came when nothing except inertia joined us to Spain: that terrible inertia of the dying person who raises his hand and claws at the air, as if to hold on to life for another moment. But life deserts him, in a last, violent convulsion. New Spain, insofar as it was a universal creation, insofar as it was a living order and not a mask, died when faith no longer nourished it. Sor Juana, incapable of resolving the conflict between her intellectual curiosity and the religious principles of her epoch in a creative and organic way, renounced life and died an exemplary death. In a less exemplary manner colonial society dragged itself through another century, defending itself with a sterile tenacity.

Independence offers us the same ambiguous image as the Conquest. The accomplishments of Hernán Cortés were preceded by a political synthesis that had been realized by the Catholic Kings in Spain and had been at least initiated by the Aztecs in Mesoamerica. Independence was likewise a phenomenon with a dual significance: the dismembering of the corpse of imperialism and the birth of a number of new nations. The Conquest and Independence seem like moments of flux and reflux in a great historical wave that gathered in the fifteenth century, flooded over America, attained a brief but splendid equilibrium in the sixteenth and seventeenth centuries, and finally receded after collapsing into a thousand fragments.

The philosopher José Gaos justifies this metaphor when he divides modern Hispanic thinking into two parts: that of the peninsula itself, which consists of one long meditation on Spanish decadence, and that of Spanish America, which is less a meditation than a petition in favor of Independence and a search for our true destiny. Spanish thought turns to the past and its own self, in order to investigate the causes of its decadence, or to isolate, among so much that is dead, the still-living elements that give meaning and reality to the fact — strangest of all, perhaps — of being Spanish. In contrast, Spanish American thought begins as a justification of Independence but transforms itself almost immediately into a project: America is not so much a tradition to be carried on as it is a future to be realized. This project and the idea of utopia are inseparable in Spanish-American thinking from the end of the eighteenth century to our own times. Elegy and criticism belong to the peninsula, and are represented by Unamuno, the elegiac poet, and Ortega y Gasset, the philosophical critic, among others.

This dualism is even more perceptible in the South American countries. The personalities of their leaders were less adulterated and their opposition to the Spanish tradition was more radical. Aristocrats, intellectuals and cosmopolitan travelers were not only familiar with the new ideas but also took an active part in the new movements and societies. Miranda participated in the French Revolution and fought at Valmy. Bello lived in London. Bolívar spent his apprentice years in the kind of atmosphere that produces heroes and princes; he was educated from early childhood to liberate and to govern. Our own Independence movement was less brilliant, less rich in ideas and phrases, more rigidly determined by local circumstances. Our leaders — humble priests and obscure captains — did not have a clear conception of what they were attempting to do. On the other hand, they had a greater sense of reality and were better able to hear the coded messages that the people were murmuring to them.

These differences influenced the later history of our countries. The Independence movement in South America began with a continent-wide victory: San Martín liberated half the continent, Bolívar the other half. They created great states and confederations. They thought that emancipation from Spain would not bring about the dismemberment of the Hispanic world. In a short while, however, reality shattered all their projects. The process of disintegration in the Spanish Empire proved stronger than Bolívar's clairvoyance.

In sum, two opposing tendencies struggled within the Independence movement: one, of European origin, liberal and utopian, conceived of Spanish America as a single whole, an assembly of free nations; the other, more traditional, broke the ties with the metropolis only to speed up the fragmentation of the Empire.

Spanish American Independence, like the whole history of our peoples, is difficult to interpret because, once again, ideas disguise reality instead of clarifying or expressing it. The groups and classes that brought about Independence in South America belonged to the native feudal aristocracy. They were descendants of the Spanish colonists, in a situation of inferiority to peninsula Spaniards. The metropolis, carrying out a protectionist policy, hindered the free commerce of the colonies and restricted their economic and social development with administrative and political checks. At the same time, it closed the way to the *criollos* who desired, justly enough, to enter into higher offices and the direction of the state. Thus the struggle for Independence tended to free the *criollos* from the mummified bureaucracy of the peninsula, though actually there was no proposal to change the social structure of the colonies. It is true that the programs and language of the Independence leaders resembled those of the revolutionaries of the epoch, and no doubt they were sincere. That language was "modern," an echo of the French Revolution and, above all, of the ideas behind the North American War of Independence. But in North America those ideas were expressed by groups who proposed a basic transformation of the country in accordance with a new political philosophy. What is more, they did not intend to exchange one state of affairs for another, but instead — and the difference is radical — to create a new nation. In effect, the United States is a novelty in the history of the nineteenth century, a society that grew and expanded naturally. Among ourselves, on the other hand, the ruling classes consolidated themselves, once Independence was achieved, as heirs of the old Spanish order. They broke with Spain but they proved incapable of creating a modern society. It could not have beeen otherwise, because the groups that headed the Independence movement did not represent new social forces, merely a prolongation of the feudal system. The newness of the new Spanish American nations is deceptive: in reality they were decadent or static societies, fragments and survivals of a shattered whole.

The division of the Spanish Empire into a multitude of republics was carried out by native oligarchies, which favored and even speeded up the process of disintegration. We should also remember the determining influence of many of the revolutionary leaders. Some of them — more fortunate in this than the conquistadors, their historical counterparts — succeeded in taking over the state as if it were medieval booty. The image of the "Spanish American dictator" appeared, in embryo, in that of the "liberator." Thus the new republics were created by the political and military necessities of the moment, not as an expression of a real historical need. "National traits" were formed later, and in many cases they were simply the result of the nationalistic preachments of the various governments. Even now, a century and a half later, no one can explain satisfactorily the "national" differences between Argentinians and Uruguayans, Peruvians and Ecuadorians, Guatemalans and Mexicans. And nothing except the persistence of local oligarchies, supported by North American imperialism, can explain the existence of nine republics in Central America and the Antilles.

Nor is this all. Every one of the new nations, on the day after Independence, had a more or less — almost always less rather than more — liberal and democratic constitution. In Europe and the United States these principles corresponded to historical reality, for they were an expression of the rise of the bourgeoisie, a consequence of the Industrial Revolution and the destruction of the old regime. In Spanish America they merely served as modern trappings for the survivals of the colonial system. This liberal, democratic ideology, far from expressing our concrete historical situation, disguised it, and the political lie established itself almost constitutionally. The moral damage it has caused is incalculable; it has affected profound areas of our existence. We move about in this lie with complete naturalness. For over a hundred years we have suffered from regimes that have been at the service of feudal oligarchies but have utilized the language of freedom. The situation has continued to our own day. Hence the struggle against the official, constitutional lie must be the first step in any serious attempt at reform. This seems to be the import of current Latin-American movements whose common objective is to realize at last the ideals of Independence; that is, to transform our countries into truly modern societies, not mere façades for demagogues and tourists. In this struggle the people must confront not only their old Spanish heritage — the Church, the army and the oligarchy — but also the dictator, the boss, with his mouth full of legal and patriotic formulas, and allied now with a power very different from Spanish imperialism: the vast interests of foreign capitalism.

Almost all of the foregoing is applicable to Mexico, with some decisive exceptions. In the first place, our Revolution of Independence was not characterized by those pretensions of universality that were both the vision and the blindness of Bolívar. Also, the insurgents vacillated between Independence (Morelos) and modern forms of autonomy (Hidalgo). The war began as a protest against the abuses of the metropolis and the Spanish bureaucracy, but it was also, and primarily, a protest against the great native landholders. It was not a rebellion of the local aristocracy against the metropolis but of the people against the former. Therefore the revolutionaries gave greater importance to certain social reforms than to Independence itself: Hidalgo proclaimed the abolition of slavery and Morelos broke up the great estates. The Revolution of Independence was a class war, and its nature cannot be understood correctly unless we recognize the fact that unlike what happened in South America, it was an agrarian revolt in gestation. This is why the army (with its *criollos* like Iturbide), the Church and the great landowners supported the Spanish crown, and these were the forces that defeated Hidalgo, Morelos and Javier Mina. A little later, when the insurgent movement had almost been destroyd, the unexpected occurred: the liberals seized power, transformed the absolute monarchy into a constitutional monarchy, and threatened the privileges of the Church and the aristocracy. A sudden change of allegiance took place: the high clergy, the great landowners, the bureaucracy and the *criollo* military leaders, confronted with this new danger, sought an alliance with the remainder of the insurgents and consummated the Independence. It was a veritable act of prestidigitation: the political separation from the metropolis was brought about in order to defeat the classes that had fought for Independence. The Viceroyalty of New Spain became the Mexican Empire. Iturbide, the former royalist general, became Agustín I. A little later he was overthrown by a rebellion. The era of pronunciamentos had begun.

For the next quarter of a century or more, in a confused struggle that included transitory alliances, changes of allegiance and even treachery, the liberals attempted to complete the break with the colonial tradition. In a certain sense they carried on the efforts of the first leaders, Hidalgo and Morelos. But their criticism of the order of things was directed less toward a change of reality than toward a change of legislation. Almost all of them believed, with an optimism inherited from the Encyclopaedia, that to transform reality it was sufficient to pass new laws. They saw the United States as a model, and thought that its prosperity was due to the excellence of its republican institutions. Hence their federalism, as opposed to the centralism of the conservatives. They all hoped that a democratic constitution, limiting the temporal power of the Church and the privileges of the landholding aristocracy, would almost automatically produce a new social class, the bourgeoisie. The liberals not only had to fight the conservatives but also take into account the military, which changed allegiance according to its own interests. While these factions struggled, the country disintegrated. The United States took advantage of the situation, and in one of the most unjust wars in the history of imperialist expansion, deprived us of over half of our territory. In the long run this defeat produced a salutary reaction, because it gave the death blow to military bossism as exemplified by the dictator Santa-Ana. (He was alternately liberal and conservative, guardian of freedom and traitor to his country. He must be considered one of the archetypes of the Latin American dictator. Toward the end of his political career he ordered solemn funeral honors for the leg he lost in battle, and also declared himself Most Serene Highness.) A popular rebellion overthrew Santa-Ana and brought the liberals into power. A new generation — heirs of José María Mora and Valentín Gómez Farías, leader of the liberal intelligensia — undertook the task of building new foundations for the nation. The cornerstone was to be a new constitution. Mexico adopted a liberal constitutional charter in 1857. The conservatives took up arms, and Benito Juárez responded with the Reform Laws, which put an end to special privileges and destroyed the material power of the Church. The defeated conservatives turned to the outside world, and with the help of troops sent by Napoleon III they installed Maximilian, second Emperor of Mexico, in the capital. (Another historical ambiguity: Maximilian was a liberal and dreamed of creating a Latin Empire in opposition to *yanqui* power. His ideas had no relation to those of the conservatives who supported him.) The reverses suffered by the Napoleonic Empire in Europe, the pressure from North America (which can be misunderstood if it is forgotten that Lincoln was President) and the rise of popular resistance — which was the original and determining cause of victory — brought about the republican triumph. Juárez had Maximilian executed, an incident that has analogies with the execution of Louis XVI: "geometric reasoning" is as hard as steel.

The Reform movement consummated the Independence movement and gave it true meaning, since it undertook to examine the bases of Mexican society and the historical and philosophical climate in which it developed. This examination ended in a triple negation: of our Spanish inheritance, of our indigenous past, and of Catholicism, which reconciled the first two in a higher affirmation. The Reform Laws and the Constitution of 1857 were a legal and political expression of this examination, and promoted the destruction of two institutions that represented the continuity of our triple inheritance: religious associations and communal indigenous landholding. The separation of Church and State, the disentailing of ecclesiastical holdings, and the freeing of education (completed with the dissolution of the religious orders that had monopolized it) were merely negative aspects of the Reform movement. The generation of 1857 affirmed certain principles with the same violence with which it rejected tradition. Its accomplishments did not consist solely in a break with the colonial world: it also projected the founding of a new society. That is to say, the historical project of the liberals was to replace the colonial tradition, based on Catholic doctrine, with an affirmation equally universal: the freedom of the individual. The Mexican nation was founded on a principle very different from that of the hierarchy which ruled in colonial times: equality before the law of all Mexicans as human, reasoning beings. The Reform movement founded Mexico and denied the past. It rejected tradition and sought to justify itself in the future.

The significance of this necessary matricide did not escape the attention of our best thinkers. Ignacio Ramírez, perhaps the outstanding figure in a group of extraordinary men, ended one of his poems with these lines:

> *Mother Nature, there are no flowers*
> *where my wandering steps advance;*
> *I was born without hope or fear;*
> *I return to you without fear or hope.*

When God — the center of colonial society — died, nature again became a mother. The atheism of Ramírez, like the later Marxism of Diego Rivera, finally became a sort of materialistic affirmation with religious overtones. An authentically scientific or merely rational conception of matter cannot regard it or nature as a mother. It is not even the stepmother of the pessimist Leopardi, but an indifferent process that creates and destroys, invents and repeats, without rest, without memory, without reflection.

If, as Ortega y Gasset said, a nation is not really a nation unless it has both a past that influences it inactively and a valid historical project that is capable of animating dissimilar spirits and of giving unity and transcendence to solitary efforts, then Mexico was born during the epoch of the Reform. She was conceived, invented, projected in it and through it. The Reform movement was the project of a very small group of Mexicans who voluntarily disengaged themselves from the passively religious and traditional masses. The Mexican nation was created by a minority that succeeded in imposing its scheme on the rest of the people, against the wishes of another minority that was actively traditional.

Like colonial Catholicism, the Reform was a movement inspired by a universal philosophy. The similarities and differences between them are significant. Catholicism was imposed by a minority of strangers after a military conquest; liberalism was imposed by a native minority, though its intellectual formation was French, after a civil war. The former was the reverse face of the Conquest: the Indians, with their own theocracy destroyed, their gods dead or exiled, and without lands to develop or other regions to which they could emigrate, embraced the Christian religion as a mother. She was a womb, a resting place, a return to origins, like all mothers; but at the same time she was a devouring mouth, a woman who punished and mutilated them: a terrifying mother. Liberalism was a critique of the old order and a projected social pact. It was not a religion but a utopian ideology; it fought rather than consoled; it replaced the notion of an other world with that of a terrestial future. It championed man but it ignored a half of his nature, that which is expressed in communion, myths, festivals, dreams, eroticism. Above all, the Reform movement was a negation, and its greatness resides in that fact. But what this negation affirmed — the principles of European liberalism — was a philosophy whose beauty was exact, sterile and, in the long run, empty. Geometry cannot take the place of myth. To convert the schemes of the liberals into a truly national project it would have been necessary to win the support of the country as a whole. This would have been supremely difficult, because the Reform was attacking a very concrete and particular affirmation: that all men are the sons of God, a creed permitting a genuinely filial relationship between the individual and the cosmos. In its place the Reform offered an abstract postulate: that all men are equal before the law. Freedom and equality were — and are — empty concepts, ideas with no other concrete historical content than that given them by social relationships, as Marx has demonstrated. We are aware, by now, of the forms into which that abstract equality can change itself, and of the true meaning of that empty freedom. Also, the founding of Mexico on a general notion of man, rather than on the actual situation of our people, sacrificed reality to words and delivered us up to the ravenous appetites of the strong.

Despite all the predictions of the clearest thinkers, the liberal revolution did not bring about the birth of that strong bourgeoisie which everyone, even Justo Sierra, saw as the only hope for Mexico. On the contrary, the sale of church properties and the disappearance of communal indigenous landholdings (which had precariously survived three and a half centuries of abuses and seizures by land agents and hacienda owners) accentuated the feudal character of our country. Those who benefited were a group of speculators, who made up the aristocracy of the new regime. Thus a new class of landowners arose. The republic, with no enemy to face now that the conservatives and imperialists had been defeated, suddenly found itself without a social basis. In breaking its ties with the past, it also broke its ties with Mexican realities. Power could belong to whoever dared reach out his hand for it. And Porfirio Díaz dared. He was the most brilliant of the generals whom the fall of the empire had left — for the first time in almost a century of battles and pronunciamentos — without a job.

The "soldier of April 2nd" became the "hero of the peace." Anarchy was overcome but liberty was sacrificed in the process. The different factions were reconciled but special privileges were restored. The country was reorganized but the regime prolonged an anachronistic feudalism with nothing to ameliorate its severity (the Laws of the Indies had contained precepts that protected the Indians). Commerce was stimulated, railroads were built, the Public Treasury was freed of debt, and the first modern industries were established, but the doors were opened wide to Anglo-American capitalism. During this period Mexico lived the life of a semicolonial country.

Despite what has usually been thought, the dictatorship of Porfirio Díaz was a return to the past. Díaz appeared to be governing according to the ideas in vogue: he believed in progress, in science and in the miracles of industry and free enterprise. His ideals were those of the European bourgeoisie. He was the most illustrious dictator in Spanish America and at times his regime recalled the years of the *belle époque* in France. The intellectuals discovered Comte and Renan, Spencer and Darwin; the poets imitated the French Parnassians and Symbolists; the Mexican aristocracy was an urbane and civilized class. But the other face of the coin was very different. Those great gentlemen who loved progress and science were not industrialists or businessmen: they were landholders who had grown rich from the purchase of Church properties or in the public affairs of the regime. The peasants on the haciendas lived like serfs, much as they had done during the colonial era. The Díaz regime claimed that ideologically it was the legitimate successor of liberalism. The Constitution of 1857 was still in effect — theoretically — and no one attempted to oppose the ideas of the Reform by offering different principles. Many persons, including the old liberals, honestly thought the Díaz regime was preparing the country for the transition from the feudal past to the modern world. In reality, however, the regime was the heir of colonial feudalism: the ownership of land was concentrated in a few hands and the landholding class grew constantly stronger. The past returned, decked out in the trappings of progress, science and republican laws, but with a complete lack of fecundity. It could produce nothing except rebellion.

We are indebted to Leopoldo Zea for a very comprehensive analysis of the ideas of this period.[1] He observes that the adoption of positivism as the official state philosophy corresponded to certain intellectual and moral necessities of the Díaz dictatorship. Liberal thought was both a critical instrument and a utopian construction and it contained some explosive principles. To have extended its sway would have been to prolong anarchy. The epoch of peace required a philosophy of order. The intel-

---

[1] Leopoldo Zea: *El positivismo en México* (Mexico: 1942).

lectuals found it in the positivism of Comte, with his law of the three states, and later in that of Spencer and in Darwin's evolutionism. The primitive, abstract and revolutionary principle of the equality of men was replaced by the theory of the struggle for existence and the survival of the fittest. Positivism offered the social hierarchies a new justification. Inequalities were now explained, not by race or inheritance or religion, but by science.

Zea's analysis is irrefutable save on one point. It is true that positivism expressed bourgeois Europe during a moment of its history; but it expressed it in a natural, organic manner. In Mexico this philosophy served a class that was relatively new insofar as the families who made it up were concerned — almost all of them had acquired wealth and power during the struggles of the Reform movement — but historically this class simply took the place of the feudal aristocracy of colonial times. Therefore, if the function of positivist philosophy was similar here and in Europe, the historical and human relationship that was established between positivism and the European bourgeoisie was quite different from that which existed in Mexico between this doctrine and the "neofeudal" class.

The Díaz regime adopted positivist philosophy; it did not father it. Thus it discovered itself in a situation of dependence even more serious than that of the liberals or the colonial theologians, for it could neither take a critical position in regard to that philosophy nor embrace it with complete good faith. In some instances it resembled one of those acts which Antonio Caso — following Tarde — has called "extralogical imitation": unnecessary, superfluous and contrary to the imitator's condition. An abyss opened up between the system and the regime that adopted it, rendering impossible any authentic relationship with ideas, which at times became mere masks. The Díaz era, then, was a period of historical falseness. Santa-Ana had happily switched disguises: he was an actor who did not believe what he said. The Díaz regime tried hard to believe, to make the adopted ideas its own. It simulated, in every sense of the word.

This simulation was especially grave because, in embracing positivism, the regime took over a system which historically did not belong to it. The landholding class did not constitute a Mexican equivalent to the European bourgeosie, and its role had no relation whatever to that of its model. The ideas of Spencer and John Stuart Mill demanded, as their historical context, the development of heavy industry, a democratic bourgeoisie and the free exercise of intellectual activity. The Díaz dictatorship, based on great rural holdings, bossism and the absence of democratic freedoms, could not make these ideas its own without either denying itself or disfiguring them beyond recognition. Thus positivism became a historical superimposition much more dangerous than those that preceded it, because it was based on a misconception. Between the landholders and their political and philosophical ideas an invisible wall of deception arose, and the expulsion of the Díaz regime followed almost inevitably.

The positivist disguise was not intended to deceive the people but to hide the moral nakedness of the regime from its own leaders and beneficiaries. It was a philosophy that could not justify social hierarchies to the disinherited, for whom liberalism guaranteed the dignity of man. It had nothing to offer the poor; its function was to salve the conscience — the *mauvaise conscience* — of the European bourgeoisie. In Mexico the guilt feelings of the European bourgeoisie took on a special cast, for a double historical reason: the neofeudalists were both the heirs of liberalism and the successors of the colonial aristocracy. Their intellectual and moral legacy — the principles of the Reform — and their enjoyment of the Church's properties necessarily produced a profound sense of guilt. Their social eminence was the result of a usurpation and a misconception, but positivism could not remedy or palliate this shameful situation. On the contrary, it aggravated it, since it never reached down to the consciences of those who adopted it. Falseness and falsehoods were thus the only psychological bases of Mexican positivism.

In its own fashion the dictatorship completed the work of the Reform movement. With the introduction of positivist philosophy the nation broke its last links with the past. The Conquest destroyed temples but the colonial world built others. The Reform denied tradition but offered us a universal image of man. Positivism gave us nothing at all. Instead, it revealed the principles of liberalism in all their nakedness, as lovely but inapplicable words. The ideals of the Reform, that great historical project by means of which Mexico was to become a nation destined to realize itself through certain universal truths, were reduced to utopian dreams. Its laws and principles became a rigid framework that stifled our spontaneity and mutilated our character. After a hundred years of struggle the people found themselves more alone than ever, with their religious life impoverished and their popular culture debased. We had lost our historical orientation.

The image that Mexico presents us at the end of the nineteenth century is one of discord. It was a discord more profound than the earlier political quarrels or even the civil war, because it consisted in the imposition of juridical and cultural forms which not only did not express our true nature but actually smothered and immobilized it. This discord fostered a caste that showed itself incapable of becoming a class in the strict sense of the word. Our national life was poisoned by lies and sterility. Our ties with the past had been broken, a dialogue with the United States — which only spoke to us in the language of force or of business — was impossible, and relationships with other Spanish-speaking countries, walled up within dead forms, were useless. We were reduced to a unilateral imitation of France, which had always ignored us. What was left to us? Asphyxiation and solitude.

If the history of Mexico is that of a people seeking a form that will express them, the history of the individual Mexican is that of a man aspiring to communion. The fecundity of colonial Catholicism resided in the fact that above all it was participation. The liberals offered us ideas, but no communion was made with those ideas, at least while they were not incarnated and turned into blood and food. Communion is festivity and ceremony. At the close of the nineteenth century the Mexican, like Mexico, was imprisoned in a rigid Catholicism or in the closed and hopeless universe of the official philosophy.

Justo Sierra was the first to understand the significance of this situation. Despite his liberal and positivist antecedents, he was the only Mexican of his epoch who concerned himself with history. The most durable and useful portion of his work is a meditation on universal and Mexican history. His attitude differed radically from that of his predecessors. To the liberals, conservatives and positivists, Mexican reality by itself had little meaning; it was something inert that only acquired meaning when it was reflected in a universal scheme. Sierra conceived of Mexico as an autonomous reality existing in time: the nation was a past that advanced, however tortuously, toward the future, and the present was full of signs and indications. Neither religion nor science did us justice. Our history, like that of any other people, had a meaning and a direction. Perhaps without fully knowing what he did, Sierra introduced the philosophy of history as a possible answer to our solitude and malaise.

He founded the National University as a consequence of these ideas. In his inaugural address he said that the new institution "has no ancestors or grandfathers . . . ; the faculty and directors of the Royal Pontifical University of Mexico are for us not predecessors but the past. Nevertheless, we remember them with a certain involuntary filial respect; involuntary, but not lacking in emotion and interest." These words reveal how completely the liberals and their heirs had broken with the colonial era. Sierra questioned the sufficiency of liberal and positivist thinking, just as he rejected religious dogmatism. He believed that science and reason were man's best hope and the only one worthy of confidence. But he conceived of them as instruments. He thought they should serve individuals and the nation, for only thus "would the University have sufficient power to coordinate the directional lines of the national character. . . ."

Truth, he said elsewhere in that address, is not a given fact, despite what the medieval scholastics or the metaphysicians of rationalism believed. Truth is to be found scattered among the true particulars of each science, and to reconstruct it was one of the tasks of the epoch. Without naming it, he invoked philosophy, which was absent from positivist teaching. Positivism was to confront new doctrines.

The words of the Minister of Education inaugurated another chapter in the history of ideas in Mexico. However, Sierra himself was not to write it; that was accomplished by a group of young men: Antonio Caso, José Vasconcelos, Alfonso Reyes and Pedro Henríquez Ureña. They undertook a critique of positivism and in the end discredited it completely. Their intellectual unrest coincided with an even more dramatic search: that of the country for its own true self during the Revolution.

The Mexican Revolution was an explosive and authentic revelation of our real nature. Many things, including our internal political history and the more secret history of our national character, had prepared the way for it, but very few voices — all of them weak and muffled — had predicted it. The Revolution had antecedents, causes and motives, but in a profound sense it lacked precursors. The Independence was not simply the result of various historical circumstances, but rather of a universal intellectual movement, which in Mexico began in the eighteenth century. The Reform was the result of the work and ideas of several intellectual generations, who predicted it, prepared it and realized it. It was the work of the Mexican intelligentsia. The Revolution began as a demand for truth and honesty in the government, as can be seen from the Plan of San Luis (Oct. 5, 1910). Gradually the movement found and defined itself, in the midst of battle and later when in power. Its lack of a set program gave it popular authenticity and originality. This fact accounts for both its greatness and its weaknesses.

It is customary to cite the names of a scattered and isolated group — Andrés Molina Enríquez, Filomeno Mata, Paulino Martínez, Juan Sarabia, Antonio Villarreal and Ricardo and Enrique Flores Magón — as being among the precursors of the Revolution.[2] None of them was a true intellectual, that is, a person who had formulated Mexico's situation as a problem to be solved and who offered a new historical project. Molina Enríquez had a clear understanding of the agrarian problem, but I doubt if his ideas would have been approved by the revolutionaries until after the period of the Plan of Ayala (November 25, 1911), a document that embodied the aspirations of Emiliano Zapata and his followers. The influence of Ricardo Flores Magón, one of the most honorable men in the Mexican labor movement, is absent from our labor laws. As an anarchist he

_____

[2] Jesús Silva Herzog: *Meditaciones sobre México* (Mexico, 1946).

was necessarily outside the Revolution, although at the beginning the Mexican labor leaders were influenced by anarchist ideas.

The Independence and Reform movements — especially the latter — reflected, extended and adapted certain ideologies of their epochs, but the Revolution did not. Silva Herzog has written: "Our Revolution had nothing in common with the Russian Revolution, not even on the surface. It took place later than ours, so how could we have imitated it? There is no use of European socialistic terminology in the revolutionary literature of Mexico from the end of the last century until 1917. The fact is that our social movement grew up out of our own soil, out of the lacerated hearts of our people, and it became a drama that was both tragic and creative."[3] This lack of ideological precursors and the scarcity of links with a universal ideology are characteristic aspects of the Revolution, and the seeds of many later conflicts and confusions.

The immediate antecedents of the movement are not difficult to find. First, there was the political and social situation. The middle class had increased due to the growth of commerce and industry, which used native personnel even though they were mostly foreign-owned. A new generation had risen, a restless generation that desired a change. The quarrel of the generations became a part of the general social discord. The Díaz regime was not only a government of the privileged but also of elderly men who could not resign themselves to giving up power. The nonconformity of the young expressed itself as an anxiety to see the principles of liberalism realized at last. The first revolutionary ideals were predominantly political. It was thought that the exercise of democratic rights would make possible a

---

[3]*Op. cit.*

change of methods and persons.

The nascent working class was equally restless. Liberal legislation had not provided any defenses against abuse by the powerful. Peasants and workers were helpless before the bosses, feudal lords and industrialists, but the Mexican peasant had a long tradition of struggle, while the workers lacked not only the most elementary rights but also the experience and theories with which to support their demands and justify their fight. Because of this lack of traditions the working class was truly disinherited. A number of strikes broke out nevertheless, and all of them were mercilessly suppressed. Later the workers took part in one of the most important episodes of the civil struggle: their leaders went over to Carranza and signed the "Pact of the House of the Workers of the World and the Constitutionalist Movement" (February 17, 1915). Instead of seeking labor legislation, the proletariat joined one of the factions into which the revolutionary movement had divided. Since then the working class has depended more or less completely on the revolutionary governments, a circumstance of the first importance — as we shall see — in understanding today's Mexico.

Another circumstance that favored the development of the Revolution was the international situation. Porfirio Díaz, following a political plan favored by liberals like Lerdo de Tejada and almost all of the conservatives, wanted to limit the economic influence of the United States in favor of European capitalism. "International relations caused deep concern during the last years of the Díaz government. The opportunities conceded to English capital provoked resentment in the United States. And there were other causes for ill feelings, such as the protection Díaz offered to the President of Nicaragua, his refusal to allow the United States fleet to remain for a longer period in Magdalena Bay, and the judgment which a Canadian arbiter handed down in favor of Mexico in the Chamizal boundary dispute."[4] There is no doubt that the United States tolerated the political activities of Mexican revolutionaries within its territory, but it is impossible to reduce the Mexican Revolution, as some conservatives would like to do, to a conspiracy by *yanqui* imperialism. The later intervention of the U. S. Ambassador in the counterrevolutionary coup d'état which defeated President Madero proves the limited extent of foreign influences in the development of the Revolution.

Strikes and peasant uprisings undermined the social structure of the dictatorship; political unrest in the cities caused Díaz to lose confidence in the popular support for his regime; and in the sphere of ideas, two young men — Antonio Caso and José Vasconcelos — undertook a critique of the regime's official philosophy. Their work forms a part of the vast intellectual renovation begun by the group known as the Ateneo de la Juventud (Athenaeum of the Young).

In 1909 Antonio Caso made an examination of positivist philosophy. In the course of seven lectures (the first three devoted to Comte and his predecessors, the remainder to "Independent Positivism," Mill, Spencer and Taine), he expounded his disagreement with official doctrine. He made particular use of Boutroux's philosophy of contingency and certain of Bergson's ideas. At the close of the series Caso made known his personal philosophy. Here is how Henríquez Ureña described this act of faith: "Caso postulated intellectualism against the imminent invasion of pragmatism and related tendencies . . . praising the great constructive metaphysicists, Plato, Spinoza, Hegel, and then declaring himself an idealist in regard

---

[4]Silvio Zavala: *Síntesis de la Historia del pueblo Mexicano*, in *Mexico en la cultura* (Mexico, 1946).

to the problem of knowledge. . . . His profession of faith ends
with a quotation ('All is thought . . .') from Henri Poincaré, the
pragmatist. . . . Caso's final lecture was a petition in favor of
philosophical speculation. Within the walls of the Preparatory
School, the old positivist stronghold, the voice of the meta-
physician was heard again, reclaiming his inalienable rights."[5]

Vasconcelos was anti-intellectual. He was a philosopher of
intuitions, holding that the emotions were the only faculties
capable of apprehending material things, and that knowledge
was a total and instantaneous vision of reality. Later Vasconcelos elaborated a "philosophy of the Iberoamerican race" which
carried forward a very important trend in Spanish-American
thought. But his influence was not to be felt at its strongest
until some years afterward, when he became Secretary of
Public Education under Alvaro Obregón.

The critique of positivism was decisive in the intellectual
history of Mexico and was one of the indispensable antecedents
of the Revolution. But it was a negative antecedent. Caso and
his associates destroyed the philosophy of the Díaz regime, but
their ideas did not offer a new project for national reform. Their
intellectual position had hardly any relation to the aspirations
of the people and the needs of the time. The difference between
the new generation and that of the liberals is significant: it
could not help but have very grave consequences in modern
Mexican history. The Revolution, without any doctrines
(whether imported or its own) to guide it, was an explosion
of reality and a groping search for the universal doctrine that
would justify it and give it a place in the history of America
and the world. But if Caso's ideas did not exercise any influence
on those of the Revolution, his unfailing love for knowledge —

---

[5]Pedro Henríquez Ureña: *Horas de estudio* (Paris, 1910).

which caused him to go on with his classes even while opposing factions were shooting each other in the street — made him a splendid example of what philosophy means: a love that nothing can buy and that nothing can pervert.

These were the most notable antecedents, then, of the Mexican Revolution. Its causes — fewer but more profound — were part of the very life of Mexico itself.

Our movement was distinguished by a lack of any previous ideological system and by a hunger for land. The Mexican peasants supported the Revolution not only to achieve better living conditions but also to recover the lands that had been taken from them during the colonial period and the nineteenth century by the royal land grants and the great haciendas and estates.

The *calpulli* was the basic form of land ownership before the Conquest. This system consisted in "dividing the populated areas into various suburbs or *calpulli*, each of them with a set amount of land; this land did not belong to the inhabitants as individuals, but rather was granted to a family or tribe. . . . The person who left his *calpulli*, or who failed to cultivate the land assigned to him, lost his right to share in the communal properties."[6] The Laws of the Indies protected this institution, and many judgments were handed down in defense of the communal indigenous lands against every sort of abuse and usurpation. The admirable precepts of the Laws of the Indies were not always respected, however, and the situation of the peasants was desperate by the end of the eighteenth century. The attitude of Morelos, one of the few Mexican leaders who was aware of the problem, shows the extent to which the agrarian crisis

---

[6]Gabino Fraga: *El derecho agrario*, in *México en la Cultura* (Mexico, 1946).

influenced the War of Independence. The Reform committed the fatal error of dissolving the communal indigenous properties, despite the opposition of Ponciano Arriaga and others. Later, through several Laws of Colonization and of Occupation and Transferral of Uncultivated Lands, the Díaz regime "put an end to what was left of communal ownership in Mexico."[7]

Almost all the programs and manifestoes of the revolutionary groups alluded to the agrarian problem, but only the Revolution of the South and its leader, Emiliano Zapata, posed the problem clearly, simply and decisively. It is no accident that Zapata, a figure who shared the plastic beauty and poetry of our popular images, has served again and again as a subject for Mexican painters. Like Morelos and Cuauhtémoc, he is one of our legendary heroes. Realism and myth are joined in this ardent, melancholy and hopeful figure who died as he had lived: embracing the earth. His image, like the earth, is made up of patience and fecundity, silence and hope, death and resurrection. His program contained few ideas, only those that were needed to break the political and economic shackles that bound us. Articles Six and Seven of the Plan of Ayala, which foresaw the restitution and distribution of the land, called for a basic change of policy regarding agrarian properties, and opened the door to modern Mexico. Zapata's program, in brief, consisted in the elimination of feudalism and the passage of legislation adjusted to Mexican realities.

Every revolution, according to Ortega y Gasset, is an attempt to make reality conform to a rational project, and therefore the revolutionary conceives of himself as an agent of reason's imperative and radical demands. This opinion may itself be a little too radical, for I have noticed that most revolutions,

---

[6]*Op. cit.*

although they are presented as an invitation to realize certain ideas in the near or not so near future, are founded on an attempt to restore a legal or social order that has been violated by the oppressor. Every revolution tries to bring back a Golden Age. The French Revolution based the viability of its program on the belief that if the ideal conditions of the Social Contract were re-established, peace would follow. Marxism points to the theory of primitive communism as the antecendent of what it promises to bring about. The "eternal return" is one of the implicit assumptions of almost every revolutionary theory.

Marx wrote that all radicalism is a form of humanism, since man is the root of both reason and society. Thus every revolution tries to create a world in which man, free at last from the trammels of the old regime, can express himself truly and fulfill his human condition. Man is a being who can realize himself, can *be* himself, only in a revolutionary society. And that society bases its hopes on man's own nature, which is not something given and static, but rather consists in a range of possibilities that the regime has suppressed or mutilated. How can we tell that man is possibility, frustrated by injustice? The mythic notion of a Golden Age enters here: at some moment in history, in some part of the world, there was once a society that permitted man to express and realize himself. It prefigured and prophesied the new society which the revolutionary proposes to create. Almost all utopias suppose the previous existence, in some remote past, of a Golden Age that justifies revolutionary action and makes it viable.

The originality of the Plan of Ayala resides in the fact that this Golden Age was not a simple creation of man's reason or a mere hypothesis. The Mexican agrarian movement insisted that the restitution of lands must be legally binding: those who received lands should also receive titles to them. If it called for a redistribution of the land, its purpose was to extend the benefits of the traditional system to all the peasants and villages that did not possess titles. The Zapatista movement attempted to rectify the history of Mexico and the very meaning of our existence as a nation — a program quite different from the historical project of the liberals. The Zapatistas did not conceive of Mexico as a future to be realized but as a return to origins. The radicalism of the Mexican Revolution consisted in its originality, that is, in its return to our roots, the only proper bases for our institutions. When the Zapatistas made the *calpulli* the basic element in our economic and social structure, they not only salvaged the valid portion of the colonial tradition but also affirmed that any political construction, if it is to be truly productive, must derive from the most ancient, stable and lasting part of our national being: the indigenous past.

Zapata's traditionalism reveals that he had a profound awareness of our history. He was isolated both racially and regionally from the journalists and theorists of the epoch, and this isolation gave him the strength and insight to grasp the simple truth. And the truth of the Revolution was actually very simple: it was the freeing of Mexican reality from the constricting schemes of liberalism and the abuses of the conservatives and neo-conservatives.

The Zapatista movement was a return to our most ancient and permanent tradition. It was a profound denial of the work of the Reform, in that it was a return to the very world from which the liberals had wanted to cut themselves loose. The Revolution became an attempt to integrate our present and our past, or — as Leopoldo Zea put it — to "assimilate our history," to change it into a living thing: a past made present. This effort at integration, this return to sources, contrasts with the attitude of the intellectuals of the time, who not only failed to understand the meaning of the revolutionary movement but even went on playing with ideas that had no function whatsoever except as masks.

The inability of the Mexican intelligentsia to formulate the confused aspirations of the people in a coherent system became obvious as soon as the Revolution ceased to be an instinctive act and was established as a regime. The Zapatista and Villista movements — twin factions, one in the south, the other in the north — were popular explosions that proved almost wholly incapable of incorporating their truths, which were more felt than thought out, in an organic plan. They were a point of departure, an obscure and stammering expression of the revolutionary will. The triumphant faction — the Carrancistas — attempted to transcend the limitations of its two enemies, but on the other hand it thwarted the spontaneous desires of the people (the only source of revolutionary health) by restoring Caesarism. Every revolution tends to worship its leaders, and Carranza, the first of the revolutionary Caesars, was a forerunner of the so-called "personality cult," which is merely a euphemism for modern political idolatry. (This cult, also fostered by Obregón and Calles, still rules our political life, though the law forbidding re-election keeps it within limits.) At the same time, the revolutionaries who gathered around Carranza — especially Luis Cabrera, one of the most lucid minds of the period — strove to articulate and give coherence to the people's instinctive wishes. But the ideological insufficiency of the Revolution became plain almost at once, and the result was a compromise: the Constitution of 1917. It was impossible to return to the pre-Cortesian world; it was equally impossible to return to the colonial tradition. The Revolution had no other recourse than to take over the program of the liberals, though with certain modifications. This adoption of the liberals' scheme was a direct consequence of the lack of ideas among the revolutionaries. The intelligentsia did have some ideas, but they were completely useless: reality had smashed them to bits even before they could be submitted to the test of history.

The revival of the liberal program, with its classical division of powers (nonexistent in Mexico), its theoretical federalism and its blindness to our realities, opened the door once again to lies and pretenses. It is scarcely very strange that a good portion of our political ideas are still nothing but words intended to hide and restrict our true selves. Also, the influence of imperialism contributed toward frustrating the development of a native bourgeoisie, which could have given meaning to the liberal plan. The restoration of communal properties entailed the destruction of feudalism and should have brought a bourgeoisie into power. Thus our evolution would have followed the same stages as that of Europe. But our progress is erratic. Imperialism has not allowed us to achieve "historical normality," and the ruling classes of Mexico have no other mission than to collaborate, as administrators or associates, with a foreign power. This situation is historically ambiguous, and there is the danger of a return to the policies of the Díaz regime. It is possible for bankers and intermediaries to take over the government. Their methods would not be much different from those of the great landholders under Díaz: they would govern from behind the mask of the Revolution, just as Díaz governed from behind the mask of liberalism. But in this case it would be difficult to find a philosophy that would serve the same function as positivism. There are no longer any tailor-made ideas in our world.

If we contemplate the Mexican Revolution in terms of the ideas outlined in this essay, we see that it was a movement attempting to reconquer our past, to assimilate it and make it live in the present. This will to return, the consequence of solitude and desperation, is one of the phases of that dialectic of solitude and communion, reunion and separation, which seems to rule our whole history. Thanks to the Revolution, the Mexican wants to reconcile himself with his history and his origins. This explains why the character of the movement is both desperate and redemptive. If these words still have any meaning for us after so many repetitions, they mean that the people refuse all outside help, every imported scheme, every idea lacking some profound relationship to their intimate feelings, and that instead they turn to themselves. This desperation, this refusal to be saved by an alien project, is characteristic of the person who rejects all consolation and shuts himself up in his private world: he is alone. At the same moment, however, his solitude becomes an effort at communion. Once again, despair and solitude, redemption and communion are equivalent terms.

It is remarkable how the Revolution has crystallized itself after its long, extremely confused search. It is not a scheme that some group imposed on reality; instead, reality manifested itself in various places and began to take form, embodied in conflicting groups and at different times. Only recently has it been possible to see that such opposite figures as Emiliano Zapata and Venustiano Carranza, Luis Cabrera and José Vasconcelos, Francisco Villa and Álvaro Obregón, Francisco I. Madero and Lázaro Cárdenas, Felipe Ángeles and Antonio Díaz Soto y Gama are all part of a single process. If we compare the protagonists of the Reform with those of the Revolution, we observe that — apart from the clear ideas of the former and the confusion of the latter — the eminence of the liberals has not redeemed them from a certain dryness which makes them respectable but official figures, heroes of Public Office, while the brutality and

uncouthness of many of the revolutionary leaders has not prevented them from becoming popular myths. Villa still gallops
through the north, in songs and ballads; Zapata dies at every
popular fair; Madero appears on the balconies, waving the
flag; Carranza and Obregón still travel back and forth across
the country in those trains of the revolutionary period, causing
the women to flutter with alarm and the young men to leave
home. Everybody follows them, but to where? Nobody knows.
It is the Revolution, the magical word, the word that is going
to change everything, that is going to bring us immense delight
and a quick death. By means of the Revolution the Mexican
people found itself, located itself in its own past and substance.
Hence the Revolution's fertility, compared with our nineteenth-
century movements. Its cultural and artistic fertility resulted
from the profound manner in which its heroes, bandits and
myths stamped themselves forever on the sensibility and
imagination of every Mexican.

The Revolution was a sudden immersion of Mexico in her
own being, from which she brought back up, almost blindly,
the essentials of a new kind of state. In addition, it was a return
to the past, a reuniting of the ties broken by the Reform and
the Diaz dictatorship, a search for our own selves, and a return
to the maternal womb. Therefore it was also a fiesta: "the fiesta
of the bullets," to use the phrase by Martín Luis Guzmán. Like
our popular fiestas, the Revolution was an excess and a squandering, a going to extremes, an explosion of joy and hopelessness,
a shout of orphanhood and jubilation, of suicide and life, all
of them mingled together. Our Revolution is the other face of
Mexico, ignored by the Reform and humbled by the dictatorship. It is not the face of courtesy, of dissimulation, of form
imposed by means of lies and mutilations; it is the brutal,
resplendent face of death and fiestas, of gossip and gunfire, of

celebration and love (which is rape and pistol shots). The Revolution has hardly any ideas. It is an explosion of reality: a return and a communion, an upsetting of old institutions, a releasing of many ferocious, tender and noble feelings that had been hidden by our fear of being. And with whom does Mexico commune in this bloody fiesta? With herself, with her own being. Mexico dares to exist, to be. The revolutionary explosion is a prodigious fiesta in which the Mexican, drunk with his own self, is aware at last, in a mortal embrace, of his fellow Mexican.

CHAPTER SEVEN

The Mexican Intelligentsia

It would be a gross oversimplification to assert that Mexican culture is a reflection of the historical changes brought about by the revolutionary movement. It would be much more accurate to say that in their own way these changes, like Mexican culture, express the sometimes contradictory aims and tendencies of the nation, or rather of that part of Mexico that has accepted the responsibilities and joys of being Mexican. In this sense it is possible to say that the history of our culture is not very different from that of our people, although the relationship is not strict. It is not strict or inevitable because culture is often in advance of history, prophesying what is to come. Either that or it fails to express it, and thus betrays it, which is what happened at certain moments during the Díaz dictatorship. Poetry, by its very nature, and by the nature of its instrument, words, always tends to abolish history, not because it disdains it but because it transcends it. To reduce poetry to its reflections of historical events and movements would be like reducing the poet's words to their logical or grammatical connotations. Poetry transcends both history and language, although they are its necessary food. The same could be said, in different ways, of painting, music, the novel, the theater and the other arts. But artistic creation is not the theme of the following pages; they are simply a description of certain attitudes of the Mexican intelligentsia, that is, of the group whose vital activity is critical

151

thinking.[1] Their books and other writings are of lesser significance than their public influence and their political actions.

If the Revolution was a search and an immersion of ourselves in our own origins and being, no one embodied this fertile, desperate desire better than José Vasconcelos, the founder of modern education in Mexico. His work was brief but fecund, and the essence of it is still alive. In part he carried on the task begun by Justo Sierra, which was to extend elementary education and to improve the quality of instruction on the higher levels, but he also tried to base education on certain principles that were implicit in our tradition but had been forgotten or ignored by the positivists. Vasconcelos believed that the Revolution was going to rediscover the meaning of our history, which Sierra had sought in vain. The new education was to be founded on "our blood, our language and our people."

The character of the educational movement was organic. It was not the isolated work of one extraordinary man — though Vasconcelos was certainly that, in several ways — but rather an accomplishment of the Revolution, and its realization expressed the finest and most secret element of the revolutionary movement. Poets, painters, prose writers, teachers, architects and musicians all collaborated in the project. All, that is, of the Mexican intelligentsia, or almost all. It was a social effort, but one that required the presence of a man who could catch fire and then transmit his enthusiasm to others. Vasconcelos, as a philosopher and a man of action, possessed that unity of vision which brings coherence to diverse plans, and although he sometimes overooked details, he never lost himself in them. His work, subject to a number of necessary and not always happy corrections, was the work of a founder, not of a mere technician.

---

[1] *Las peras del olmo* (Mexico, 1956) gives the author's position on Mexican art, particularly poetry and painting.

Vasconcelos conceived of instruction as active participation. Schools were established, readers and the classics were published, institutes were created, and cultural missions were sent to the remotest parts of the country. At the same time, the intelligentsia turned toward the people, discovering their true nature and eventually making them the center of its activities. The popular arts emerged again, after centuries of having been ignored; the old songs were sung once more in schools and concert halls; the regional dances with their pure and timid movements, combining flight and immobility, fire and reserve, were danced for a wider audience. Contemporary Mexican painting was born. Some of our writers turned their eyes to the colonial past, and others used Indian themes; but the most courageous faced up to the present, and created the novel of the Revolution. After the lies and pretences of the dictatorship, Mexico suddenly discovered herself, with astonished and loving eyes: "We are the prodigal sons of a homeland which we cannot even define but which we are beginning at last to observe. She is Castilian and Moorish, with Aztec markings."

As a member of the Ateneo group and as a participant in the battle against positivism, Vasconcelos knew that all education entails an image of the world and a program for living. Hence his efforts to base the Mexican schools on something more concrete than Article 3 of the Constitution, which stated that education was to be secular. Of course, secularism had never been neutral, and its pretended indifference toward ultimate questions was an artifice that deceived nobody. Vasconcelos, who was neither a Catholic nor a Jacobin, was not a neutral either. He wanted to base our school system on tradition, in the same way that the Revolution attempted to create a new economy on the basis of the *ejido*.[2] To do so meant to formulate

---

[2] *Ejido:* common, public land. — *Tr.*

the impulses behind the Revolution in an explicit way, since up till then they had only expressed themselves in a kind of instinctive stammering. Our tradition, if it was really still alive, would link us to a universal tradition that would enlarge and justify our own.

Every time we return to tradition we are reminded that we are part of the universal tradition of Spain, the only one that Spanish Americans can accept and carry on. There are two Spains: the Spain that is closed to the outside world, and the open, heterodox Spain that breaks out of its prison to breathe the free air of the spirit. Ours is the latter. The former — pure-blooded and medieval — never accepted us, never discovered us, and our whole history, like a part of the history of the Spaniards themselves, has been a struggle against it. Now the universal tradition of Spain in America, as we have already noted, consists above all in conceiving of the continent as a unit superior to national divisions. A return to the Spanish tradition, therefore, can have no other meaning than a return to the unity of Spanish America. The philosophy of the "cosmic race" (that is, of the new American man who would resolve all racial conflicts and the great opposition between East and West) was the natural and ultimate consequence of Spanish universality. The ideas expounded by Vasconcelos had little or no relation to the caste-conscious traditionalism of the Mexican conservatives: he saw our continent, as did the founders of America, as futurity and newness. "Spanish America is magnificently new, not only as a geographical region but also as a realm for the spirit." His traditionalism did not look to the past for support: it was to be justified in and by the future.

This Ibero-American philosophy was the first attempt to resolve the conflict that had been latent in the Revolution from the beginning. The revolutionary movement was an instinctive explosion, a longing for communion, a revelation of our being; it was a search for, and discovery of, the ties that had been broken by liberalism. But that rediscovered tradition was not enough to feed the hunger of a newborn country; it lacked the universal elements necessary for the building of a new society now that Catholicism and liberalism, the two great universal forces which had shaped our culture, could no longer serve us. In fact, the Revolution was unable to justify itself even to itself, because it had scarcely any ideas. The only choice left, then, was between feeding on itself and inventing a new system. Vasconcelos tried to resolve the question by offering his philosophy of the Ibero-American race. The motto of positivism, "Love, Order and Progress," was replaced by a proud boast: "The Spirit Shall Speak through My Race."

Unfortunately his philosophy was a personal creation, the very opposite of that of the liberals and positivists, who had been part of a vast ideological current. The work that Vasconcelos created has all the poetic coherency of the great philosophical systems, but not their rigor. It is an isolated monument and has not originated any schools or movements. As Malraux said, "Myths do not enlist the complicity of our reason, but rather that of our instincts." The philosophy of Vasconcelos contains fragments that are still alive and fecund, portions that still illuminate and even prophesy, but it does not contain the essentials of our being or our culture.

During the period that Lázaro Cárdenas directed the country, the Revolution tried to realize itself more amply and profoundly. The reforms announced by the preceding regimes were finally carried out. Cárdenas completed the work begun by Zapata and Carranza. The necessity of giving the people something more than liberal secularism caused a revision of Article 3 of the Constitution: "Education will be socialistic . . .

it will combat fanaticism and prejudice, creating in the young a rational and accurate conception of the Universe and of society." Even the Marxists who proposed it agreed that the new text was defective. How could socialistic education be established in a country whose Constitution made private property almost sacred, and whose working class had no share in the directing of public affairs? The idea became a mere political weapon, causing the regime a good deal of unnecessary trouble and providing the conservatives with ready criticisms. Most important of all, it could not remedy the shortcomings of the Revolution: if revolutions cannot be made with words, neither can ideas be implanted by decrees. The philosophy implicit in Article 3 did not invite creative participation nor re-establish the bases of the nation, as colonial Catholicism had done in its time. Socialistic education was a trap that caught only its inventors, to the delight of all the conservatives. The conflict between the universality of our tradition and the impossibility of returning to the forms that had expressed it could not be resolved by the adoption of a philosophy which was not — and could not be — the philosophy of the Mexican nation.

The same conflict damages the political and economic forms created by the Revolution. In all aspects of Mexican life there is a vital awareness of the authenticity and originality of our Revolution, but at the same time there is a desire for wholeness and coherence, and these the Revolution did not offer us. The *calpulli* was an economic, social, political and religious institution that grew up naturally at the very center of pre-Cortesian life. It managed to survive during the colonial period alongside other forms of land ownership, thanks to the nature of the world founded by the Spaniards, a universal order that permitted various conceptions of property in much the same way that it included a variety of races, castes and classes. But how could a system of communal land ownership be incorporated into a society that had already entered a capitalistic phase and involved itself, unintentionally, in the conflicts of the imperialist world? The same problem confronted our writers and artists: to find a whole and organic solution that would not sacrifice the particulars of our being to the universal of a system, as had happened with liberalism, and that would not reduce our participation to the passive attitude of the mere believer or imitator. For the first time the Mexican saw his life and his history as something he must invent from head to foot. This was impossible, and therefore our culture and our politics have swung from one extreme to another. We have not been able to realize a synthesis and have ended by accepting a whole series of compromises, in the sphere of education as well as in that of social problems. These compromises have allowed us to defend the gains we have already made, but it would be dangerous to consider them as definitive. The present text of Article 3 reflects this situation. The revisions that were made in it have brought certain benefits, but there are questions that have still not been answered: What is the meaning of Mexican tradition and what is its current value? What program for living do our schools offer the young? The answers to these questions cannot be arrived at by any one man. If we have not answered them, the reason is that history itself has not resolved the conflict.

Once the military phase of the Revolution had ended, many young intellectuals who had not been able to participate in it, because of their age or for other reasons, now began to work with the revolutionary governments. The intellectuals became the secret or public advisors of the illiterate generals, the labor or peasant leaders, the political bosses. It was an immense task and everything had to be improvised. The poets studied economics; the jurists, sociology; the novelists, international law or pedagogy or agronomy. Except for the painters — who were supported in the best possible manner, by being given public walls to cover with murals — all of the intelligentsia was enlisted for specific and immediate ends: legal projects, governmental plans, confidential missions, educational work, the founding of schools and agrarian banks, etc. The diplomatic service, foreign trade, public administration, all opened their doors to an intelligentsia that came from the middle class. Within a short time the country possessed a considerable group of technicians and experts, thanks to the new professional schools and the opportunity to study abroad. Their participation in the work of government has made it possible to continue the efforts that were initiated by the first revolutionaries. However, their situation is extremely difficult. In their anxiety not to surrender either their material or ideological positions, they have made compromise both an art and a way of life. Many aspects of their work have been admirable, but they have lost their independence and their criticism has become excessively diluted, out of prudence or Machiavellism. The Mexican intelligentsia as a whole has not been able to use the weapons of the intellectual — criticism, examination, judgment — or has not learned how to wield them effectively. As a result, the spirit of accommodation — a natural product, it would appear, of all revolutions that turn into governments — has invaded almost every area of public activity. In addition, government service has become a sort of cult or sect, with the usual bureaucratic rituals and "state secrets." Public affairs are not discussed, they are whispered. It should be remembered, however, that in serving the government a number of men have made genuine personal sacrifices. The demon of efficiency (rather than of ambition), the desire to contribute to the collective effort, and even an ascetic view of civic duty as a form of self-abnegation, have caused some of them to suffer the unhappiest of all losses: that of a sense of personal accomplishment. This situation is very different from that of the European intellectual. In Europe and the United States, the intellectual has been deprived of power. He lives in exile, so far as the state is concerned, and wields his influence from outside the government, with criticism as his principal mission. In Mexico, the intellectual's mission is political action. The Mexican intelligentsia has not only served its country, it has also defended it, honestly and effectively. But in so doing, has it not ceased to be an intelligentsia? That is, has it not renounced its proper role as the critical conscience of its people?

A number of factors have caused the people to grow sceptical and the intelligentsia to lose confidence in its work. Among these factors are the varying aims of the Revolution, the international pressures that began to be felt as soon as the first social reforms were undertaken, the demagoguery that quickly became a chronic illness of our political system, and the political corruption that has made it impossible for us to realize our liberal, democratic ideals. Although the Mexican intelligentsia is united in a common cause, it also has its heterodox and solitary figures, its critics and its zealots. Some of them have withdrawn from government service to found opposition groups or parties. For instance, Manuel Gómez Morín — who formulated the Revolution's property laws — is now the head of the right-wing National Action Party. Others, like Jesús Silva Herzog, have shown that technical efficiency and spiritual independence are not necessarily at odds: Herzog has succeeded in bringing together all the independent writers of Latin America in his magazine *Cuadernos Americanos*. Vicente Lombardo Toledano and Narciso Bassols are among those who turned to Marxism in the belief that it was the only philosophy capable of reconciling the particulars of Mexican history with the universality of the Revolution. Their work should be judged above all in the field of social action. Unfortunately their efforts have been vitiated for many years now by the docility with which they have followed the party line from Moscow, even at its worst moments.

If a part of the intelligentsia embraced Marxism (almost always in its official, bureaucratic form) in the hope of breaking out of their solitude to join the international labor movement, other men took up the task of revision and criticism. The Revolution had discovered the true character of Mexico, and Samuel Ramos began to ask his country questions: he tore away its masks, hoping to find out what the Mexican is really like. It has been said that his *Profile of Man and Culture in Mexico* — our first serious attempt at self-knowledge — suffers from a variety of limitations: for example, that the Mexican described in its pages is an isolated type, or that the instruments he used to penetrate reality (the theory of resentment as expounded by Scheler and Adler, especially the latter) reduce the significance of his conclusions. But the book remains our only point of departure. The majority of its observations are still valid, and the central idea — that the Mexican hides himself when he expresses himself, that his words and gestures are almost always masks — is as true as ever. Ramos has given us an extremely penetrating description of the attitudes that make each one of us a closed, inaccessible being.

At about the same time that Ramos was studying our personality, Jorge Cuesta was investigating the meaning of our tradition. His results are scattered among articles on politics and aesthetic criticism, but nevertheless his ideas are unified and coherent. Whether he was discussing classicism in Mexican poetry or French influence on our culture, the Mexican muralists or the poetry of López Velarde, Cuesta reiterated his belief that Mexico is a self-created country and therefore lacks a past. Or, to put it more exactly, that Mexico has re-created itself in opposition to its past, repudiating the inert, parochial, caste-conscious nature of its Indian and Spanish inheritance. The true Mexican tradition does not carry on the colonial tradition; on the contrary, it denies it, because it is a free election of certain universal values, those of French rationalism. Cuesta believed that our "Frenchification" was not accidental, and was not the result of mere historical circumstances. The Mexican discovers in French culture — which is also free election — his universal vocation. The models of our poetry, like those of our political systems, are universal, with little interest in time, space and local color. Our poets tend to ignore our national particulars in favor of a universal conception of mankind. They are ruled by Method and Form. Hence our poetry is Romantic or national only when it is weak or self-betraying. The same is true, in various ways, of the rest of our artistic and political forms.

Cuesta was scornful of historical examinations. He saw the Spanish tradition as nothing but inertia, conformity and passivity, because he ignored the other side of the coin. He also neglected to analyze the influence of the indigenist tradition. As for our preference for French culture, is it not the result of various circumstances in both Mexican and world history rather than a supposed affinity? Cuesta was influenced by Julian Benda, and forgot that French culture is nourished by French history and is inseparable from the reality that sustains it.

Despite the limitations in his intellectual position, we are indebted to Cuesta for a number of valuable observations.

Mexico's self-discovery or self-definition takes the form of a negation of her past. Cuesta's error, like that of the liberals and positivists, was in supposing that this negation required her to adopt French radicalism and classicism in her politics, art and poetry. History refutes this hypothesis, because the revolutionary movement, contemporary poetry and painting, and the very development of the country have all tended to emphasize our individuality and to break out of the intellectual geometry we imported from France. Mexican radicalism, as we have seen, is something quite different.

Although Ramos and Cuesta disagree in many things, there is still an important resemblance between them: they both reflect our profound desire for self-knowledge. The former represents our search for the intimate particulars of our nature, a search that was the very essence of our Revolution, while the latter represents our anxiety to incorporate these particulars in a universal tradition.

The economist and historian Daniel Cosío Villegas was another solitary figure. He established the Fondo de Cultura Económica, a money-losing publishing house whose main object was to provide Spanish Americans with the basic texts of economics, from Adam Smith to Keynes. Thanks to Cosío and his successors, the Fondo broadened its aims considerably, and published works of philosophy, sociology and history that have revitalized the intellectual life of the Spanish-speaking countries. Cosío Villegas also gave us the most complete and serious examination of the Díaz regime that has yet been produced. But perhaps his finest contribution is the spirit that animates his criticism: unbiased opinions, independent judgments. I believe his best book is *American Extremes,* a far from pious study of our real situation, written with irony, courage and a most admirable impertinence.

President Cárdenas opened Mexico's doors to those who had supported the losing side in the Spanish civil war. Among them were writers, poets and professors, and they have played an important part in the renascence of Mexican culture, especially in the sphere of philosophy. Mexico owes a debt of gratitude to the Spanish philosopher José Gaos, the teacher of the young intelligentsia. The new generation is capable of using the instruments which every intellectual enterprise must have, and a Mexican intelligentsia can now be formed within the classroom for the first time since the Independence period. Our new teachers do not offer the young a ready-made philosophy, but rather the opportunity and means to create one. This, of course, is a teacher's true mission.

Alfonso Reyes was another source of stimulation. His work, which we can now begin to appreciate in its full dimensions, is an invitation to rigorous clarity and coherence. His classicism is equidistant from the academicism of Ignacio Ramírez and Justo Sierra's Romanticism. It is not a mere imitation or adaptation of universal forms: it seeks its own form and becomes its own best model. It is simultaneously a mirror and a clear spring, in which man can recognize himself but can also surpass himself.

To Reyes, literature was more than a vocation or a profession, it was a religion. He was a complete writer, for whom language was everything that language can be: sounds and symbols, inanimate design and sheer magic, clockworks and a living organism. As poet, critic and essayist he was a Man of Letters in the highest sense: a miner, artificer, peon, gardener, lover and priest of words. His work is history and poetry, reflection and creation. Reyes was a whole group of writers and therefore his work is a Literature in itself. Is it a lesson in form? No, it is a lesson in expression. In a world of eloquent rhetoric and studious silences, Reyes instructs us in the dangers and responsibilities of language. He is sometimes accused of not having given us a philosophy or an orientation. His accusers forget that his writings clarify many of the historical situations confronting us in the Americas. But his greatest contribution, I think, is the fact that to read him is to receive a lesson in clarity. By teaching us how words should be used, he also teaches us how to think. Hence the significance of his thoughts on the American intelligentsia and the responsibilities of the present-day writer and intellectual.

Reyes tells us that the writer's first obligation is fidelity to his language. The writer has no other instrument but words. Unlike the tools of the artisan or painter or musician, words are full of ambiguous and even contradictory meanings. Using them should mean clarifying them, purifying them, making them true instruments of our thinking rather than masks or approximations. Writing implies a profession of faith and an attitude that transcends rhetoric and grammar. The roots of language are entwined with those of morality, and thus the criticism of language is moral and historical criticism. Every literary style is something more than a way of speaking. It is a way of thinking, an implicit or explicit judgment of reality. Language is by nature social, while the writer must work in solitude, and therefore they establish a very strange relationship: thanks to language the modern writer participates in the life of the community, although the other means of communication with his people and his times have broken down.

Alfonso Reyes offers us not only a criticism of language but also a philosophy and an ethics. It is not surprising, then, that while he defends the clarity of words and the universality of their meanings, he also points out a duty. The Mexican writer has certain specific obligations beyond that fidelity to language which should characterize every writer. The first and most important of these is to express our own nature – or, as Reyes put it, "to seek the soul of our nation." This is an extremely arduous task, because we have only a received language, not one we created ourselves, to express the thoughts and feelings of our confused, inarticulate people. That is, we must use the language of Góngora and Quevedo, Cervantes and St. John of the Cross to express a very different world. For us, writing means breaking down the Spanish language and re-creating it in such a way that it becomes Mexican without ceasing to be Spanish. Our fidelity to language thus implies fidelity to our people and to a tradition that is ours only through an act of intellectual violence. Both terms of this immense obligation are vitally present in the writings of Alfonso Reyes, and for this reason his best work consists in the invention of a universal language and form that can contain all our unexpressed conflicts without smothering or disfiguring them.

Reyes considered language an artistic and ethical problem. His work is not a model or lesson but a stimulus. Our attitude toward language cannot be different from that of our predecessors, and our responsibilities are even greater than theirs because we have fewer illusions about the ideas that Western civilization once dreamed were eternal. The life and history of our people demand the creation of a form that will express this demand and that will also transcend it without betraying it. Solitude and communion, individuality and universality are still the extremes that devour every Mexican. This conflict characterizes our most intimate selves and gives a special color – alternately dark and bright – to our private conduct and our relationships with others; at the same time it has a profound effect on all our political, social and artistic efforts. Mexican life is a continual, lacerating swing between extremes, or else an unstable and painful equilibrium.

The whole history of Mexico, from the Conquest to the Revolution, can be regarded as a search for our own selves, which have been deformed or disguised by alien institutions, and for a form that will express them. The pre-Cortesian societies achieved rich and diversified creations, as we can see from what the Spaniards left standing and from what the archaeologists and anthropologists are bringing to light almost daily. The Conquest destroyed those forms and imposed Spanish substitutes. There are two different aspects to Spanish culture, reconciled but never wholly united by the Spanish state: the medieval tradition based on castes, which is still alive in Spain today, and a universal tradition which Spain adopted and made her own before the Counter Reformation. Through Catholicism Spain arrived at a synthesis of both elements in the realm of art. The same is true of some of the institutions and some of the conceptions of political rights which had so decisive an effect on the structure of colonial society and on the status assigned to the Indians and their communities. Due to the universal nature of the Catholic religion — which was a religion for everyone, especially orphans and the disinherited, although this is often forgotten by its followers as well as its opponents — colonial society managed to become a true order, if only for a brief while. Form and substance were one. There was no wall or abyss between reality and institutions, the people and the law, art and life, the individual and society; on the contrary, everything harmonized and everyone was guided by the same concepts and the same will. No man was alone, however humble his situation, and neither was society: this world and the next, life and death, action and contemplation were experienced as totalities, not as isolated acts or ideas. Every fragment participated in the whole, which was alive in each one of its parts. The pre-Cortesian order was replaced by a universal form that was open to the participation and communion of all the faithful.

The paralysis of colonial society, and its eventual hardening into a pious or ferocious mask, seems to have been the result of a circumstance that has rarely been examined: the decadence of European Catholicism as the source of Western culture coincided with its expansion and apogee in New Spain. The religious life — a source of great creativity in an earlier epoch — became mere inert participation for the vast majority. For the minority, wavering between faith and curiosity, it became a sort of ingenious game and, finally, silence and sleep. Or to state it another way, Catholicism was a refuge for the great mass of Indians. The Conquest had left them orphans, and they escaped this condition by returning to the maternal womb. Colonial religion was a return to prenatal life, passive, neutral and self-satisfied.[3] The small minority who wanted to emerge into the fresh air of the world were either smothered into silence or forced to retreat.

The Independence movement, the Reform movement and the Díaz dictatorship were distinct and contradictory phases of one continuing effort to break free. The nineteenth century was a complete break with form. At the same time, the liberal movement was an attempt to create a utopia, and thus provoked the vengeance of reality. Our independent history, from the time we were first aware of ourselves as individuals and of our geographical area as an individual nation, has been a break with tradition, with form, and a search for a new form that would contain all our native particulars and would also be open to the future. Catholicism was closed to the future; liberalism replaced the concrete Mexican with an inanimate abstraction;

---

[3] See Jorge Carrión: "La ruta psicológica de Quetzalcóatl," in *Cuadernos Americanos,* No. 5, Sept.-Oct. 1949, Mexico.

neither could express both our individual desires and our universal longings.

The Revolution began as a discovery of our own selves and a return to our origins; later it became a search and an abortive attempt at a synthesis; finally, since it was unable to assimilate our tradition and to offer us a new and workable plan, it became a compromise. The Revolution has not been capable of organizing its explosive values into a world view, and the Mexican intelligentsia has not been able to resolve the conflict between the insufficiencies of our tradition and our need and desire for universality.

This recapitulation helps to define the problem of a Mexican philosophy, a problem recently brought up by Ramos and Zea. The conflicts that have been examined in the course of this chapter remained hidden until a short while ago, covered over by foreign ideas and forms that have served to justify our actions but have also hindered our self-expression and obscured the nature of our inner controversy. Our situation resembles that of the neurotic, for whom moral principles and abstract ideas have no practical function except as a defense for his privacy — that is, as a complex system he employs to deceive both himself and others regarding the true meaning of his inclinations and the true character of his conflicts. But when these latter are clearly and accurately revealed to him, he must then confront them and resolve them himself. Much the same thing has happened to us. We have suddenly discovered that we are naked and that we are confronted by an equally naked reality. Nothing can justify us now: we alone can answer the questions reality is asking us. Philosophical reflection thus becomes an urgent necessity. It is not enough to examine our intellectual past or describe our characteristic attitudes. What we desperately need is a concrete solution, one that will give meaning to our presence on earth.

How could a philosophical project of this sort be Mexican? If it examined our tradition, it would be a philosophy of Mexican history and a history of Mexican ideas. But our history is only a fragment of world history, by which I mean that — except for the Revolution — we have always lived our history as a minor episode in the history of the world as a whole. As for our ideas, they have never been really ours: they have been either impositions or importations from Europe. Therefore a philosophy of Mexican history would simply be a consideration of the various ways in which we have reacted to the themes proposed to us by world history: the Counter Reformation, rationalism, positivism, socialism. Any historical meditation would require an answer to the following question: In what way have we Mexicans "lived" these universal ideas?

The question implies a concept of the Mexican as a distinctive individual, a concept that makes up the second theme of this projected Mexican philosophy. We have never succeeded in creating a form that would express our individuality. As a result, "Mexicanism" has never been identifiable with any specific form or tendency: it has always veered from one universal project to another, all of them foreign to our nature and all of them useless in our present crisis. Mexicanism is a way of not being ourselves, a way of life that is not our own. Sometimes it is a mask; sometimes it is a sudden determination to find ourselves, to gash open our breasts in order to release our true and most secret voices. A Mexican philosophy would have to take into account not only the ambiguity of our tradition but also that of our will-to-be, which demands recognition of our individuality but only if that recognition is joined with a universal solution to our problems.

A number of writers have undertaken the task of examining

our intellectual past. The studies by Leopoldo Zea and Edmundo O'Gorman are especially important. The question that preoccupies O'Gorman is how to define the historical entity we call America. It is not a geographical region, and it is not a past; perhaps it is not even a present. It is an idea, an invention of the European spirit. America is a utopia, a moment in which the European spirit becomes universal by freeing itself of its historical particulars and conceiving of itself as a universal idea. Almost miraculously, this idea finds its embodiment and home in a specific land and also in a specific time: the future. European culture conceives of itself in America as a superior unity. O'Gorman is correct when he sees our continent as an actualization of the European spirit, but what happens to America as an autonomous historical entity when it confronts the realities of Europe? This questions seems to be Leopoldo Zea's essential concern. As a historian of Spanish-American thought, and as an independent critic even when discussing everyday politics, Zea declares that until recently America was Europe's monologue, one of the historical forms in which its thought was embodied. Lately, however, this monologue has become a dialogue, one that is not purely intellectual but is also social and political. Zea has studied American alienation, but although alienation is more basic to our character than our individual traits, it is now a condition shared by all men. We Mexicans have always lived on the periphery of history. Now the center or nucleus of world society has disintegrated and everyone — including the European and the North American — is a peripheral being. We are all living on the margin because there is no longer any center.

Other younger writers are studying the meaning of our attitudes toward life. The greatest virtue of many of these efforts lies in the writers' anxiety to understand what we are, and to understand clearly and without complacency. Nevertheless, most of the members of this group — especially Emilio Uranga, its leader — have realized that the theme of Mexicanism can only be a part of a larger meditation on a much vaster theme: the historical alienation of dependent peoples and of mankind in general.

For the first time, Mexico does not have at her disposal a set of universal ideas that can justify her situation. Europe, once a storehouse of ready-to-use ideas, now lives as we do, from day to day. Strictly speaking, the modern world no longer possesses any ideas. Hence the Mexican must face reality in the same way as everyone else: alone. But in his nakedness he will discover his true universality, which previously was a mere adaptation of European thought. His philosophy will be Mexican only in its accent or emphasis or style, not in its content. Mexicanism will become a mask which, when taken off, reveals at last the genuine human being it disguised. Under the present circumstances, then, our need to develop a Mexican philosophy becomes a need to think out for ourselves certain problems which are no longer exclusively ours but pertain to all men. That is, Mexican philosophy, to be truly that, must be philosophy plain and simple.

This conclusion can be corroborated by a historical examination of the problem. The Mexican Revolution placed an injunction on our intellectual tradition. The revolutionary movement showed that all the ideas that had justified us in the past were either dead or were deforming our nature. Also, world history has forced us to struggle with many problems and questions which affected our predecessors only indirectly. Despite our national differences — historical superimpositions, an ambiguous tradition, semicolonialism, etc. — our situation is now no different from that of other countries. Our cultural crisis, for perhaps the first time in history, is the same as the crisis of our species. We are no longer moved by Valéry's melancholy reflections on vanished civilizations, because it is not Western culture that is in danger of being destroyed tomorrow, as the cultures of the Greeks and the Arabs, the Aztecs and the Egyptians were destroyed in the past: it is man himself. The old plurality of cultures, postulating various and contrary ideals, and offering various and contrary views of the future, has been replaced by a single civilization and a single future. Until recently, history was a meditation on the many truths proposed by many cultures, and a verification of the radical heterogeneity of every society and archetype. Now history has recovered its unity and become what it was at the beginning: a meditation on mankind. And mankind, too, has recovered its unity. All of today's civilizations derive from that of the Western world, which has assimilated or crushed its rivals. The decisions we make in Mexico now affect all men, and vice versa. The differences that separate the Communists and the West are much less profound than those that separated the Persians and the Greeks, the Romans and the Egyptians, the Chinese and the peoples of Europe. Communists and bourgeois democrats brandish opposing ideas, but those ideas have a common source and are phrased in a common language which both sides understand. The contemporary crisis is not a struggle between two diverse cultures, as the conservatives would have us believe, but rather an internal quarrel in a civilization that no longer has any rivals, a civilization whose future is the future of the whole world. Each man's fate is that of man himself. Therefore, every attempt we make as Mexicans to resolve our conflicts must have universal validity or it will be futile from the outset.

The Mexican Revolution forced us to emerge from ourselves, to confront the truths of history, and to recognize that we must invent new institutions and a new future. But the Revolution has expired without resolving our contradictions. Ever since World War II we have been aware that the self-creation demanded of us by our national realities is no different from that which similar realities are demanding of others. The past has left us orphans, as it has the rest of the planet, and we must join together in inventing our common future. World history has become everyone's task, and our own labyrinth is the labyrinth of all mankind.

CHAPTER EIGHT

The Present Day

The revolutionary movement, as a search for — and momentary finding of — our own selves, transformed Mexico and made her "other." To be oneself is always to become that other person who is one's real self, that hidden promise or possibility. In one sense, then, the Revolution has recreated the nation; in another sense, of equal importance, it has extended nationality to races and classes which neither colonialism nor the nineteenth century were able to incorporate into our national life. But despite its extraordinary fecundity, it was incapable of creating a vital order that would be at once a world view and the basis of a really just and free society. The Revolution has not succeeded in changing our country into a community, or even in offering any hope of doing so. By community, I mean a world in which men recognize themselves in each other, and in which the "principle of authority" — that is, force, whatever its origin and justification — concedes its place to a responsible form of liberty. It is true, however, that no known society has ever achieved this state, and it is no accident, of course, that the Revolution has not given us a vision of man comparable to that of colonial Catholicism or the liberalism of the last century. It is our own phenomenon, but many of its limitations result from circumstances that have been determined by contemporary world history.

The Mexican Revolution was chronologically the first of the great revolutions of the twentieth century. To understand it correctly, it is necessary to see it as part of a general process that is still going on. Like all modern revolutions, it proposed to liquidate feudalism, transform the country by means of industry and technology, put an end to our economic and political dependence, and establish a genuinely democratic society. In other words, to make the leap that our most forward-looking liberals had dreamed about, consummate at last the Independence and Reform movements, and convert Mexico into a modern nation. And to do all this without betraying ourselves. On the contrary, the changes were to reveal our true being, the face that was both known and unknown to us. The Revolution was going to invent a Mexico that would be faithful to itself.

The most advanced countries, except for Germany, turned from the *ancien régime* to modern bourgeois democracy in a way that could almost be called natural. Their political, economic and technical transformations seemed to be inspired and guided by some superior coherency. History has its own logic, and if we can discover the secret of its functionings, we can control the future. This notion, false as it is, still causes us to regard the history of the great powers as the unfolding of some majestic logical proposition. In fact, capitalism gradually developed from a sort of primitive accumulation into more and more intricate forms, until it reached the stage of high finance and world imperialism. The transition from primitive to international capitalism produced radical changes within each country and in the world as a whole. On the one hand, the differences between a worker and his boss (after the colonial and semicolonial peoples had been exploited for a century and a half) were less great than the differences between that same worker and a Hindu pariah or Bolivian peon. On the other hand, imperialist expansion unified the planet: it seized all its riches, converted them into merchandise, and cast them into the stream of international trade; it universalized human labor (the textile worker, perhaps thousands of miles away, continues the work done by the cotton-picker), making real for the first time, as a fact rather than a moral postulate, the oneness of the human condition; and it destroyed the eccentric cultures and civilizations, forcing all the world's peoples to orbit around two or three suns, from which radiated all political, economic and social power. At the same time, the peoples thus annexed were assigned a merely passive role. Economically, they were nothing but cheap manual labor and producers of raw materials; politically, they were colonials or semicolonials; spiritually, they lived in barbarous or picturesque societies. "Progress" brought them certain material benefits, but it also required them to accede to historical "normality": to be, that is, mere phantoms. This was the background of the Mexican Revolution and, in general, of the revolutions of the twentieth century.

We can now see more clearly what the Revolution undertook to accomplish. It tried, within a short time and with a minimum of human sacrifices, to complete a task that had taken the European bourgeoisie more than a hundred and fifty years. To do so, first we had to secure our political independence and recover control of our natural resources. And it had to be done without infringing on the social rights guaranteed by the Constitution of 1917, especially the rights of the workers. In Europe and the United States these conquests were the result of over a century of proletarian struggle, and to a considerable extent they represented (and represent) participation in earnings from abroad. In Mexico we had no colonial income to distribute; we did not even own the oil, minerals, electric power and other resources with which we had to transform the country. Therefore the Revolution's problem was not merely one of beginning at the beginning: we had to begin from before the beginning.

The Revolution made the new state the principal agent of social change. Its first job was to recover and divide up the land, open other lands to cultivation, and establish irrigation projects, rural schools and agrarian banks. There are experts who hold forth on the technical errors that have been committed, and moralists who decry the continuing power of our traditional rural bosses and greedy politicians. They are quite right. And it is also true that the danger of a return to monopolization of the land still exists. Our gains have to be defended constantly. But at least the feudal regime has disappeared: to forget that is to forget much too much. Also, the agrarian reforms not only benefited the rural population but also broke up the old social structure, making possible the birth of new and productive forces.

Despite these accomplishments, however, thousands of our rural citizens live in dire misery, and other thousands have no recourse but to emigrate to the United States each year as temporary laborers. Our population increase — a circumstance the first revolutionary governments failed to take into account — is partially responsible for the present imbalance. Incredible as it may seem, the greater part of the country suffers from rural overpopulation. Or to be more exact, we simply do not have enough cultivable land. New farming areas have been opened up, and new industries and centers of production have been established, but they have not been sufficient to absorb the growth in population. With our present resources we are unable to create even the minimum amount of industrial and agricultural employment required by our excess of hands and mouths. It is clear that the problem is not only one of increased population but also of insufficient economic progress. It is equally clear, however, that we are faced with a situation that is beyond the capabilities of the government and even of the nation as a whole. Where and how can we obtain the necessary economic and technical resources? This question, which I will attempt to answer a little later, should not be asked in isolation, but rather

in connection with the whole vast problem of economic development. Industry is not growing with the speed which our growing
population demands, and the result is underemployment. At the
same time, rural underemployment is retarding industrial development, because it is not increasing the number of consumers.

The Revolution also proposed, as noted earlier, to recover
our natural wealth. The revolutionary governments, that of
Cárdenas in particular, called for the nationalization of oil, the
railroads and other industries. This policy brought us into conflict with economic imperialism, and the state had to back down
and suspend its expropriations, though without surrendering
what had already been recovered. (It should be mentioned in
passing that our industrial growth would have been impossible
without the nationalization of the petroleum industry.) The
Revolution did much more than expropriate: it created new
state industries by means of a network of banks and credit
institutions, gave financial and technical assistance to others
(private and semiprivate), and in general tried to guide our
economic development rationally and for the benefit of the
public. All these things, and many others, were accomplished
slowly and not without a certain amount of blundering and
corruption. Yet the face of Mexico began to change, despite the
difficulties and contradictions, Little by little a new working
class and a bourgeoisie arose. Both classes lived in the shadow
of the state and have only now begun to achieve an autonomous
life.

Government protection of the working class began with a
popular alliance: the workers supported Carranza in exchange
for a more advanced social policy. They also supported Obregón
and Calles for the same reason. The state rewarded them by
protecting the labor unions. Unfortunately the alliance became
a surrender on the part of the union leaders, who were given

high political offices. The process reached its zenith, strange as it may seem, during the Cárdenas administration, which was the most radical period of the Revolution. And the leaders who surrendered their unions to the government were the very same leaders who had fought hardest against all forms of corruption in the labor movement. As for the objection that since the policies of the Cárdenas administration were revolutionary, it was very natural for the unions to support them, the fact is that the labor leaders permitted their unions to become merely one more segment of the Party of the Revolution, that is, of the government party. This frustrated any possibility of a workers' party or, at the very least, of a labor movement like that in the United States, apolitical but autonomous, and free of governmental meddling. The only persons to gain anything were the leaders, who became professional politicians: representatives, senators, governors. In the last few years, however, there has been something of a change. The labor groups are winning more and more autonomy; they are getting rid of their corrupt leaders and are fighting for more democratic unions. This new movement could be one of the decisive forces in the rebirth of democracy in Mexican life. Considering, though, our country's social characteristics, the labor movement cannot be effective unless it avoids the sectarianism of some of its new leaders and seeks an alliance with the rural workers and with a sector that was also born during the Revoution: the middle class. Until recently the middle class was a very limited group made up of small businessmen and the members of the traditional "liberal professions": lawyers, doctors, teachers, etc. Our industrial and commercial development, along with the increase in public works, has caused the middle class to expand considerably. It is still crude and ignorant from a cultural and political viewpoint, but it is full of vitality.

Now that the bourgeoisie has grown more powerful and is more in command of itself, it is attempting to enter the government, not as a protected group but as its sole director. The banker is replacing the revolutionary general; the industrialist hopes to replace the technician or politician. They are trying to change the government more and more exclusively into a political expression of their interests. But the bourgeoisie does not form a homogeneous whole. Some of its members, heirs of the Revolution (though sometimes they do not know it), are striving to create a national capitalism; others are simply agents or intermediaries of international capital. Finally, the government contains many technicians who still champion — with varying success — a policy respectful of the revolutionary past and dedicated to the public interest. All this explains the rather zigzag progress of the state, as well as the desire of its leaders not to upset the "equilibrium." Since the Carranza epoch, the Mexican Revolution has been a compromise between opposing forces: nationalism and imperialism, the labor movement and industrial development, a regulated economy and "free enterprise," democracy and state paternalism.

None of our gains could have been won within the framework of classical capitalism. What is more, without the Revolution and its leaders we would not even have any Mexican capitalists. National capitalism was not merely a natural consequence of the Revolution: to a great extent it was actually a creation of the revolutionary state. If it had not been for land redistribution, major public works, government-formed enterprises, public investments, direct or indirect subsidies to industry and, in general, state intervention in the economy, our bankers and businessmen would not have had the opportunity to perform their work or to become part of the "native personnel" of foreign-owned companies. It was indispensable, in a country whose economy had been stagnant for over two centuries, to accelerate the "natural" growth of our productive powers. This acceleration took the form of state intervention in the economy and partial direction of it. Thanks to this policy, our evolution has been the most rapid and constant of any in America. It was not brought about by some temporary bonanza or by the prosperity of one isolated industry — such as oil in Venezuela or sugar in Cuba — but rather by a fuller and more general development. Perhaps the most significant sign is the attempt to create a "diversified economy" and an "integrated" industrial structure (that is, one which takes into account our resources and their limitations).

It must be added, however, that we are still far from achieving everything that is needed. We do not have any basic industries except for the beginnings of a steel industry; we do not make machines that make machines, and do not even make tractors; we are still short of roads, bridges and railways; we have turned our backs on the sea, and lack ports, vessels and a fishing industry; our foreign exchange is balanced only because of tourism and the dollars our seasonal workers send back from the United States. And the fact that North American capital, despite our nationalistic legislation, is increasingly more powerful in the vital centers of our economy is even more decisive. Essentially, then, we are still a country producing raw materials, despite a certain amount of industrial growth. This means that in foreign trade we are subject to the fluctuations of the world markets, and that at home we suffer from instability, poverty and a cruel difference in the lives of the rich and the poor.

The question of whether our social and economic policies have succeeded is an almost standard topic of debate. There is no doubt that it has to do with more than techniques or the errors and corrupt practices of certain groups. The truth is that the resources of our nation as a whole are insufficient to "finance" our development or even to create what the experts call an "economic infrastructure," the only solid basis for real progress. We lack capital, and the rhythm of internal capitalization and reinvestment is still too slow. Thus our essential problem, according to the experts, is to obtain the resources vital to our growth. But where, and how?

One of the facts that characterize world economy is the imbalance between the low cost of raw materials and the high cost of manufactured products. Countries like Mexico — which is to say, the greater part of the world — suffer from the continual and unforeseen changes in the world market. As our delegates have stated in many inter-American and international conferences, it is impossible even to sketch out any long-range economic programs until this instability is remedied. Also, the growing gap between the "advanced" and "underdeveloped" countries cannot be lessened if the former refuse to pay a just price for raw materials. These materials are our principle source of income, and thus constitute our best chance of financing our economic development. For obvious reasons, we have made practically no gains whatever in this field. The "advanced" nations reply very calmly that it is all a matter of "natural economic laws" over which human beings have very little control. They talk as if we were living at the beginning of the last century. Actually, of course, the law they are talking about is the law of the lion's share.

One of the remedies most frequently offered to us by the "advanced" nations — especially the United States — is that of private foreign investments. In the first place, everyone is aware that the earnings from these investments leave the country, in the form of dividends or other benefits. In the second place, the result is bound to be economic dependence and, in the long run, political interference in our domestic affairs. There is also the fact that private capital is not interested in the sort of investments we need: those offering long terms and accepting small profits. On the contrary, it searches for opportunities that promise better and more rapid earnings. The capitalist cannot and will not involve himself in a general plan for economic development.

No doubt the best — and perhaps only — solution lies in the investment of public capital, either as direct government loans or through international organizations. The former entail political and economic conditions, hence the latter are preferable. One of the purposes for which the United Nations and its specialized organizations were founded was to assist the economic and social development of the "underdeveloped" countries, and the charter of the Organization of American States includes analogous principles. Considering the unstable situation in the world today (basically a reflection of the imbalance between the "great" and "underdeveloped" countries), it might seem that a good deal would be accomplished in this area. But in reality the sums devoted to these ends have been a mockery, above all in the light of what the great powers spend for military preparations. They are so busy winning the next war by means of military pacts with ephemeral or unpopular governments, so busy conquering the moon, that they forget what is happening in the rest of the world. Clearly we are faced with a wall that we by ourselves can neither leap over nor break down. Our foreign policy has been a just one, but doubtless we could have achieved more if we had joined with other countries whose problems are similar to our own. In this regard, Mexico's situation is no different from that of the majority of countries in Latin America, Asia and Africa.

Our lack of capital could be remedied in another way. As we

know, there is a method whose efficacy has been proved. Capital, after all, is simply accumulated human labor, and the extraordinary development of the Soviet Union is nothing but an application of this formula. By means of a controlled economy, which avoids the waste and confusion inherent in the capitalist system, and the "rational" use of an immense work force, directed to the exploiting of equally vast resources, the Soviet Union has become, in less than half a century, the only rival of the United States. In Mexico, however, we have neither the population nor the natural and technical resources required by an experiment of such proportions (not to mention our proximity to the United States and other historical circumstances). Above all, the "rational" use of workers and a controlled economy signify — among other things — forced labor, concentration camps, the displacing of races and nationalities, the suppression of the workers' basic rights, and the rule of a bureaucracy. The methods of "socialist accumulation," to use Stalin's phrase, have turned out to be much more cruel than the systems of "primitive accumulation" which aroused the justified anger of Marx and Engels. No one doubts that totalitarian "socialism" can change the economy of a nation: what is doubtful is whether it can give men freedom. And this last is all that interests us, and all that can justify a revolution.

It is true that certain authors — Isaac Deutscher, for instance — believe that as soon as abundance has been achieved, the state will almost imperceptibly move in the direction of true socialism and democracy. They forget that classes or castes with absolute political and economic power have been created in the meanwhile. History demonstrates that no class has ever voluntarily surrendered its gains and privileges. The notion of an "imperceptible" turning toward socialism is as fantastic as the myth of the "gradual disappearance of the state" on the lips of Stalin and his successors. There is always the possibility of changes in Soviet society, of course. Every society is historical, by which I mean that it is subject to transformation. But, at the moment, both systems are characterized by their resistance to change, their unwillingness to respond to external or internal pressures. The danger in this situation is that they will choose war in preference to change.

From the viewpoint of traditional revolutionary thinking, or even from that of nineteenth-century liberalism, the existence of historical anomalies like the "underdeveloped" countries or a totalitarian "socialist" regime, here in the middle of the twentieth century, is absolutely scandalous. Many of the prophecies and even dreams of the nineteenth century have been realized (the great revolutions, progress in science and technology, the transformation of nature etc.), but in a paradoxical or unexpected manner, defying the well-known logic of history. From the time of the utopian socialists it was claimed that the working class would be the principal agent of world history. Its function was to consist in bringing about a revolution in the most advanced countries, thus creating the bases for the liberation of mankind. True, Lenin thought it was possible to take a historical leap and assign the traditional task of the bourgeoisie — industrial development — to the dictatorship of the proletariat. He probably believed that revolutions in the backward countries would precipitate revolutionary changes in the capitalist world. It was a matter of breaking the capitalist chain at its weakest link. . . . The efforts of an "underdeveloped" country to industrialize itself are in a certain sense anti-economic, and demand great sacrifices from the people; but there is no other way of raising the standard of living. Also, national self-sufficiency is a costly experiment that must be paid for by the workers, consumers and peasants. However, the nationalism of the "under-developed" countries is not a logical response: it is the inevitable explosion of a situation which the "advanced" countries have made unbearable. In contrast, rational direction of world economy — that is, socialism — would have created complementary economies instead of rival systems. Once imperialism had disappeared and prices in the world market had been regulated to eliminate excess profits, the "underdeveloped" nations would have been able to obtain the resources they needed for their economic transformation. A socialist revolution in Europe and the United States would have facilitated the transition of all the "backward" countries to the modern world, and in this case in a truly rational and almost imperceptible way.

The history of the twentieth century causes some doubt (to say the least) as to the validity of these revolutionary theses and especially as to the role of the working class as the embodiment of the world's destiny. Nor is it possible to claim that the proletariat has been the decisive agent in this century's historical changes. The great revolutions of our time, not excluding the Russian, have taken place in backward countries, and the workers have represented only one segment — almost never the determining one — of the great popular masses made up of peasants, soldiers, the bourgeoisie and thousands of other persons harassed by wars and crises. These formless masses have been organized by professional revolutionists or specialists in coup d'état. Even the counterrevolutions like Fascism and Nazism fit into this scheme. The most disconcerting fact of all is the absence of a socialist revolution in Europe, the very center of the contemporary crisis. It hardly seems necessary to underline the aggravating circumstances: the European proletariat is the best educated and best organized of all, with the oldest revolutionary tradition, and the "objective conditions" favorable to a seizure of power have existed in Europe on a variety of occasions. At the same time, several isolated revolutions — in Spain, for example, and more recently in Hungary — have been mercilessly suppressed, without the international solidarity of the workers having manifested itself. On the contrary, we have witnessed a barbarous regression, that of Hitler, and a general rebirth of nationalism in all of the Old World. Finally, instead of a rebellion by a democratically organized proletariat, the twentieth century has seen the birth of the "party," that is, of a national or international grouping that combines the spirit and organization of two forces in which discipline and hierarchism are the predominant values: the Church and the Army. These "parties" are unlike the old political parties in every way. And they have been the effective agents of almost all the changes that have taken place since the first World War.

The contrast with the periphery is very revealing. The colonial and "backward" countries, since before World War I, have undergone a whole series of disturbances and revolutionary changes, and the tide, far from ebbing, rises year after year. Imperialism is withdrawing from Asia and Africa, and its place is being occupied by new states. Their ideologies are confused, but they share two ideas that once seemed irreconcilable: nationalism and the revolutionary aspirations of the masses. In Latin America, which was tranquil until recently, we have seen the fall of various dictatorships and a new revolutionary spirit. Almost everywhere — Indonesia, Venezuela, Egypt, Cuba, Ghana — the ingredients are the same: nationalism, agrarian reform, better conditions for the workers and, at the top, a state determined to complete the process of industrialization and thus leap from the feudal era to the modern. It is of little importance, in a general definition of the phenomenon, whether the state allies itself with certain sectors of the native bourgeoisie or, as in Russia and China, abolishes the old classes and entrusts the imposition of economic changes to a bureaucracy. The distinctive — and decisive — characteristic is that this is not a proletarian revolution in the "advanced" nations but an insurrection of the masses and peoples who live on the periphery of the Western world. Imperialism linked them to the destiny of the West, but now they are turning to themselves, discovering their identity and participating at last in world history.

The men and the political forms that have embodied the insurrection of the "backward" nations are widely varied. At one extreme, Gandhi; at the other Stalin; and then there is Mao Tse-tung. There are martyrs like Madero and Zapata, buffoons like Péron, intellectuals like Nehru. It is a portrait-gallery with very different types: Cárdenas, Tito, Nasser. Most of these men would have been inconceivable as political leaders during the past century or even during the first third of the present. As for their language, they combine messianic formulas with the ideology of democracy and revolution. They are "strong men" and political realists, but they are also inspired leaders, and dreamers, and — sometimes — demagogues. The masses identify with them and follow them. The political philosophy of these movements has the same variegated character. Democracy as the West understands it is mixed with new and sometimes barbarous ideas, from the "directed democracy" of Indonesia to the idolatrous "personality cult" of the Soviet Union. And we should not forget the respect — the veneration, even — which Mexicans show for the figure of the President.

Along with the cult of the leader there is the official party. In some countries, including Mexico, it is an open group to which almost anyone who wants to participate in public affairs can belong, and which includes great sectors of both the left and the right. This is true of the Congress Party in India. We should mention here that one of the healthiest traits of the Mexican Revolution — due, no doubt, to the lack of an orthodox political creed as well as to the open nature of the party — is the absence of organized terrorism. Our lack of an "ideology" has saved us from committing those tortuous persecutions which characterize the exercise of power in certain countries. True, we have suffered from violence, repression, caprices, arbitrarinesses, brutality, the "heavy hand" (*mano dura*) of certain generals, etc., but even at the worst moments it has always been human, that is, the result of passions, of circumstances, even of chance and fantasy. It is very different from the spiritual aridity of a closed system with its syllogistic, police-state morality. In the Communist countries the party is a minority, an exclusive and omnipotent sect; it is at once an army, an administration and an inquisition, combining both spiritual and secular power. Thus a wholly new type of state has arisen, in which various revolutionary traits — a directed economy, for example, or the disappearance of private property — are inseparable from such archaic traits as the sacred nature of the state or the deification of its leaders. Past, present and future; technical progress and the basest of political magic, economic development and slave labor, science and a state theology: this is the prodigious and terrifying visage of the Soviet Union. Our century is a huge cauldron in which all historical eras are boiling and mingling.

How is it possible that the contemporary intelligentsia — I am thinking especially of the heirs of Europe's revolutionary tradition — has failed to make an anlysis of the present situation, not from the perspective of the last century but from that of the new reality confronting us? For example, the debate between Rosa Luxemburg and Lenin regarding the "spontaneous revolution of the masses" and the function of the Communist Party as the "vanguard of the proletariat" would perhaps gain new meaning in light of the respective conditions in Germany and Russia. In the same way, there is no doubt that the Soviet Union hardly resembles what Marx and Engels thought a workers' state should be. Nevertheless, this state exists; it is not an aberration or "historical error." It is a vast reality, which manifests itself in the only way possible to living things: by the solidity and fullness of its existence. Even so eminent a philosopher as Lukacs, who has devoted so much energy to denouncing the "irrationality" of bourgeois philosophy, has never seriously attempted to analyze Soviet society from the point of view of reason. Can anyone assert that Stalinism was rational? Was the Communists' use of "dialectic" rational, or was it merely a rationalization of certain obsessions, as happens in other neuroses? And the "theory of collective rule," and that of "different roads to Socialism," and the Pasternak scandal . . . were these rational? Also, not one left-wing European intellectual, not one "Marxologist," has studied the blurred and shapeless face of the agrarian and nationalistic revolution in Latin America and Asia in an attempt to understand them for what they are: a phenomenon of world-wide importance which demands a new interpretation. Of course the silence of the Latin American and Asiatic intelligentsia, who live in the center of the whirlwind, is even more discouraging. It should be clear that I am not suggesting we abandon the old methods or reject Marxism, at least as an instrument for historical analysis. But new facts, radically contrary to the predictions of theory, demand a new set of instruments or at least a sharpening of those we already possess. A little before he died, Trotsky wrote — with greater humility and perception — that if revolution did not break out in the advanced nations after the second World War, the Marxist view of world history would perhaps require a complete revision.

The Mexican Revolution is a part of world history. Despite certain differences in degree, in methods and in "historical time," our situation is much like that of many other countries in Latin America, Africa and the Orient. We have freed ourselves from feudalism, military bosses and the Church, but our problems are essentially the same. They are immense problems, difficult to resolve. We are surrounded by many dangers, and also by many temptations, from "government by the bankers" (that is, the intermediaries) to Caesarism, along with nationalistic demagoguery and other spasmodic political forms. Our material resources are few and we have still not learned how to use them effectively. Our intellectual instruments are even poorer. We have done very little thinking on our own account; most of our ideas have been borrowed from the United States or Europe. The grand words that gave birth to our peoples now have equivocal values and no one knows exactly what they mean. Franco is democratic and forms a part of the "free world." The word "Communism" is associated with Stalin. "Socialism" means a group of gentlemen defending the colonial order. Everything seems to be one gigantic mistake. We console ourselves by saying that everything has happened as it should not have happened. But it is we who are mistaken, not history. We must learn to look reality in the face; if necessary, we must invent new words and new ideas for these new realities that are challenging us. Thinking is the first obligation of the intelligentsia, and in certain cases it is the only one.

Meanwhile, what can we do? There are no prescriptions any longer. But there *is* a valid point of departure: our problems are our own, and we are responsible for solving them, but at the same time they are also everyone's. Our situation in Latin America is that of the majority of the peripheral countries. For the first time in over three hundred years, we have ceased to

be an inert material which the strong could use as they wished
We were objects before, but now we have begun to be the
agents of historical changes, and our acts and omissions affect
the great powers. The image of the present-day world as a
struggle between two giants, with the rest of us as their friends,
supporters, servants and followers, is very superficial. The background — and, indeed, the very substance — of contemporary
history is the revolutionary wave that is whelming in the peripheral countries. For Moscow, Tito is a disagreeable reality,
but he is a reality. The same can be said of Nassar or Nehru for
the West. A third front, then? A new club of nations, a club
made up of the poor? Perhaps it is too soon. Or perhaps it is too
late: history is moving swiftly and the great powers expand
more rapidly than we are able to grow. But before the flow of
historical life congeals completely — and the "draw" between
the great powers is leading to this — there are still opportunities
for intelligent concerted action.

We have forgotten that many others are as isolated as ourselves. We Mexicans must acquire a new awareness of Latin
America. These countries are waking up now. Are we going to
ignore them? We have many unknown friends in the United
States and Europe. The struggles in the Orient are related in
one way or another to our own. Our nationalism, to be more
than a mental illness or self-adulation, must search the whole
world. We must recognize that our alienation is not unique, that
it is shared by a majority of the world's peoples. To be ourselves
would be to oppose the freezing of history with the mobile
features of a living human face. It is better that we have no
prescriptions or patent medicines for our ills. At least we can
think and work soberly and resolutely.

The object of these reflections is no different from that which
troubles other men and other peoples: How can we create a

society, a culture, that will not deny our humanity but will also not change it into an empty abstraction? The contradictory violence of our reactions and the explosions of our intimate selves and our history all began as a rejection of the petrified forms oppressing us; now we are attempting to resolve them by creating a society which is not ruled by lies and betrayals, by avarice and violence and dissimulation. A society that does not make man an instrument of the state. A human society.

The Mexican hides behind a variety of masks, but he tears them away during a fiesta or a time of grief or suffering, just as the nation has cast off all the forms that were stifling it. However, we have not yet found a way of reconciling liberty with order, the word with the act, and both with the evidence — not supernatural now, but human — of our fellowship with others. We have retreated now and then in our search, only to advance again with greater determination. And suddenly we have reached the limit: in these few years we have exhausted all the historical forms Europe could provide us. There is nothing left except nakedness or lies. After the general collapse of Faith and Reason, of God and Utopia, none of the intellectual systems — new or old — is capable of alleviating our anguish or calming our fears. We are alone at last, like all men, and like them we live in a world of violence and deception, a world dominated by Don No One. It protects us but also oppresses us, hides us but also disfigures us. If we tear off these masks, if we open ourselves up, if — in brief — we face our own selves, then we can truly begin to live and to think. Nakedness and defenselessness are awaiting us. But there, in that "open" solitude, transcendence is also waiting: the outstretched hands of other solitary beings. For the first time in our history, we are contemporaries of all mankind.

CHAPTER NINE

The Dialectic of Solitude

Solitude — the feeling and knowledge that one is alone, alienated from the world and oneself — is not an exclusively Mexican characteristic. All men, at some moment in their lives, feel themselves to be alone. And they are. To live is to be separated from what we were in order to approach what we are going to be in the mysterious future. Solitude is the profoundest fact of the human condition. Man is the only being who knows he is alone, and the only one who seeks out another. His nature — if that word can be used in reference to man, who has "invented" himself by saying "No" to nature — consists in his longing to realize himself in another. Man is nostalgia and a search for communion. Therefore, when he is aware of himself he is aware of his lack of another, that is, of his solitude.

The foetus is at one with the world around it; it is pure brute life, unconscious of itself. When we are born we break the ties that joined us to the blind life we lived in the maternal womb, where there is no gap between desire and satisfaction. We sense the change as separation and loss, as abandonment, as a fall into a strange or hostile atmosphere. Later this primitive sense of loss becomes a feeling of solitude, and still later it becomes awareness: we are condemned to live alone, but also to transcend our solitude, to re-establish the bonds that united us with life in a paradisiac past. All our forces strive to abolish our solitude. Hence the feeling that we are alone has a double significance: on the one hand it is self-awareness, and on the other it is a longing to escape from ourselves. Solitude — the very condition of our lives — appears to us as a test and a purgation, at the conclusion of which our anguish and instability will vanish. At the exit from the labyrinth of solitude we will find reunion (which is repose and happiness), and plenitude, and harmony with the world.

Popular language reflects this dualism by identifying solitude with suffering. The pangs of love are pangs of solitude. Communion and solitude are opposite and complementary. The redemptive power of solitude clarifies our obscure but vivid sense of guilt: the solitary man is "forsaken by the hand of God." Solitude is both a sentence and an expiation. It is a punishment but it is also a promise that our exile will end. All human life is pervaded by this dialectic.

Death and birth are solitary experiences. We are born alone and we die alone. When we are expelled from the maternal womb, we begin the painful struggle that finally ends in death. Does death mean a return to the life that precedes life? Does it mean to relive that prenatal life in which rest and motion, day and night, time and eternity are not opposites? Does dying mean to cease existing as a being and finally, definitively, to be? Is death the truest kind of life? Is birth death, and is death birth? We do not know. But although we do not know, our whole being strives to escape the opposites that torment us. Everything — self-awareness, time, reason, customs, habits — tends to make us exiles from life, but at the same time everything impels us to return, to descend to the creative womb from which we were cast out. What we ask of love (which, being desire, is a hunger for communion, a will to fall and to die as well as to be reborn) is that it give us a bit of true life, of true death. We do not ask it for happiness or repose, but simply for an instant of that full life in which opposites vanish, in which life and death, time and eternity are united. In some obscure way we realize that life and death are but two phases — antagonistic but complementary — of a single reality. Creation and destruction become one in the act of love, and during a fraction of a second man has a glimpse of a more perfect state of being.

In our world, love is an almost inaccessible experience. Everything is against it: morals, classes, laws, races and the very lovers themselves. Woman has always been for man the "other," his opposite and complement. If one part of our being longs to unite itself with her, another part — equally imperious — rejects and excludes her. Woman is an object, sometimes precious, sometimes harmful, but always different. By converting her into an object and by subjecting her to the deformations which his interests, his vanity, his anguish and his very love dictate, man changes her into an instrument, a means of obtaining understanding and pleasure, a way of achieving survival. Woman is an idol, a goddess, a mother, a witch or a muse, as Simone de Beauvoir has said, but she can never be her own self. Thus our erotic relationships are vitiated at the outset, are poisoned at the root. A phantasm comes between us, and this phantasm is her image, the image we have made of her and in which she clothes herself. When we reach out to touch her, we cannot even touch unthinking flesh, because this docile, servile vision of a surrendering body always intrudes. And the same thing happens to her: she can only conceive of herself as an object, as something "other." She is never her own mistress. Her being is divided between what she really is and what she imagines she is, and this image has been dictated to her by her family, class, school, friends, religion and lover. She never expresses her femininity because it always manifests itself in forms men have invented for her. Love is not a "natural" thing. It is something human, the most human trait of all. Something that we have made ourselves and that is not found in nature. Something that we create — and destroy — every day.

These are not the only obstacles standing between love and ourselves. Love is a choice . . . perhaps a free choosing of our destiny, a sudden discovery of the most secret and fateful part of our being. But the choosing of love is impossible in our society. In one of his finest books — *Mad Love* — Breton has said that two prohibitions restrict it from the very outset: social disapproval and the Christian idea of sin. To realize itself, love must violate the laws of our world. It is scandalous and disorderly, a transgression committed by two stars that break out of their predestined orbits and rush together in the midst of space. The romantic conception of love, which implies a breaking away and a catastrophe, is the only one we know today because everything in our society prevents love from being a free choice.

Women are imprisoned in the image masculine society has imposed on them; therefore, if they attempt a free choice it must be a kind of jail break. Lovers say that "love has transformed her, it has made her a different person." And they are right. Love changes a woman completely. If she dares to love, if she dares to be herself, she has to destroy the image in which the world has imprisoned her.

A man is also prevented from choosing. His range of possibilities is very limited. He discovers femininity as a child, in his mother or sisters, and from then on he identifies love with taboos. Our eroticism is conditioned by the horror and attraction of incest. Also, modern life stimulates our desires excessively, while it also frustrates them with all sorts of prohibitions: social, moral, even hygienic. Guilt is both the spur and rein of desire. Everything restricts our choice. We have to adjust our profoundest affections to the image of what our social group approves of in a woman. It is difficult to love persons of other races, cultures or classes, even though it is perfectly possible for a light-skinned man to love a dark-skinned woman, for her to love a Chinese, for a "gentleman" to love his maid. And vice versa. But these possibilities make us blush, and since we are prevented from choosing freely, we select a wife from among the women who are "suitable." We never confess that we have married a woman we do not love, a woman who may love us, perhaps, but who is incapable of being her true self. Swann says: "And to think that I have wasted the best years of my life with a woman who was not my type." The majority of modern men could repeat that sentence on their deathbeds. And with the change of one word, so could the majority of modern women.

Society denies the nature of love by conceiving of it as a stable union whose purpose is to beget and raise children. It identifies it, that is, with marriage. Every transgression against this rule is punished, the severity of the punishment depending on the time and place. (In Mexico the punishment is often fatal if the transgressor is a woman, because — like all Hispanic peoples — we have two sets of morals: one for the "señor," another for women, children and the poor.) The protection given to marriage would be justifiable if society permitted free choice. Since it does not, it should accept the fact that marriage is not the supreme realization of love, but rather a legal, social and economic form whose purposes are different from love's. The stability of the family depends upon marriage, which becomes a mere protection for society with no other object but the reproducing of that same society. Hence marriage is by nature profoundly conservative. To attack it is to attack the very bases of society. And love, for the same reason, is an antisocial act, though not deliberately so. Whenever it succeeds in realizing itself, it breaks up a marriage and transforms it into what society does not want it to be: a revelation of two solitary beings who create their own world, a world that rejects society's lies, abolishes time and work, and declares itself to be self-sufficient. It is hardly strange, then, that society should punish love and its testimony — poetry — with equal malevolence, condemning them to the confused, clandestine world of the forbidden, the absurd, the abnormal. Nor it is strange that both love and poetry explode in strange, pure forms: a scandal, a crime, a poem.

As a result of this protection afforded to marriage, love is persecuted and prostitution is either tolerated or given official blessing. Our ambiguous attitude toward prostitution is quite revealing. Some peoples consider the institution to be sacred, but among us it is alternately contemptible and desirable. The prostitute is a caricature of love, a victim of love, a symbol of the powers that are debasing our world. But even this travesty of love is not enough: in some circles the bonds of marriage are loosened so much that promiscuity is the general rule. The person who goes from bed to bed is no longer considered a libertine. The seducer — the man who cannot transcend himself because women are always instruments of his vanity or anxiety — is a figure as outmoded as the knight errant. There is no longer anyone to seduce, just as there are no maidens to rescue or ogres to destroy. Modern eroticism has a different meaning from that of Sade, for example. Sade was a tragic character, a man who was completely possessed, and his work is an explosive revelation of the human condition. There are no heroes as desperate as his. Modern eroticism, on the other hand, is almost always rhetorical, a complacent literary exercise. It is not a revelation of man; it is simply one more document describing a society that encourages crime and condemns love. Freedom of passion? Divorce has ceased to be a conquest. It is not so much a way of casting off established ties as it is of permitting men and women to choose more freely. In an ideal society, the only basis for divorce would be the disappearance of love or the appearance of a new love. In a society in which everyone could choose, divorce would become an anachronism or a rarity, like prostitution and promiscuity and adultery.

Society pretends to be an organic whole that lives by and for itself. But while it conceives of itself as an indivisible unit, it is inwardly divided by a dualism which perhaps originated when man ceased to be an animal, when he invented his self, his conscience and his ethics. Society is an organism that suffers the strange necessity of justifying its ends and appetites. Sometimes its ends — disguised as moral precepts — coincide with the desires and needs of those who comprise it. But sometimes they deny the aspirations of important minorities or classes, and too often they even deny man's profoundest instincts. When this last occurs, society lives through a period of crisis: it either explodes or stagnates. Its components cease to be human beings and are converted into mere soulless instruments.

The dualism inherent in every society, and which every society tries to resolve by transforming itself into a community, expresses itself today in many ways: good and evil, permission and taboo, the ideal and the real, the rational and the irrational, beauty and ugliness, dreams and vigils, poverty and wealth, bourgeoisie and proletariat, innocence and knowledge, imagination and reason. By an irresistible movement of its own being, society attempts to overcome this dualism and to convert its hostile, solitary components into a harmonious whole. But modern society attempts to do this by suppressing the dialectic of solitude, which alone can make love possible. Industrial societies, regardless of their differing "ideologies," politics and economics, strive to change qualitative — that is, human — differences into quantitative uniformity. The methods of mass production are also applied to morality, art and the emotions. Contradictions and exceptions are eliminated, and this results in the closing off of our access to the profoundest experience life can offer us, that of discovering reality as a oneness in which opposites agree. The new powers prohibit solitude by fiat . . . and thus they also prohibit love, a clandestine and heroic form of communion. Defending love has always been a dangerous, antisocial activity. Now it is even beginning to be revolutionary. The problem of love in our world reveals how the dialectic of solitude, in its deepest manifestation, is frustrated by society. Our social life prevents almost every possibility of achieving true erotic communion.

Love is one of the clearest examples of that double instinct which causes us to dig deeper into our own selves and, at the same time, to emerge from ourselves and to realize ourselves in another: death and re-creation, solitude and communion. But it is not the only one. In the life of every man there are periods that are both departures and reunions, separations and reconciliations. Each of these phases is an attempt to transcend our solitude, and is followed by an immersion in strange environments.

The child must face an irreducible reality, and at first he responds to its stimuli with tears or silence. The cord that united him with life has been broken, and he tries to restore it by means of play and affection. This is the beginning of a dialogue that ends only when he recites the monologue of his death. But his relations with the external world are not passive now, as they were in his prenatal life, because the world demands a response. Reality has to be peopled by his acts. Thanks to games and fantasies, the inert natural world of adults — a chair, a book, anything — suddenly acquires a life of its own. The child uses the magic power of language or gesture, symbol or act, to create a living world in which objects are capable of replying to his questions. Language, freed of intellectual meanings, ceases to be a collection of signs and again becomes a delicate and magnetic organism. Verbal representation equals reproduction of the object itself, in the same way that a carving, for the primitive man, is not a representation but a double of the object represented. Speech again becomes a creative activity dealing with realities, that is, a poetic activity. Through magic the child creates a world in his own image and thus resolves his solitude. Self-awareness begins when we doubt the magical efficacy of our instruments.

Adolescence is a break with the world of childhood and a pause on the threshold of the adult world. Spranger points out that solitude is a distinctive characteristic of adolescence. Narcissus, the solitary, is the very image of the adolescent. It is during this period that we become aware of our singularity for the first time. But the dialectic of the emotions intervenes once more: since adolescence is extreme self-consciousness, it can only be transcended by self-forgetfulness, by self-surrender. Therefore solitude is not only a time of solitude but also of great romances, of heroism and sacrifice. The people have good reason to picture the hero and the lover as adolescents. The vision of the adolescent as a solitary figure, closed up within himself and consumed by desire or timidity, almost always resolves into a crowd of young people dancing, singing or marching as a group, or into a young couple strolling under the arched green branches in a park. The adolescent opens himself up to the world: to love, action, friendship, sports, heroic adventures. The literature of modern nations — except Spain, where they never appear except as rogues or orphans — is filled with adolescents, with solitaries in search of communion: of the ring, the sword, the Vision. Adolescence is an armed watch, at the end of which one enters the world of facts.

Solitude is not characteristic of maturity. When a man struggles with other men or with things, he forgets himself in his work, in creation or in the construction of objects, ideas and institutions. His personal consciousness unites with that of others: time takes on meaning and purpose and thus becomes history, a vivid, significant account with both a past and a future. Our singularity — deriving from the fact that we are situated in time, in a particular time which is made up of our own selves and which devours us while it feeds us — is not actually abolished, but it is attenuated and, in a certain sense, "redeemed." Our personal existence takes part in history, which becomes, in Eliot's phrase, "a pattern of timeless moments." During vital and productive epochs, therefore, a mature man suffering from the illness of solitude is always an anomaly. This type of solitary figure is very frequent today, and indicates the gravity of our ills. In an epoch of group work, group songs, group pleasures, man is more alone than ever. Modern man never surrenders himself to what he is doing. A part of him — the profoundest part — always remains detached and alert. Man spies on himself. Work, the only modern god, is no longer creative. It is endless, infinite work, corresponding to the inconclusive life of modern society. And the solitude it engenders — the random solitude of hotels, offices, shops and movie theaters — is not a test that strengthens the soul, a necessary purgatory. It is utter damnation, mirroring a world without exit.

The dual significance of solitude — a break with one world and an attempt to create another — can be seen in our conception of heroes, saints and redeemers. Myth, biography, history and poetry describe a period of withdrawal and solitude — almost always during early youth — preceding a return to the world and to action. These are years of preparation and study, but above all they are years of sacrifice and penitence, of self-examination, of expiation and purification. Arnold Toynbee gives many illustrations of this idea: the myth of Plato's cave, the lives of St. Paul, Buddha, Mahomet, Machiavelli, Dante. And all of us in our own lives, and within our limitations, have lived in solitude and retirement, in order to purify ourselves and then return to the world.

The dialectic of solitude — "the twofold motion of withdrawal-and-return," to use Toynbee's words — is clearly revealed in the history of every people. Perhaps the ancient societies, less complex than ours, are better illustrations of this double motion.

It is not difficult to imagine the extent to which solitude is a dangerous and terrifying condition for the persons we refer to — complacently and inaccurately — as "primitives." In archaic societies, a complex and rigid systems of prohibitions, rules and rituals protects the individual from solitude. The group is the only source of health. The solitary man is an invalid, a dead branch that must be lopped off and burned, for society as a whole is endangered if one of its components becomes ill. Repetition of secular beliefs and formulas assures not only the permanence of the group but also its unity and cohesion; while religious ritual, and the constant presence of the dead, create a center of relationships which restrict independent action, thus protecting the individual from solitude and the group from dissolution.

To the primitive man, health and society are synonymous terms, and so are death and dispersion. Lévy-Bruhl says that anyone who leaves his native region "ceases to belong to the group. He dies, and receives the customary funeral rites."[1] Permanent exile, then, is the same as a death sentence. The social group's identification with the spirits of its ancestors, and its identification of these with the land, is expressed in this symbolic African ritual: "When a native brings back a wife from Kimberley, they carry with them a little dirt from his home place. Every day she has to eat a bit of this dirt . . . to accustom herself to this change of residence." The social solidarity of these people has "a vital, organic character. The individual is literally part of a body." Therefore individual conversions are rare. "No one is either saved or damned on his own account," and each person's actions affect the entire group.

Despite all these safeguards, the group is not immune to dispersion. Anything can break it up: wars, religious schisms, changes in the systems of production, conquests. . . . As soon as the group is divided, each of its fragments is faced with a drastic new situation. When the source of health — the old, closed society — is destroyed, solitude is no longer merely a threat or an accident: it is a condition, the basic and ultimate condition. And it leads to a sense of sin — not a sin resulting from the violation of some rule, but rather one that forms a part of their nature. Or, to be more precise, one that now *is* their nature. Solitude and original sin become one and the same. Also, health and communion again become synonymous, but are located in a remote past. They constitute the golden age, an era which preceded history and to which we could perhaps return if we broke out of time's prison. When we acquire a sense of sin, we also grow aware of our need for redemption and a redeemer.

A new mythology and a new religion are then created. The new society — unlike the old — is open and fluid, since it is made up of exiles. The fact of having been born within the

---

[1] Lucien Lévy-Bruhl: *La mentalité primitive* (Paris: 1922).

group no longer assures a man that he belongs: he has to be worthy of belonging. Prayer begins to take the place of magic formulas, and initiation rites put more and more emphasis on purification. The idea of redemption fosters religious specula-tion, theology, asceticism and mysticism. Sacrifice and com-munion cease to be totem feasts (if that is what they actually were) and become means of entering the new society. A god — almost always a god who is also a son, a descendant of ancient creation-gods — dies and is resurrected at fixed periods. He is a fertility god but he is also a redeemer, and his sacrifice is a pledge that the group is an earthly prefiguration of the perfect society awaiting us on the other side of death. These hopes concerning the next life are in part a nostalgic longing for the old society. A return to the golden age is implicit in the promise of salvation.

Of course it is difficult to discover all these factors in the his-tory of any one society. Nevertheless, there are various societies that fit the scheme in almost every detail. Consider, for instance, the birth of Orphism. The Orphic cult arose after the destruction of Achaean civilization, which caused a general dispersion of the Greek world and a vast reaccommodation of its peoples and cultures. The necessity of reforging the ancient links, both social and sacred, created a number of secret cults in which the only participants were "uprooted, transplanted beings . . . who dreamed of fashioning an organization from which they could not be separated. Their only collective name was that of 'orphans.'"[2] (I should mention that *orphanos* means both "orphan" and "empty." Solitude and orphanhood are similar forms of emptiness.)

The Orphic and Dionysiac religions, like the proletarian

---

[2] Amable Audin: *Les Fêtes Solaires* (Paris, 1945).

religions that flourished during the collapse of the ancient world, show very clearly how a closed society becomes an open one. The sense of guilt, of solitude and expiation, plays the same dual role as it does in the life of an individual.

The feeling of solitude, which is a nostalgic longing for the body from which we were cast out, is a longing for a place. According to an ancient belief, held by virtually all peoples, that place[3] is the center of the world, the navel of the universe. Sometimes it is identified with paradise, and both of these with the group's real or mythical place of origin. Among the Aztecs, the dead returned to Mictlán, a place situated in the north, from which they had emigrated. Almost all the rites connected with the founding of cities or houses allude to a search for that holy center from which we were driven out. The great sanctuaries — Rome, Jerusalem, Mecca — are at the center of the world, or symbolize and prefigure it. Pilgrimages to these sanctuaries are ritual repetitions of what each group did in the mythical past before establishing itself in the promised land. The custom of circling a house or city before entering it has the same origin.

The myth of the labyrinth pertains to this set of beliefs. Several related ideas make the labyrinth one of the most fertile and meaningful mythical symbols: the talisman or other object, capable of restoring health or freedom to the people, at the center of a sacred area; the hero or saint who, after doing penance and performing the rites of expiation, enters the labyrinth or enchanted palace; and the hero's return either to save or redeem his city or to found a new one. In the Perseus myth

---

[3] On the idea of "sacred place," see Mircia Eliade: *Histoire des Religions* (Paris, 1949).

the mystical elements are almost invisible, but in that of the Holy Grail asceticism and mysticism are closely related: sin, which causes sterility in the lands and subjects of the Fisher King; purification rites; spiritual combat; and, finally, grace — that is, communion.

We have been expelled from the center of the world and are condemned to search for it through jungles and deserts or in the underground mazes of the labyrinth. Also, there was a time when time was not succession and transition, but rather the perpetual source of a fixed present in which all times, past and future, were contained. When man was exiled from that eternity in which all times were one, he entered chronometric time and became a prisoner of the clock and the calendar. As soon as time was divided up into yesterday, today and tomorrow, into hours, minutes and seconds, man ceased to be one with time, ceased to coincide with the flow of reality. When one says, "at this moment," the moment has already passed. These spatial measurements of time separate man from reality — which is a continuous present — and turn all the presences in which reality manifests itself, as Bergson said, into phantasms.

If we consider the nature of these two opposing ideas, it becomes clear that chronometric time is a homogeneous succession lacking all particularity. It is always the same, always indifferent to pleasure or pain. Mythological time, on the other hand, is impregnated with all the particulars of our lives: it is as long as eternity or as short as a breath, ominous or propitious, fecund or sterile. This idea allows for the existence of a number of varying times. Life and time coalesce to form a single whole, an indivisible unity. To the Aztecs, time was associated with space, and each day with one of the cardinal points. The same can be said of any religious calendar. A fiesta is more than a date or anniversary. It does not celebrate an event: it *repro-*

duces it. Chronometric time is destroyed and the eternal present
— for a brief but immeasurable period — is reinstated. The fiesta
becomes the creator of time; repetition becomes conception.
The golden age returns. Whenever the priest officiates in the
Mystery of the Holy Mass, Christ descends to the here and
now, giving himself to man and saving the world. The true
believers, as Kierkegaard wished, are "contemporaries of Jesus."
And myths and religious fiestas are not the only ways in which
the present can interrupt succession. Love and poetry also offer
us a brief revelation of this original time. Juan Ramón Jiménez
wrote: "More time is not more eternity," referring to the eternity of the poetic instant. Unquestionably the conception of
time as a fixed present and as pure actuality is more ancient
than that of chronometric time, which is not an immediate
apprehension of the flow of reality but is instead a rationalization of its passing.

This dichotomy is expressed in the opposition between history and myth or between history and poetry. In myth — as in
religious fiestas or children's stories — time has no dates: "Once
upon a time . . ." "In the days when animals could talk . . ." "In
the beginning . . ." And that beginning, which is not such-and-
such a year or day, contains all beginnings and ushers us into
living time where everything truly begins every instant. Through
ritual, which realizes and reproduces a mythical account, and
also through poetry and fairy tales, man gains access to a world
in which opposites are reconciled and united. As Van der Leeuw
said, "all rituals have the property of taking place in the now,
at this very instant."[4] Every poem we read is a re-creation, that
is, a ceremonial ritual, a fiesta.

The theater and the epic are also fiestas. In theatrical perform-

---

[4] Van der Leeuw: *L'homme primitif et la Religion* (Paris, 1940).

ances and in the reciting of poetry, ordinary time ceases to operate and is replaced by original time. Thanks to participation, this mythical time — father of all the times that mask reality — coincides with our inner, subjective time. Man, the prisoner of succession, breaks out of his invisible jail and enters living time: his subjective life becomes identical with exterior time, because this has ceased to be a spatial measurement and has changed into a source, a spring, in the absolute present, endlessly re-creating itself. Myths and fiestas, whether secular or religious, permit man to emerge from his solitude and become one with creation. Therefore myth — disguised, obscure, hidden — reappears in almost all our acts and intervenes decisively in our history: it opens the doors of communion.

Contemporary man has rationalized the myths, but he has not been able to destroy them. Many of our scientific truths, like the majority of our moral, political and philosophical conceptions, are only new ways of expressing tendencies that were embodied earlier in mythical forms. The rational language of our day can barely hide the ancient myths behind it. Utopias — especially modern political utopias (despite their rationalistic disguises)— are violently concentrated expressions of the tendency that causes every society to imagine a golden age from which the social group was exiled and to which man will return on the Day of Days. Modern fiestas — political meetings, parades, demonstrations and other ritual acts — prefigure the advent of that day of redemption. Everyone hopes society will return to its original freedom, and man to his primitive purity. Then time will cease to torment us with doubts, with the necessity of choosing between good and evil, the just and the unjust, the real and the imaginary. The kingdom of the fixed present, of perpetual communion, will be re-established. Reality will tear off its masks, and at last we will be able to know both it and our fellow men.

Every moribund or sterile society attempts to save itself by creating a redemption myth which is also a fertility myth, a creation myth. Solitude and sin are resolved in communion and fertility. The society we live in today has also created its myth. The sterility of the bourgeois world will end in suicide or a new form of creative participation. This is the "theme of our times," in Ortega y Gasset's phrase; it is the substance of our dreams and the meaning of our acts.

Modern man likes to pretend that his thinking is wide-awake. But this wide-awake thinking has led us into the mazes of a nightmare in which the torture chambers are endlessly repeated in the mirrors of reason. When we emerge, perhaps we will realize that we have been dreaming with our eyes open, and that the dreams of reason are intolerable. And then, perhaps, we will begin to dream once more with our eyes closed.

The
Other
Mexico

TRANSLATED BY LYSANDER KEMP

Note

These pages develop and amplify the Hackett Memorial Lecture that I delivered at the University of Texas at Austin on October 30, 1969. Their theme is a reflection upon what has taken place in Mexico since I wrote *The Labyrinth of Solitude*. It is a continuation of that book, but, as I scarcely need to add, it is a critical and self-critical continuation; not only does it extend it and bring it up to date, but it is also a new attempt to decipher reality. Perhaps it would be worth the trouble to explain (once again) that *The Labyrinth of Solitude* was an exercise of the critical imagination: a vision and, simultaneously, a revision—something very different from an essay on Mexican-ness or a search for our supposed being. The Mexican is not an essence but a history. Neither ontology nor psychology. I was and am intrigued not so much by the "national character" as by what that character conceals: by what is behind the mask. From this perspective, the Mexican character performs its function in the same way as that of other peoples and societies: on the one hand, it is a shield, a wall; on the other, a symbol-covered surface, a hieroglyph. As the former, it is a rampart that protects us from the stranger's glance, at the cost of immobilizing and imprisoning us; as the latter, it is a mask that at the same time expresses and suffocates us. Mexican-ness is no more than another example, another variety, of that changing, identical, single, plural creature that each is, all are, none is. Man/ men: perpetual oscillation. The diversity of characters, temperaments, histories, civilizations makes of man, men. And the plural is resolved, is dissolved, in the singular: I, you, he, vanishing as soon as pronounced. Pronouns, like nouns, are masks, and there is no one behind them—except, perhaps, an instantaneous we which is a twinkling of an equally fleeting it. But while we live we can escape neither masks nor nouns and pronouns: we are inseparable from our fictions, our features. We are condemned to invent a mask and to discover afterward that the mask is our true visage. In *The Labyrinth of Solitude* I tried hard (without wholly succeeding, of course) to avoid both the pitfalls of abstract humanism and the illusions of a philosophy of Mexican-ness: the mask that changes into a face, the petrified face that changes into a mask. In those days I was not interested in a definition of Mexican-ness but rather, *as now,* in criticism: that activity which consists not only in knowing ourselves but, just as much or more, in freeing ourselves. Criticism unfolds the possibility of freedom and is thus an invitation to action.

These pages are both a postscript to a book I wrote some twenty years ago and, equally, a preface to another, unwritten book. I have alluded in two of my works, *The Labyrinth of Solitude* and *Corriente alterna* [*Alternating Current*], to that unwritten book: the theme of Mexico leads to a reflection upon the fate of Latin America. Mexico is a fragment, a part, of a vaster history. I do not know whether I am the most appropriate person to write that book, or, if I am, whether I will someday be able to do so. On the other hand, I know that that reflection should be a recovery of our true history, from the time of Spanish domination and the failure of our revolution of independence—a failure that corresponds to those of Spain in the nineteenth and twentieth centuries—to our own day. I also know that the book should deal with the problem of development, taking it as its central theme. The contemporary revolutions in Latin America have been, and are, responses to insufficient development, and both their historical justification and their obvious and fatal limitations derive from this fact. According to the classics of nineteenth-century revolutionary thought, revolution would be the consequence of development: the urban proletariat would put an end to the inequality between technological and economic development (the way of industrial production) and little or no social progress (the way of capitalist ownership). The twentieth-century revolutionary *caudillos* in the underdeveloped or marginal countries have changed revolution into a way toward development, with the results we are all familiar with. On the other hand, the models of development that the West and East offer us today are compendiums of horrors. Can we devise more humane models that correspond to what we

are? As people on the fringes, inhabitants of the suburbs of history, we Latin Americans are uninvited
guests who have sneaked in through the West's back
door, intruders who have arrived at the feast of modernity as the lights are about to be put out. We arrive
late everywhere, we were born when it was already
late in history, we have no past or, if we have one,
we spit on its remains, our peoples lay down and slept
for a century, and while asleep they were robbed and
now they go about in rags, we have not been able to
save even what the Spaniards left us when they departed, we have stabbed one another . . . Despite
all this, and despite the fact that our countries are
inimical to thought, poets and prose writers and
painters who equal the best in the other parts of the
world have sprung up here and there, separately but
without interruption. Will we now, at last, be capable of thinking for ourselves? Can we plan a society
that is not based on the domination of others and
that will not end up like the chilling police paradises
of the East or with the explosions of disgust and
hatred that disrupt the banquet of the West?

The theme of development is intimately linked
to that of our identity: who, what, and how we are.
I repeat that we are nothing except a relationship:
something that can be defined only as a part of a history. The question of Mexico is inseparable from the
question of Latin America's future, and this, in turn,
is included in another: that of the future relations
between Latin America and the United States. The
question of ourselves always turns out to be a question of others. For more than a century that country
has appeared to our eyes as a gigantic but scarcely

human reality. The United States, smiling or angry, its hand open or clenched, neither sees nor hears us but keeps striding on, and as it does so, enters our lands and crushes us. It is impossible to hold back a giant; it is possible, though far from easy, to make him listen to others; if he listens, that opens the possibility of coexistence. Because of their origins (the Puritan speaks only with God and himself, not with others), and above all because of their power, the North Americans are outstanding in the art of the monologue: they are eloquent and they also know the value of silence. But conversation is not their forte: they do not know how to listen or to reply. Although most of our attempts at a dialogue with them have thus far been unsuccessful, in the last few years we have witnessed certain events that may prefigure a change of attitude. If Latin America is living through a period of revolts and transformations, the United States is also experiencing an upheaval no less violent and profound: the rebellion of Blacks and Chicanos, of women and the young, of artists and intellectuals. The causes that originate and the ideas that inspire these upheavals make them different from those that agitate our own countries, and therefore we would be committing a new error if we attempted to imitate them blindly. But it would not be an error to take note of the capacity for criticism and self-criticism that is unfolding within them—a capacity it would be futile to search for in Latin America. We still have not learned how to think with true freedom. The fault is not intellectual but moral: the worth of a spirit, Nietzsche said, is measured by its capacity for enduring the truth. One of the causes of our incapacity for democratic government is our correlative in-capacity for critical thinking. The North Americans —at least the best of them, the conscience of the na-tion—are trying now to see the truth, their truth, without shutting their eyes. For the first time in the history of the United States (earlier, only a few poets and philosophers voiced it), there is a powerful cur-rent of opinion that places under judgment the very values and beliefs on which Anglo-American civili-zation has been built. Is that not unprecedented? This criticism of progress is a portent, a promise of other changes. If I asked myself, "Can the United States carry on a dialogue with us?" my answer would be yes—on condition that first they learn to speak with themselves, with their own *otherness*: their Blacks, their Chicanos, their young people. And something similar must be said to Latin Americans: criticism of others begins with criticism of oneself.

OCTAVIO PAZ
Austin, 14 December 1969

Translator's Note

This version in English was made from the pub-lished text (*Postdata,* Mexico City: Siglo XXI Edi-tores, 1970) but it incorporates the minor emenda-tions the author made after that publication and after reading the translation in typescript.   L.K.

Olympics
and Tlatelolco

1968 was a pivotal year: protests, disturbances, and riots in Prague, Chicago, Paris, Tokyo, Belgrade, Rome, Mexico City, Santiago. Just as the epidemics of the Middle Ages respected neither religious frontiers nor social hierarchies, so the student rebellions annulled ideological classifications. The spontaneous universality of the protest caused a reaction no less spontaneous and universal: the governments invariably attributed the disorders to a conspiracy from without. Although the alleged and secret instigators were almost the same everywhere, their names were shuffled differently in each country. Sometimes there were curious, involuntary coincidences: for example, both the Mexican government and the French Communist party claimed that the students were motivated by agents of Mao and the

CIA. And the absence or, in the case of France, the reticence of the class traditionally considered revolutionary per se—the proletariat—was also notable: up to now, the students' only allies have been the marginal groups which the technological society has not been able, or has not wanted, to integrate. Clearly, we are not facing a recrudescence of the class war but rather a revolt of those sectors to which the technological society has assigned a marginal position, either permanently or temporarily. The students pertain to the second of these categories. In addition, they are the only truly international group: all of the young people of the developed countries pertain to the international subculture of the young, which is produced by a technology that is equally international.

Of all the disaffected sectors, that of the students is the most restless and, with the exception of the North American blacks, the most exasperated. Their exasperation does not spring from particularly hard living conditions but from the paradox that being a student entails: during the long years in which young men and women are isolated in schools of higher education, they live under artificial conditions, half as privileged recluses, half as dangerous irresponsibles. Add to this the extraordinary overcrowding in the universities and the other well-known circumstances that operate as factors of segregation:

real beings in an unreal world. It is true that the alienation of the young is but one of the forms (and among the most benevolent) of the alienation imposed upon everyone by the technological society. It is also true that, because of the very unreality of their situation as inhabitants of a laboratory in which some of the rules of outside society do not apply, the students can reflect on their state and likewise on that of the world around them. The university is at once the object and the condition of student criticism. It is the object of their criticism because it is an institution that segregates the young from the collective life and is thus, in a way, an anticipation of their future alienation. They discover that men are fragmented and separated by modern society: the system, by its very nature, cannot create a true community. And it is the condition of their criticism because, without the distance that the university establishes between the young and the society outside, their criticism would not be possible and the students would immediately enter into the mechanical cycle of production and consumption. The contradiction is irresolvable. If the university were to disappear, so would the possibility of criticism; at the same time, its existence is a proof—and more, a guarantee—of the permanence of the object of criticism, that is, of what it is wished would disappear. The student rebellion oscillates between these two extremes:

its criticism is real, its actions are unreal. The criticism is on target but the actions cannot change society—and in some cases, far from attracting or inspiring other sectors, they even provoke regressions such as that of the French elections of 1968.

Government actions, for their part, have the opacity of all those short-term "realistic" measures that produce, in the long run, cataclysms or decadence. To strengthen, the *status quo* is to strengthen a system that grows and spreads at the expense of the people who feed it: as its reality increases, so does our unreality. The technological society distributes ataraxia—that state of equanimous lack of anxiety which the Stoics believed would be achieved by control of the passions—as a panacea for everyone. It does not cure us of the misfortune of being men, but it gratifies us with a stupor that is made up of contented resignation and that does not exclude febrile activity. Yet reality reappears, each time more quickly and more fiercely: crises, violence, explosions. The pivotal year, 1968, showed the universality of the revolt and its ultimate unreality: ataraxia and explosion, but an explosion that dissipates itself, violence that is a new alienation. If the explosions are part of the system, so are the repressions and the lethargy, enforced or voluntary, that follow them. The sickness corroding our societies is constitutional and congenital, not something that comes from without. It is a sickness that has defied all the diagnosticians, both those who call themselves Marxists and those who call themselves heirs of Tocqueville. It is a strange ailment, one that condemns us to incessant development and prosperity—by means of which we multiply our contradictions, inflame our sores, and exacerbate our tendencies toward destruction. And at last the philosophy of progress shows its true face: a featureless blank. We know now that the kingdom of progress is not of this world: the paradise it promises us is in the future, a future that is impalpable, unreachable, perpetual. Progress has peopled history with the marvels and monsters of technology but it has depopulated the life of man. It has given us more things but not more being.

The deeper meaning of the protest movement—not overlooking its reasons and its immediate, circumstantial aims—consists in its having opposed the implacable phantasm of the future with the spontaneous reality of the now. This outbreak of the now signifies the apparition, in the midst of contemporary life, of that forbidden, that damned word "pleasure." A word no less explosive and no less beautiful than the word "justice." When I say "pleasure" I am not thinking of the elaboration of a new hedonism nor of a return to ancient sensual wisdom—although the former would not be calamitous and the latter would be desirous—but rather of the revelation of that dark half of man that has been humiliated and buried by the morality of progress: the half that reveals itself in the images of art and love. The definition of man as a being that works should be changed to that of a being that desires. This is the tradition which extends from Blake to the surrealist poets and which the young have taken up: the prophetic tradition of Western poetry since the German Romantic movement. For the first time since the philosophy of progress grew from the ruins of the medieval universe, the young are questioning the validity and meaning of the very principles that underlie the modern age—and they are doing so within the most advanced and progressive society in the world, the United States. This questioning reflects neither hatred for reason and science, nor nostalgia for the Neolithic age (although Lévi-Strauss and other anthropologists tell us that the Neolithic was probably the only happy age that man has known). On the contrary, the question they ask is one that only a technological society can ask itself, and the answer to it will determine the fate of the world we have made. Past, present, or future—which is the true time of man, in which is his kingdom? And if his kingdom is in the present, how can the now, by nature explosive and orgiastic, be inserted in historical time? Modern society must answer these questions about the now—*right now*. The other alternative is to perish in a suicidal explosion or to sink deeper and deeper into the current process in which the production of goods is in danger of becoming less than the production of refuse.

The universality of youthful protest has not prevented it from assuming specific characteristics in each region of the world. As I have said, the youth movement in the United States and Europe poses implicit, unformulated questions about the very foundations of the modern age and that which has been, since the eighteenth century, its guiding principle. These questions arise in the countries of Eastern Europe in a very diluted form, and in Latin America they never rise at all except as empty slogans. The reason for this is clear: the North Americans and Europeans are the only ones who have a really complete experience of what progress is and of what it means. In the West the young rebel against the mechanisms of the technological society, against its tantalizing world of objects that wear out and vanish almost as soon as we possess them (as if they were an involuntary and conclusive confirmation of the illusory character that the Buddhists attribute to reality), against the overt or covert violence which that society brings to bear upon its minorities or, in foreign affairs, upon other peoples. In the countries of Eastern Europe, on the other hand, the struggle of the young presents two features that are absent in the West: nationalism and democracy. Nationalism in opposition to Soviet domination of and interference in those countries, and democracy in opposition to the Communist bureaucracies governing political and economic life. It is significant that the latter seems the immediate and primordial means of recovery to the youth of the East: in the West, the word "democracy" has lost almost all of its magnetism. This symptom is terrifying: whatever may be the limitations of Western democracy (which are many and grave: bureaucratic rule by parties, monopolies of information, corruption, et cetera), there can be no political life without freedom of criticism and a variety of opinions and groups. For us, as modern men, political life is synonymous with rational, civilized life. This is true even for nations that have inherited a high civilization and that, like ancient China, never knew democracy. The young fanatics who recite the catechism of Mao—by the way, a mediocre academic poet—commit not only an aesthetic and intellectual error but also a moral one. Critical thinking cannot be sacrificed on the altars of accelerated economic development, the revolutionary idea, the leader's prestige and infallibility, or any other mirage of that sort. The experiences of Russia and Mexico are conclusive: without democracy, economic development has no meaning, even though that development has been gigantic in the former and far more modest —though proportionally no less remarkable—in the latter. Every dictatorship, whether of man or of party, leads to the two forms that schizophrenia loves most: the monologue and the mausoleum. Moscow and Mexico City are full of gagged people and monuments to the Revolution.

The student movement in Mexico was in some ways like those in other countries, both of the West and of Eastern Europe. It seems to me that the closest affinities were with those in the latter countries: nationalism, reacting not against Soviet intervention but against North American imperialism; aspirations for democratic reform; and protest, not against Communist bureaucracies but against the Institutional Revolutionary Party. But this revolt of Mexican youth was singular, as is the country itself. There is not any dubious nationalism in this statement. Mexico is a country that occupies an eccentric position in Western civilization—it is "Castilian streaked with Aztec," as the Mexican poet López Velarde wrote—and within Latin America its historical situation is also unique: Mexico lives in a post-revolutionary period while the majority of the other Latin American countries are going through a prerevolutionary stage. Finally, its economic development has been exceptional. After a prolonged and bloody period of violence, the Mexican Revolution was able to create original institutions and a new state. For the last forty years, and especially for the last two decades, the nation's economy has made such strides that economists and sociologists point to Mexico as an example for other underdeveloped countries. The statistics are indeed impressive, especially if one keeps in mind the condition of the nation when the Revolution broke out in 1910, as well as the material and human destruction it suffered during more than ten years of civil strife. In order to gain international recognition of its transformation into a modern or semi-modern country, Mexico requested, and was granted, the designation of its capital as the site of the 1968 Olympic Games. The organizers of the Games not only passed the test successfully, they even added an original program to that of the sports events, a program underlining the pacific, noncompetitive nature of the Mexican Olympics: exhibits of international art; concerts, plays, and dance presentations by orchestras and companies from all over the world; an international meeting of poets; and other events of a similar nature. But, in the context of the student revolt and the repression that ensued, these celebrations seemed nothing but gaudy gestures designed to hide the realities of a country stirred and terrified by governmental violence. Thus, at the very moment in which the Mexican government was receiving international recognition for forty years of political stability and economic progress, a swash of blood dispelled the official optimism and caused every citizen to doubt the meaning of that progress.

The student movement began as a street brawl between rival groups of adolescents. Police brutality united them. Later, as the repression became more severe and the hostility of the press, radio, and television—almost all pro-government —increased, the movement strengthened, expanded, and grew aware of itself. In the course of a few weeks it became clear that the young students, without having expressly intended it, were the spokesmen of the people. Let me emphasize that they were not the spokesmen of this or that class but of the collective conscience. From the very beginning an attempt was made to isolate the movement by placing it in quarantine, in order to prevent the spread of ideological infection. The leaders and officials of the labor unions hastened to condemn the students in menacing terms; so did the official political parties of the left and of the right, though with less vehemence. Despite the mobilization of all the means of propaganda and moral coercion, not to mention the physical violence of the police and the army, the people spontaneously joined the student demonstrations, and one of them, the famous "Silent Demonstration," brought together about 400,000 people, something never before seen in Mexico.

Unlike the French students in May of the same year, the Mexican students did not propose violent and revolutionary social changes, nor was their program as radical as those of many groups of German and North American youths. It also lacked the orgiastic and near-religious tone of the "hippies." The movement was democratic and reformist, even though some of its leaders were of the extreme left. Was this a tactical maneuver? I think it would be more sensible to attribute that moderation to the circumstances themselves and to the weight of objective reality: the temper of the Mexican people is not revolutionary and neither are the historical conditions of the country. Nobody wants a revolution. What the people do want is reform: an end to the rule of privilege initiated by the National Revolutionary Party forty years ago. The students' demands were genuinely moderate: derogation of one article in the Penal Code, an article that is completely unconstitutional and that contains the affront to human rights called "crime of opinion"; the freeing of various political prisoners; the dismissal of the chief of police; et cetera. All of their petitions could be summed up in a single word that was both the crux of the movement and the key to its magnetic influence on the conscience of the people: *democratization*. Again and again the demonstrators asked for "a public dialogue between the government and the students" as a prelude to a dialogue between the people and the authorities. This demand was an echo of that which a group of us writers had made in 1958, during similar but less widespread disturbances that foretold much worse ones to come—as we warned the government at the time.

The attitude of the students gave the government an opportunity to correct its policies without losing face. It would have been enough to listen to what the people were saying through their student spokesmen. They were not expecting a radical change, but they did expect greater flexibility and a return to the tradition of the Mexican Revolution, a tradition that was never dogmatic and that was very sensitive to changes in popular feeling. In this way the government could have broken out of the prison of words and concepts in which it had enclosed and isolated itself, the prison of all those formulas that nobody believes in any longer and that are summed up in the grotesque expression with which the official family describes the only political party: the Institutional Revolution. By freeing itself from its prison of words, the government could also have broken out of another prison—a realer one—that surrounded and paralyzed it: the prison of business and of the interests of bankers and financiers. A return to com-

municating with the people would have meant a
recovery of the authority and freedom to carry
on a dialogue with the right, the left, and the
United States. With great clarity and concision,
Daniel Cosío Villegas, one of the keenest and
most honest minds in Mexico, pointed out what,
in his opinion (and, I should add, in the opinion
of most thinking Mexicans), was "the only remedy: to make public life truly public." The government preferred to resort, alternately, to physical force and institutional-revolutionary rhetoric.
This oscillation probably reflected a struggle between the technocrats, desirous of saving what
little was left of the revolutionary tradition, and
the political bureaucracy, which favored a strong
hand. But at no time did the government show
any desire to "make public life truly public," and
to begin a dialogue with the people. The authorities did propose negotiations, but behind the
scenes, and the talks aborted because the students
refused to accept this immoral procedure.

Near the end of September the army occupied the University and the Polytechnical Insti-
tute. This action was so widely criticized that the
troops withdrew from both institutions. There
was a breathing spell. The students, full of hope,
gathered for a meeting—not a demonstration—
in the Plaza of Tlatelolco on the second of October. At the end of the meeting, when those
attending it were about to leave, the plaza was

surrounded by the army and the killing began.
A few hours later it was all over. How many
died? No newspaper in Mexico dared to print
the number of deaths. Here is the figure that the
English newspaper *The Guardian,* after a care-
ful investigation, considered the most probable:
325. Thousands must have been injured, thousands must have been arrested. The second of
October, 1968, put an end to the student movement. It also ended an epoch in the history of
Mexico.

Although student uprisings are a world-wide
phenomenon, they break out with the greatest
virulence in the most advanced societies. It could
be said, therefore, that the student movement and
the Olympic Games in Mexico were complementary events: both of them were signs that the
country was relatively developed. What was dis-
cordant, and anomalous, and unforeseen, was the
attitude of the government. How can it be explained? On the one hand, the students' petitions
did not endanger the regime, and it was not faced
with a revolutionary situation. On the other hand,
no action by any government—not even that of
France, which was menaced by a revolutionary
tide—had the ferocity, there is no other word for
it, of the repression in Mexico. The world press,
in spite of the daily ration of horrors it dispenses,
was shocked. A popular North American magazine, rather appalled but in a maidenly way, said

that what happened in Mexico was a typical case of "overreaction," a symptom of "the sclerosis of the Mexican regime." A curious understatement. In any living organism, an exaggerated or excessive reaction indicates fear and insecurity, and sclerosis is a sign not only of old age but also of an inability to change. The regime showed that it was neither willing nor able to examine its own conscience; but without criticism, above all without self-criticism, there is no possibility of change.

This mental and moral weakness led to the physical violence. Like those neurotics who retreat when confronted with new and difficult situations, who swing from fear to rage, who commit insensate acts in a regression to the instinctive behavior of infants or animals, the government regressed to earlier periods in the history of Mexico. Aggression is synonymous with regression. It was an instinctive repetition that took the form of an expiatory ritual. Its resemblances to Mexico's past, especially to the Aztec world, are fascinating, frightening, and repellent. The massacre at Tlatelolco shows us that the past which we thought was buried is still alive and has burst out among us. Each time it appears in public it is both masked and armed, and we cannot tell what it is, except that it is vengeance and destruction. It is a past that we have not been able to recognize, to name, to unmask. But before discussing this theme—which is the central and secret theme of our history—I must describe in its broad outlines the development of modern Mexico, that paradoxical development in which the simultaneous existence of contradictory elements is symbolized by those two words, "Olympics" and "Tlatelolco."

Development
and Other Mirages

Mexico, 1920: the military overthrow of the old regime had hardly been accomplished when the country had to face the danger that threatens every victorious revolution—anarchy. The quarrels among the different factions that made up the revolutionary movement were no less violent than the armed rebellion of the people against the autocracy of Porfirio Díaz and his professional army. Those factions were more personalistic than ideological, but in a rudimentary form they already represented the interests and tendencies of the country's different classes and groups: peasants, farmers, the petite bourgeoisie, the growing working class, et cetera. Although the recently adopted Constitution of 1917 foresaw a peaceful transference of power by means of democratic elections, the reality was very different: there were no political parties and the country was ruled by the revolutionary dictatorship, that is, by the dictatorship of the military chieftains of the Revolution. The struggle among factions was never democratic; political supremacy was achieved, not by the number of votes, but by the number of soldiers and guns. Each presidential election degenerated into an armed struggle that ended with the death of one or various of the aspirants to power and of many of their followers, not to mention the innocent people dragged into the conflict. After the fall of Porfirio Díaz, it seemed as if the country was condemned to repeat again—and forever—the monotonous, bloody cycle of dictatorship followed by anarchy, anarchy followed by dictatorship. But the progressive and violent elimination of military chieftains led to a regime which, if not democratic, was also not self-destructive. The first measure—a negative one—was the constitutional prohibition of presidential re-election. This ruled out personal dictatorship. The second measure—a positive one—was the founding, in 1929, of the National Revolutionary Party. That established the revolutionary dictatorship—or, to be more exact, the dictatorship of the group that won in the struggle among factions.

The National Revolutionary Party was an association of military and political leaders gathered around General Plutarco Elías Calles. As an agent and civil branch of revolutionary power, the party had no strength by itself; its power was a reflection of the power of the *caudillo* and of the bosses and military men who ruled in the provinces. Nevertheless, as peace spread and as the country began to return to normal, the party gained strength—not at the expense of the *caudillo* but of the generals. The dual political structure of contemporary Mexico was already there in embryo: the president and the party. The function of the new organism was above all negative: not so much to set up a program as to reduce the clashes among factions and to put down troublemakers. Although it was not a seed of democracy, it was the beginning of a national political structure, tightly bound to the new state. The most significant of the words that formed its name was the first: the National Revolutionary Party fought against and debilitated the power of the regional bosses.

In 1938, President Lázaro Cárdenas changed not only the party's name but also its composition and its program. The social base of the Party of the Mexican Revolution was wider than that of the National Revolutionary Party and it brought together four groups: the workers, the peasants, the popular sector, and the military. It was an attempt to create a functional democracy rather than a political democracy. The party became an efficient instrument: it was the eyes and ears of a fine and generous president, Lázaro Cárdenas. Although its slogan was "For a democracy of workers," the Party of the Mexican Revolution was not democratic either. If no one remembers its debates, that is because there were none; its policies never were the product of public deliberation but rather of what was dictated by President Cárdenas. Even the inclusion in the party of the worker and peasant groups, far from strengthening them, contributed to their eventual servitude. According to most historians, the Revolution as such ended in the decade between 1940 and 1950. Since then, economic development and industrialization have become the immediate and primordial objectives of the regime. This policy was initiated by Miguel Alemán, a president no less energetic than Cárdenas. In 1946, Alemán changed the name of the party once again, to that by which it is now known, a name that courageously illustrates the paradoxes of politics rather than those of logic: the Institutional Revolutionary Party.

The three names of the party reflect the three stages of modern Mexico: creation of a new state, social reform, and economic development. But none of the tendencies that characterize these three stages arose from the party; they came down from above, from the president and his advisors. The party has produced not a single idea, not a single program, in its forty years of existence! It is not a political organization in the proper sense of the term; its recruiting methods are not democratic, and it develops neither programs nor strategies for realizing them. It is a bureaucratic organism that performs political-administrative functions. Its principal mission is political domination, not by physical force but by the control and manipulation of the people through the bureaucracies that direct the labor unions and the associations of the peasants and the middle class. In this task it has the support of the government and the benevolent neutrality or outright partisanship of almost all of the information media: political monopoly entails control not only of popular organizations but also of public opinion. At the same time, the party is an organ for exploring the conscience of the people and their tendencies and aspirations. This is a prime function, one which, in the past, gave the party flexibility, vitality, even popularity, but which now, because of its hierarchical organization and the sclerosis that for some years has paralyzed it more and more, it performs with increasing inefficiency. The party's deafness increases in direct proportion to the increase in popular dissent.

In its ways of functioning and its immoderate use of revolutionary jargon, the party could be thought to resemble the Communist parties of Eastern Europe: both it and they are political bureaucracies affixed to the national economy, although the economies of those countries are state economies and ours is mixed. But the party is not an ideological party, it is one of groups and interests—a circumstance which, if it has favored venality, has also saved us from the terrors of any sort of orthodoxy. The variety of tendencies that exist within it—I should say, that until recently existed within it—could make it resemble the Congress Party of India, except for this important difference: the Mexican party has no internal democracy and is dominated by a group of hierarchs who, for their part, give blind obedience to each president in turn. This has been especially unfortunate because the diversity of currents and opinions within the party—a reflection of those that divide the nation and make up its political and social reality—would have allowed it to attempt an experiment which, besides vitalizing and regenerating the regime, would have offered a solution to the crisis in which the country has been living for more than ten years: initiating democratic reform within the party itself. But perhaps now it is too late: the massacre of October 2 wiped out that possibility with blood.

By safeguarding the continuity of the government, the party has been a force for peace and stability. The revolutionary leaders, confronted with the nightmare of personal dictatorship limited only by the power of the *caudillo* and ending almost always in a bloody explosion, conceived an institutional dictatorship that was both limited and impersonal. The president has immense power but can occupy the post for only a single term; the power he wields comes to him from his investiture and disappears when he leaves office. The principles of rotation and selection operate within the party: to be president, or governor, or senator, or deputy, one must work through the party ranks, carry out one's assignments, move upward step by step. For political and governmental leaders the Institutional Revolutionary Party is a school, a laboratory, and a sieve. Promotions are achieved as in any other bureaucracy: the requirements are discipline, *esprit de corps,* respect for the hierarchies, seniority, administrative capacity, dedication, efficiency, quickness, smoothness, and desperate energy. One is promoted by consent of one's superiors. Although the party is contemptuous of democratic elections, it does respect the aristocratic veto power: the president has the unquestioned right to choose his successor, though first he must consult the former presidents and the high functionaries. The unwritten law is that his candidate will at least not provoke the opposition of these leaders. Each of them represents powerful interests, from those of private enterprise to those of the bureaucracies of the labor unions and the peasant organizations. The veto power pertains especially to former presidents. They are the voice of tradition and represent revolutionary continuity. They are something akin to a council of the elders.

Veto power, then—but not the power to criticize. The Institutional Revolutionary Party has never been critical of presidential actions; on the contrary, it has given them its unconditional support. In Mexico there is a horror—it would not be too much to call it a sacred horror—of anything like intellectual criticism and dissidence. A difference of opinion instantly and unconsciously becomes a personal quarrel. This is particularly true with regard to the president: criticism of his policies becomes a sacrilege. I should add that this veneration disappears when he steps down. His civic attributes are venerated, but not his person. Those attributes cover him up like the masks that hid the faces of the ancient Mexican deities, and they transform him, literally, into an image. Fanatical respect for the person of the *caudillo* is of Arabic origin and can be found throughout the Hispanic world; among the Méxicans, the religious reverence inspired by the impersonal attributes of the president has its roots in the Aztec world. I will return to this point later; for the moment I will only remark that the Senate and the Chamber of Deputies have been, and still are, two groups of chatterers and flatterers who never offer any criticism whatsoever; that the judicial power is mute and impotent; that freedom of the press is more a formality than a reality; and that radio and television are in the hands of two or three families who are more interested in earning money by brutalizing the audience than in analyzing the country's problems honestly and objectively. Furthermore, as proprietor of the party and the information media, the president enjoys an almost unlimited authority to use federal funds. It is really extraordinary that with such powers in their hands our presidents have not been Caligulas and Neros. Perhaps the reason lies in the long years of self-control which the party imposes on the faithful. Once again we see the organic relationship between the presidency and the party. From the very beginning they have been complementary realities; they were a response to a crisis situation, and represented a compromise between the personal dictatorship of the *caudillos* and the democratic program of the Mexican Revolution.

The virtues and defects of the Institutional Revolutionary Party are obvious. Among the former, the most important is its gradually achieved independence from the military. The party stands for the principle of separation be-

tween the nation's military and its political leaders, something that most Latin American countries have not yet accomplished. Can it preserve
that independence in the future? I doubt it very
much. Most of the writers concerned with modern Mexican history believe that the party has
outlived itself, but they point out that, whatever
its defects, it made a powerful contribution to
the country's peace and stability, without which
economic development would have been impossible. Although I agree with this opinion, I
ask myself whether many of the defects in our
development are not the direct fault of the party.
If it is true that it preserved the continuity of
governmental action, it is likewise true that it
stifled both analysis and criticism of that action.
Furthermore, and above all, it protected the irre-
sponsible and venal bureaucrats in charge of
carrying out the programs of economic development. And there is something else: although the
party was conceived as a desperate remedy for
a seemingly chronic illness that threatened to
destroy the country—that is, the danger of continuing the cycle of dictatorship, anarchy, dictatorship—it now perpetuates a regime of transi-
tions and exceptions. The only dictatorship in
Mexico is that of the Institutional Revolutionary
Party, and the only danger of anarchy is that
which is provoked by the unnatural prolongation
of its political monopoly.

It was during the Second World War that the actual revolutionary period of modern Mexico came to an end and the period of economic development began. The process has been similar, though not identical, in every country in which revolutionary movements have triumphed without first having an economic base capable of financing social reforms. This is the great limitation—it would be more exact to say condemnation—of every revolution in the underdeveloped countries, not excluding, of course, either Russia or China. There is an inescapable contradiction between development and social reform, a contradiction that is always resolved in favor of the former. In Mexico's case the change in orientation was due mainly to these three circumstances: the regime's decision to go ahead with industrialization, if only on a small scale, as the only cure for the country's ailments; the influence of the United States; and the appearance of a new capitalist class. The first of these was the determining factor. During the course of the war, Mexico discovered that although the prices for its raw materials had risen considerably on the international market, it could not purchase anything in that market; a little later, in the postwar period, it discovered that a downward fluctuation in the prices for those materials, along with a rise in the prices for manufactured products, not only devoured all of its savings but also impeded capitalization and, therefore, development. In order to counteract, insofar as possible, the disadvantageous conditions imposed by the international market, the government set about to diversify production so as to make our economy less vulnerable and dependent. Thanks to our resources—and our efforts—we have been more fortunate in this than other countries. Cuba, for example, still depends on sugar. Our rapid development in the last twenty years would not have been possible without that diversification of production and the bonanza of 1940–1950—without those economic circumstances and, I should add, without the government's determination to change the country's economic structure: the political decision was no less important than the economic opportunity.

The influence of the United States was considerable but not central. Its economic presence was no less powerful in other countries, yet they have not undergone the structural changes that Mexico has. Since this topic has provoked and still provokes many arguments, I should analyze it briefly. The only way that weak countries can defend themselves against the strong ones is to take maximum advantage of the quarrels among the great powers. This has been the policy of Mexico's governments. The rules of the game are simple: the greater the number of world powers, the greater the freedom of movement for small and middle-sized countries. But the game has become more difficult since World War II. First, all the intermediate positions were wiped out by an alliance between the North Americans and the Russians; immediately afterward, the alliance was replaced by a rivalry that polarized nations into two irreconcilable groups. The absence of an independent international policy in the countries of Western Europe (the alternative of Gaullism arrived too late for Mexico), the expansionist and nationalistic character of Stalinist Russia, and the aggressive and intransigent attitude of John Foster Dulles accentuated the defensive nature of Mexico's international politics. And it should not be forgotten that since 1840 Mexico's policy toward the United States has been and is essentially defensive. In spite of difficulties and contradictions, the government maintained our tradition on the international front, though each time with greater timidity, greater formality: the change that took place was internal. Although external pressures favored that change, considerations of an internal nature were decisive. The government had either to accommodate itself to industrialization or resign itself to stagnation, and it chose the former alternative. This decision led it to another, that of making the private sector an essential part of the development program and, therefore, of favoring it as much as possible. Since Mexican capitalism was in its infancy, it was decided—not without much hesitation and internal dispute—that the international private sector (North American) should also participate in the task of economic development. As a result, Mexico's economic dependence was accentuated.

Here I must insert a digression, not on economics—I am no expert in such matters—but on historical evidence. The reality of the United States' economic and political imperialism is a fact that needs no demonstrating: it has been analyzed again and again. But the opposition between the United States and Latin America is not only of an economic and political nature: the dichotomy is both older and more profound. Imperialism could vanish tomorrow, either because of a change of regime in the United States or, more likely, because science and technology will have discovered substitutes for our raw materials and because the economies of the most advanced countries will have become progressively more self-sufficient. In the near future, perhaps, the developed countries will not even bother to fleece the underdeveloped: they will leave them to their poverty and their convulsions. But this does not mean that we will cease to be what we are now, the scene of their disputes and the field of their battles. What I want to emphasize is that the disappearance of economic imperialism would not imply a leveling of power:

as long as this inequality of forces exists, so will the United States' domination over the rest of the hemisphere. The inequality is the same among capitalist countries as among those that call themselves socialist. Witnesses: Santo Domingo and Prague. Let us suppose that even this inequality disappears: the opposition would persist because it lives in strata more profound than economic and political organization. I am speaking of realities that the modern world has stubbornly forgotten or denied but that now reappear with still greater force: the whole complex of attitudes toward the world and the otherworld, life and death, the I and the other, that make up what we call a civilization.

Although the Russians, Chinese, and Japanese have embraced the cause of modernity and progress—two Western ideas—with the same frenzy, they are still, and will continue to be, Russians, Chinese, Japanese: they will be different and the same, like the gryphon Dante saw in Purgatory. Duzemil has shown that the tripartite structure of Indo-European ideology has endured for millenniums, despite the fact that those societies experienced changes even more profound than those which modern nations have suffered. The change from a nomadic society to great urban civilizations during the second millennium before Christ was no less radical than the leap from feudalism to the modern age; nonetheless, the ideological substratum, as Duzèmil calls it, persisted and persists. The example of psycho-analysis saves me from wasting time on a boring proof: the persistence of infantile traumas and psychic structures in the life of an adult is equivalent to the permanence of certain historical—or better, intrahistorical—structures in societies. Those structures are the origin of the bundles of distinctive traits that are civilizations. Civilizations: styles of living and dying.

True, the opposition between the United States and Latin America is not an opposition between civilizations: it pertains instead to the subgenus of contradictions within the same civilization. But, having admitted this, I want to point out that the differences are fundamental, as I tried to demonstrate at some length in *The Labyrinth of Solitude.* This opposition could be fecund, of course, if the arrogance of one party and the anxiety of the other did not muffle and vitiate the dialogue. But even under the best of conditions these dialogues are difficult: as soon as a conversation between North Americans and Latin Americans moves beyond informative and quantitative matters, it becomes a hazardous walking-in-circles among quibbles, ambiguities, and errors. The truth is that they are not dialogues at all, they are monologues: neither of us ever hears what the other is saying—or, if we do hear, we always think the other was saying something else. Even poetry and other literary forms do not escape from this tangle of confusions. The majority of North American poets and writers ignore or look down on the culture and/or people of Latin America. An example of the former: in the *Cantos* of Ezra Pound, that great monument to the encyclopedic voracity of the United States, all civilizations and all peoples make a showing except the pre-Columbian world and Spanish-Portuguese America: no Mayan temples or baroque churches, no *Popul Vuh* or Sor Juana de la Cruz. An example of the latter: almost all of the North Americans who have written about Latin America, not excepting so distinguished a poet as Wallace Stevens, have invariably been exalted by our indigenous past or by our landscapes but, just as invariably, have considered the contemporary Latin American to be insignificant. Latin America: ruins and scenery, with here and there a dim, bungling human being—the waiter and manager at the hotel. As for the Latin American vision of the United States, it is colossal and chimerical: to Rubén Darío, the first Roosevelt was none other than a reincarnation of Nebuchadnezzar; when Jorge Luis Borges visited Texas, the first thing that occurred to him was to write a poem in honor of the defenders of the Alamo. Exaggerated wrath, or envy, or obsequiousness: we think of the United States, simultaneously and without contradiction, as Goliath, Polyphemus, and Pantagruel.

In his lucid essay, "The Mexican Revolution, Then and Now," the historian Daniel Cosío Villegas asserts that the Mexican government has become a prisoner of the new capitalist class and is thus paying for its initial mistake, which was that of giving the private sector a central role in the program of industrialization and development.* This assertion, though basically correct, should be slightly modified. I will begin by underlining a fact that has been little commented on: that the new class is a deliberate creation of the revolutionary regime, much as the capitalist class in Japan was created by the movement toward modernization following the Meiji restoration. In both cases, the relationship that Marxism had made familiar to us—and whose real nature it had oversimplified—was turned upside down: the state is less an expression of the dominant class, at least in origin, than the dominant class is a result of the actions of the state. Another factor to take into consideration is the existence of the Institutional Revolutionary Party as a relatively autonomous bureaucratic-political organization that includes bureaucracies of the worker and peasant organizations. This characteristic is not found in other countries,

---

* Daniel Cosío Villegas, *Change in Latin America* (Lincoln: University of Nebraska Press, 1960).

except those that call themselves socialist. The Institutional Revolutionary Party is bound up with Mexican capitalism but it is not Mexican capitalism itself. In analyzing the new class of entrepreneurs, Frank R. Brandenburg said that the "Alemán regime originated a dual class; some of its members headed private companies and the others took over the direction of government enterprises." * Among the latter there is that large group of technocrats who have taken it upon themselves to defend, with varying success, the legacy of the Mexican Revolution. This sector is distinct from that of the party, and it constitutes the other bureaucracy of the new state, a bureaucracy of technicians and administrators, as the party is a bureaucracy of politicians. Brandenburg remarks that the new class of private entrepreneurs "rarely occupies official positions, although many politicians move on from managing public affairs to managing private businesses." Hence, not only is there a margin of independence between the private sector and the public, but also the party maintains considerable autonomy. The official left wing, the technocrats within the government, and many groups of intellectuals, have always speculated on the possibility that the government, taking courage from the strength of the party and of the popular sectors it controls,

---

* Frank R. Brandenburg, *The Making of Modern Mexico* (Englewood Cliffs: Prentice-Hall, 1964).

will some day stand up to private enterprise and
to imperialism. It seems to me that the second
of October dissipated those hopes. To stand up
to the bankers and financiers, the party would
first have to recover its influence over the popular
classes, and to do that it would have to transform
and democratize itself, something it cannot and
does not wish to do. Furthermore, since the party
is beginning to show an alarming inability to
control the waves of discontent and protest, the
private sector will sooner or later be tempted to
free itself from the party. Here again are the alternatives arising from the student movement, the
alternatives that conclude any analysis of the
present situation in Mexico: democratization or
political immobility and, afterwards, violence.

The economic development of Mexico would
have been impossible without the three circumstances—industrialization, the influence of the
United States, and the new capitalist class—
which I have just described. There is still another
one, equally important: the revolutionary reforms,
though they failed to create a new social order,
did break up the great landholdings of the old
regime, thus freeing the social forces that have
changed the face of Mexico in the last twenty
years. I will mention only the most outstanding
changes: the rate of economic growth has been
constantly higher than the rate of demographic

growth, even though the latter is one of the highest in the world; real per capita income has also increased throughout this period; the construction of a communications network has ended the traditional isolation of the towns and villages; a relatively solid economic infrastructure has been created; the country has completed the first stage of industrialization—that is, it needs to import fewer and fewer consumer goods—and is now preparing, with some difficulty, for the second stage; important advances have been made in agriculture— thanks to agrarian reform, irrigation, the creation of new types of seeds, and other factors, Mexico is now able to feed itself; and important progress has been made in public health and public education, although the latter is still sadly inadequate, especially in the area of secondary and higher education. All of these facts can be summed up in the following: the emergence of a working class, a middle class, and a capitalist class. It would seem as if the old dream of the Mexican liberals of the nineteenth century has been realized: Mexico at last is a modern country. The trouble is that if you look at the picture carefully enough, you can see vast areas of shadow. It is a disturbing sort of modernity.

Mexico's economic development did not follow a long-range national plan. Some regions have been favored with the government's solicitude and credits, while others have been almost completely neglected. This appalling horizontal inequality is matched by another that is vertical: although the index of poverty has continuously gone down during the last thirty years, the decrease has been far from proportional to economic growth. In absolute numbers there are more rich people today than there were thirty years ago, but also many more poor people, though the proportion of the latter has diminished. Hence the country's economic development has been notable but its social development most certainly has not. Mexico continues to be a country of scandalous inequalities. In the light of this, it is not difficult to infer the principal defect in our industrialization, a defect which the North American economist Sanford Mosk pointed out almost twenty years ago: the weakness of our internal market. If the government does not attack this problem by enlarging the present market and strengthening the people's buying power, the rhythm of development will slow down and even halt. To launch this attack, it must implement a policy of social reform and it must re-establish freedom within the labor unions, which at present are controlled by an affluent bureaucracy. Without a policy of social integration and without real freedom of negotiation for the workers, Mexico's development will be interrupted. The relationship has been turned around. At first it was imperative to achieve economic progress; but now, for this progress to continue, it is equally imperative to achieve social development—that is, justice.

In a recent book, James W. Wilkie sums up the three stages of evolution of modern Mexico in this way: "Political revolution destroyed the old institutional order; it did not create a democratic state. Social revolution attacked the old structure of society; it did not bring about a new one, either economically or socially. Economic revolution brought industrialization to a high point; it did not create balanced economic growth or a large internal market." * These conclusions are essentially correct, but they overlook one fundamental characteristic of the contemporary situation: the existence of two Mexicos, one modern and the other underdeveloped. This duality is the result of the Revolution and of the development that followed it: thus, it is the source of many hopes and, at the same time, of future threats. Here is the dilemma: either the developed Mexico will absorb and integrate the other, or the underdeveloped Mexico, by the sheer dead weight of demographic increase, will end up by strangling the developed Mexico. Until now, the first Mexico has grown and the second has di-

---

* James W. Wilkie, *The Mexican Revolution: Federal Expenditure and Social Changes Since 1910* (Berkeley: University of California Press, 1967).

minished, though not with the speed and in the proportions that are desirable and, above all, possible. According to Pablo González Casanova, the positive element in the present situation is social mobility: "The peasants of yesterday are the workers of today and the sons of those workers can be the professionals of tomorrow." But the same sociologist warns that it is urgently necessary to reorient the country's economic development, which should fulfill a social and national function, for otherwise the distance between the two Mexicos will continue to increase. I believe we all agree in thinking that any attempt at reform or transformation must be preceded by a democratic reform of the regime. Only in an atmosphere of freedom and openness to criticism can the true problems of Mexico be defined and discussed. Some of them are immense—for instance, the population explosion—but the government has not even attempted to discuss them.

When we consider what is happening both in our country and in other parts of the world, we are forced to take another look at the idea of development at top speed and at any cost. Let us forget for a moment the crimes and stupidities that have been committed in the name of development from Communist Russia to India, from the Argentina of Perón to the Egypt of Nasser, and let us look at what is happening in the United States and Western Europe: the destruction of the ecological balance, the contamination of lungs and of spirits, the psychic damage to the young, the abandoning of the elderly, the erosion of the sensibilities, the corruption of the imagination, the debasement of sex, the accumulation of wastes, the explosions of hatred. Faced as we are by all this, how can we not turn away and seek another mode of development? It is an urgent task that requires both science and imagination, both honesty and sensitivity; a task without precedence, because all of the modes of development that we know, whether they come from the West or the East, lead to disaster. Under the present circumstances the race toward development is mere haste to reach ruin. But we are forbidden to speak of these themes while we still have not achieved the minimal requirement: that free atmosphere that is the natural space in which both critical thought and the imagination unfold.

Political crises are moral crises. In 1943, in a well-known article, Jesús Silva Herzog declared that the Revolution was suffering a crisis, perhaps a mortal crisis, and that the illness was more moral than physical. Those years saw the beginnings of the third period of our contemporary history, a stage that the North American historian Stanley R. Ross has called the Mexican Thermidor: ideas were transformed into formulas and the formulas into masks. Although moralists are scandalized by the fortunes amassed by the old revolutionaries, they have failed to observe that this material flowering has a verbal parallel: oratory has become the favorite literary genre of the prosperous. More than a style, it is a stamp, a class distinction. And alongside oratory, with its plastic flowers, there is the barbarous syntax of our newspapers, the foolishness of North American television programs with the Spanish dubbed in by persons who know neither English nor Spanish, the daily dishonoring of the language on loudspeakers and the radio, the loathsome vulgarities of advertising—all that asphyxiating rhetoric, that sugary, nauseating rhetoric, of satisfied people whose gluttony has made them lethargic. Seated at Mexico, the new lords and their courtesans and parasites lick their lips over a gigantic platter of choice garbage. When a society decays, it is language that is first to become gangrenous. As a result, social criticism begins with grammar and the re-establishing of meanings. This is what has happened in Mexico. Criticism of the present state of affairs was begun, not by the moralists, not by the radical revolutionaries, but by the writers (a handful of the older but a majority of the younger). Their criticism has not been directly political—though they have not shied away from treating political themes in their works—but instead verbal: the exercise of criticism as an exploration of language and the exercise of language as an exploration of reality.

The new literature, poetry as well as the novel, began by being at once a reflection on language and an attempt at creating a new language: a system of transparencies, to provoke reality into making an appearance. But to realize this proposal it was indispensable to cleanse the language, to flush away the official rhetoric. Hence these writers had to deal with two tendencies inherited from the Revolution and now thoroughly corrupt: nationalism and an "art of the people." Both tendencies had been protected by the revolutionary regimes and their successors. The resemblances between the official aesthetics of Stalinism and the officious aesthetics of Mexican politicians and hierarchs are instructive. Mexican mural painting—originally a vigorous movement—was a prime example of this mutual accommodation between the regime and the "progressive" artists. The criticism directed at a showy nationalism and an art of patriotic or revolutionary slogans was more moral than aesthetic: it criticized imposture and servility. This criticism ranged from mural painting (painted oratory) to the verse oratory (mural poetry) that has become something of a vice among many Latin American poets—and not only among the lesser ones: witness the great Neruda. Setting art free was the beginning of a wider freedom.

Their criticism of "revolutionary" and/or patriotic art lead these writers, along with the young painters, to criticism of the society created by the Revolution and the epigonic regimes. Again, their criticism was not and is not direct; it contains no explicit message and is not inspired by an established doctrine. The form it adopts is neither moral nor political but exploratory; it is not criticism in the name of this or that principle nor is it a judgment on reality: *it is a vision*. Criticism of the language is an active operation that means digging into the language to discover what is hidden there: the worm-eaten foundations of institutions, the mire of the subsoil, the slimy creatures therein, the endless underground galleries like prisons, those Mexican prisons in which so many of the young are now locked up . . . The advent of this critical and passionate art, obsessed with double images of daily marvels and banalities, of humor and passion, surprised and disturbed the new class in power. This was natural enough. That class, made up of entrepreneurs, bankers, financiers, and political bosses, is only now taking its first steps along the path which their counterparts in Europe and the United States have been walking for more than a hundred years; it takes them at precisely the moment when the nations that have been its models and the object of its admiration and envy are beginning to suffer substantial changes in both technology and economics, in both the social sphere and the spiritual, in both thought and feeling. What is sunrise in

Mexico is sunset there; what is daybreak there is still nothing at all in Mexico. The modernity in which the regime's hierarchs believe is not modern any longer; hence the horror and panic with which they react to the writers and artists, who in their eyes represent those tendencies toward dissolution, criticism, and negation that are undermining the West. The long-kept truce between the intellectuals and those in power, a truce initiated by the Revolution and prolonged by the necessities (the mirage) of development, has now ended. Mexican culture has recovered its vocation as critic of society.

The institutions of higher learning in the capital and the states have been the great centers of political independence during recent years. The ideology and phraseology of Mexico's students and professors reflect those of analogous groups in the United States and Western Europe, but actually their demands reveal an attitude that expresses the aspirations of the new social forces created by the Revolution and industrial development. I am referring in particular to those groups that make up what is called, vaguely enough, the middle class. It contains a good many individuals whose jobs are technical or intellectual in nature; since they are the most active and independent members of their class, they exercise considerable influence over the others. Our

middle class is not yet that new class of intellectual workers which the technological society
has created in the developed countries, but at
the same time it is not the traditional middle
class. It constitutes a mobile stratum which,
though relatively satisfied from an economic point
of view, is aware that the situation could change
overnight. This insecurity inspires an aggressiveness and unrest that is not found among the
workers, because the latter hold jobs that have
been won and then protected by their own unions
and the labor laws. In addition to social insecurity,
there is another feeling that is no less powerful:
the middle class is a product of the post-revolutionary society and no one assigned it a place in
the new order of things, with the result that it
lacks both an explicit status like that of the
proletariat and an implicit status like that of the
new bourgeoisie: it has neither union nor club.
Finally, it is sensitive to the inequalities it discerns
among the functions it performs (considerable),
its economic situation (mediocre), and its political influence (nil). All of this explains how it
has become the proponent and defender of the
desire for democratic change: writers, professors,
intellectuals, artists, and students pertain to the
middle class. But it has no organization of its
own and I doubt if it could create one. Its historic function is not to express itself as a class
but to exercise its role as critic in many places

and ways, just as it is doing now in the universities, in the groups of workers who serve the state, and even in the labor organizations and the Institutional Revolutionary Party. It is a diffuse national force, active and critical. Because it sows nonconformity and rebelliousness, it is destined to awaken and inspire the other groups and classes to the extent that, in the near future, the persistence of the crisis aggravates the political struggles. These are certain to come, and it is not worth asking whether or not there will be great political battles in Mexico but rather whether they will be public or clandestine, pacific or violent. It is a question that only the regime has the privilege—and the responsibility—of answering.

The Mexican proletariat is not the satisfied and arrogant class that deserted the students in Paris and demonstrated against the blacks in Pittsburgh. Nor is it actively critical and nonconforming like certain sectors of the middle class. Although its material conditions leave a great deal to be desired, its standard of living makes it a privileged group in comparison with the rural population and, in particular, with that immense and wretched floating mass of the semi-unemployed which has emigrated from the countryside to the urban centers. This sector is extremely numerous and its helplessness is almost absolute. Their lack of roots in either the countryside or the city makes all of these ragged, humiliated Mexicans a potential source of rebellion, but they constitute an amorphous group, still bound, though lightly, to the traditional culture, and with rudimentary notions about politics and the world. Nevertheless, it would be a mistake to exaggerate their passivity or scorn their dormant strength. I should say something else about the proletariat: the indifference with which it listens to the radical formulas and watchwords of the young extremists does not imply that it is equally indifferent to the program for democratization. On the contrary: the workers have been dominated and mocked by the corrupt bureaucracies that run the labor unions, bureaucracies which are the strongest pillar of the Institutional Revolutionary Party. I am convinced that one of the regime's most vulnerable points is there in the workers' organizations. The aspirations of the middle class and the working class coincide in this matter: both of them demand greater political participation and a real autonomy. The workers have got to free themselves from their leaders, a caste made up of cynics who have turned their proper function into a business and a politico-bureaucratic career. The political criticism directed at the regime demands, as a first step, the re-establishing of democratic methods within the unions.

Some government spokesmen—journalists, labor and rural leaders, former presidents, and a few ingenuous souls—responded to the student movement by raising two scarecrows: a "Marxist-Leninist" revolution and a military coup. For some, the student revolt was the prelude to a social revolution; for others, a treacherous conspiracy by Yankee imperialism, aimed at provoking a pandemonium that would justify the army's intervention and the liquidation of constitutional order. I note that the army did indeed intervene —to liquidate, not the reigning order, but several hundreds of boys and girls who had gathered in a public place. True, one cannot and should not discount a regression into militarism; I believe, however, that it is not an immediate eventuality. The presidentialist regime and the Institutional Revolutionary Party were created as means of preventing the reoccurrence of military uprisings. If, in the near future, the possibility of a democratic solution to the present crisis is cut off, then the tensions, disorders, and violence would be such that eventually they would open the door to the military; but so far we have not reached that point. The possibility of a social revolution is even more remote. The analysis I have been making throughout these pages excludes the hypothesis of an impending revolution in the cities. The necessary social class, the historical protagonist, is lacking: under present circumstances none of the urban popular sectors combines the conditions that demand revolutionary action. And in the countryside, that other Mexico, the under-developed Mexico? In vast areas of that Mexico there exist the causes which, according to the general idea, produce revolutions. I call the idea "general" because it is one of the extremely few points on which observers on both the right and the left almost always agree. I disagree with both sides, as I will explain.

There is unrest and discontent in the country-side. In many places this unrest has now become exasperation; in other places the discontent is often translated into acts of desperate violence. This is natural: industrialization and develop-ment have been paid for, in great part, by our rural population. While its own very low standard of living scarcely changed, new and relatively prosperous classes, such as the working and mid-dle classes, were created and given the oppor-tunity to increase. For years now, half of Mexico —poorly clothed, illiterate, and underfed—has watched the progress of the other half. Popular violence has broken out here and there, but none of these outbursts was really revolutionary in character: they were, and are, local conflicts. Be-sides, the regime has two weapons of dissuasion: the army and social mobility. The former is odious but real; the latter is a decisive factor, a true safety valve. Because of this social mobility and other circumstances no less positive—distri-bution of lands, irrigation projects, et cetera—it would be absurd to say that the situation in the countryside is revolutionary. It is far from absurd to say that the situation is grievous, but my disagreements with the prophets of rural revolution are not based on economic and social considerations. Agrarian movements (Marx saw this better than anyone) suffer under a double sentence: either they dissipate in a series of local rebellions or they simply halt along the way—whereupon they are destroyed or taken over by other forces that transform them into true revolutions. There is a contradiction of some sort between the exercise of power and the peasant class: there has never been, and there will never be, a peasant state. Peasants have never wanted and do not want to take power; and, when they *have* taken it, they have not known what to do with it. Beginning with Sumer and Egypt there has been an organic relation between the state and the city; the same relation exists, but in the opposite sense of conflict and contradiction, between rural society and the state. Our only link with the Neolithic, that happy age when kings and priests were hardly known, is the countryman.

A clear example of this strong distaste for power—or of this inability to seize it—may be found in 1811, during the movement of Mexican independence, in the actions of Hidalgo and his army of peasants on the outskirts of Mexico City.

They knew that the city was helpless and deserted, but they did not and could not take it; instead, they retreated, and a few months later the army was annihilated and Hidalgo executed. During the Revolution, when the capital was occupied by the forces of Villa and Zapata, the two chieftains visited the National Palace; it is well known that Zapata looked with horror on the presidential chair and, unlike Villa, refused to sit in it. Later he said: "We should have burned it so as to put an end to ambitions." (An observation in passing: the superstitious veneration that is inspired in most Mexicans by the Presidential Chair—the capital letters are *de rigueur* here—is one more indication of the permanence of Aztec and Hispanic-Arabic traits in our make-up. We worship power, and that worship is comprised of terror and adoration: the ambiguous feelings of the lamb as it faces the knife.) Zapata was correct: power corrupts and we should burn every such chair and every throne. Yet, in the inhuman context of history, and especially during a revolutionary period, Zapata's attitude was little different in meaning from Hidalgo's failure to take Mexico City: he that refuses power is condemned, by a fatal process of reversion, to be destroyed by that power. Zapata's visit to the National Palace illustrates the nature of the agrarian movement and its ultimate fate: isolation in the southern mountains, then encirclement, then liquidation at the hands of the Carranza faction. The victories of Carranza and, later, of Obregón and Calles were due to the fact that the three *caudillos,* although they represented conservative tendencies (Carranza in particular), also and above all stood for national aspirations and programs. Villa was dispersion and Zapata was isolation, segregation; the others, once the peasant armies had been beaten, integrated the demands of the rural movement into a larger, a national, program.

Peasants are tied to the land; their viewpoint is not national, much less international; and they conceive of political organizations in traditional terms, which is to say that their models of organization are blood ties, religious ties, and patrimonial ties. When rebellions break out in the countryside they are always local and provincial; if they are to become a revolutionary movement, at least two conditions are indispensable: a central power crisis and the emergence of revolutionary forces capable of transforming isolated rural uprisings into national revolutions. The latter is achieved, in general, through a process that essentially consists in the uprooting of the peasants and their consequent militarization: the countryman is turned into a soldier and the soldier into a revolutionary. This process must coincide with the central power crisis and with the collapse of that power in the cities because of a military defeat (Russia) or an internal conflict together with an external war (China). If these two conditions are not present, the rural rebellion is a mere flare-up that is soon extinguished; Zapata would have been an obscure figure lost in the solitudes of the south if his insurgency had not coincided with the nation's general insurrection and the fall of the Díaz regime in the capital. The case of Cuba also fits the scheme I have just outlined, though with the radical difference that in Cuba there was not even a peasant rebellion: a small army of revolutionaries liquidated a rotten regime, one which at the end lacked all popular support, even that of the bourgeoisie. The theories about guerrilla warfare of the unfortunate Comandante Guevara (intellectual disagreement precludes neither respect nor admiration) were and are a strange renascence of the ideology of Blanqui in the midst of the twentieth century. Strange because unexpected and desperate. But Blanqui at least based his actions on the homogeneity of the urban masses, whereas the theory of guerrilla warfare ignores the heterogeneity between the city and the countryside. Finally, I repeat that if a rural rebellion does not become part of a wider revolutionary process, national in character, it becomes immobilized. The rebellion of the Yellow Turbans, at the close of the Han period in ancient China, was able for years to withstand the combined attacks of the imperial power and the Confucian bureaucracy. The Yellow Turbans were peasant soldiers; they dominated an extensive territory and organized themselves into a communal type of society with tighter and stouter ties than those of any modern ideology: a popular Taoism with a strong magical-religious coloration. All of these circumstances gave them the energy to resist the central power, but not to defeat it; and, since the rebellion could not progress, it became so immobilized that it was surrounded and pitilessly destroyed. The rebellion of the Yellow Turbans did not offer a national alternative. To sum up, then: if a rural uprising is to prosper, it is indispensable that it coincide with a profound power crisis in the cities. In Mexico this conjunction has not come about—not yet.

Three conclusions may be derived from my analysis: first, the crisis in Mexico is the consequence of changes in the social structure and the emergence of new classes—in other words, a crisis of the developed Mexico; second, the country's grave social problems—especially that of integrating the underdeveloped or marginal Mexico into the other—require a democratic solution, one that is truly national in both its domestic and its foreign policies; and, finally, if the regime rejects that democratic solution, the result will not be the *status quo* but rather a state of enforced immobility that will end with an explosion and a return to the old cycle of anarchy and personal dictatorship.

Of course some people will say that this scheme leaves out the other solution, the extreme one—that is, the revolutionary solution. But it depends on what one means by the word "revolution." If one means what the West has meant by it since the birth of the modern age, I have already said elsewhere that in my opinion we are witnessing the end of the epoch of revolutions, at least in the developed countries. And in the underdeveloped countries? No doubt we will see a period of great changes and upheavals, but I am not sure that these transformations will be revolutions in the strictest sense of the word. In fact, I am equally uncertain about the revolutions that took place during the first half of our century. This is more than a semantic quibble. Modern history would seem to demonstrate that there are two kinds of revolutions: on the one hand, those that are the result of historical, economic, social, and cultural development, with the French Revolution as the classical example; and, on the other hand, those that are the result of insufficient development. It is this second kind, I believe, to which the word "revolution" should not be applied. But whatever they are called, it is certain that they are movements which, once they have triumphed, must face the problem of development, and which, to solve it, must sacrifice their other social and political objectives. In this case, revolution is not a result of development but a means of speeding it up. All such revolutions, from the Russian to the Mexican, and whether national or international, degenerate into bureaucratic regimes that are more or less paternalistic and oppressive.

Here I should repeat, at the risk of tedium, that the distinctive feature of the Mexican situation is the existence of a political bureaucracy set up in a state party and composed of specialists in the manipulation of the masses. The Institutional Revolutionary Party, made in the image of Mexico's political and social reality, is a hierarchical bureaucracy, a true pyramid. As I propose to demonstrate in the third part of this essay, that pyramid, besides constituting a social and political reality, also embodies an imaginary reality; the party and the president, without ceasing to be political realities, are mythic projections, forms in which the image we have made of power is condensed. By this, I am not saying that the party is an exclusively Mexican phenomenon, although the myths that nourish it are. I have already noted the universality of the phenomenon and the cause that probably explains it. The emergence of political bureaucracies in the twentieth century may be the consequence of social revolutions in insufficiently developed countries;

the imposition of advanced models of development on archaic societies, and the forced acceleration of the process, explain the institution of
regimes of exception. The contradiction between
those two words, "institution" and "exception,"
expresses the basic contradiction, one that is economic in nature but is likewise social and historical. It is frequently forgotten that only a portion
of the West—a portion that does not include
Spain, Portugal, Latin America, and the majority of the Balkan and Slavic countries, not to
mention the cases of Germany and Italy—really
possesses the double tradition of political democracy and critical thought, the two central and
complementary elements of what we call "modernity."

Modern social thinking did not foresee the
emergence of bureaucratic regimes, and until recently it was too disdainful of the phenomenon
to analyze it. Both liberals and revolutionaries
were possessed by the idea that the state is a
secondary reality, devoid of a life of its own,
merely the expression of the dominant class
or of the fundamental groups that make up a
given society. The liberals thought that through
democratic controls the state would become
weaker and less dehumanized; the Marxists, more
radical, asserted that in socialist societies the
state would begin to extinguish itself, until it
vanished completely on the advent of commu-

nism. Not only has the exact opposite occurred, but also we are beginning to suspect that the state is a relatively autonomous reality. We lack a true analysis—that is, an objective and critical analysis—of the modern state. For example: although the Institutional Revolutionary Party is intimately linked to the Mexican bourgeoisie and North American imperialism, it is not a mere agent of either one, and neither of them explains its existence. As for the countries of Eastern Europe: if it is obvious that their Communist parties do not "express" their respective proletariats, what social classes do they "represent"? The theory of the "Asiatic way" of production and the so-called hydraulic theory have been used, with no great success, to explain the ancient Oriental despotisms, all of them characterized by the predominance of immense bureaucracies. But what theory can explain the emergence of bureaucracies in the technological era? In the circles close to Trotsky, during the years immediately preceding his assassination, there was much discussion about the "true nature" of the Soviet state; this led to the elaboration of various hypotheses concerning the function and character of the bureaucracy within that system. Trotsky, loyal to Marx, always denied that the bureaucracy was a class. But what is it, then? Not only have we failed to answer this question, we have not even succeeded in formulating it in a rigorous way. Bureaucracy continues to be a ghostly, elusive concept.

The fusion of the state and what the North Americans call the "military-industrial complex" is one of the most disquieting aspects of the evolution of the capitalist countries. The phenomenon seems to consist in the following: it is not a matter of the domination of the state by financial and economic groups but rather of the emergence of almost institutional formations which, through control of economic, military, and political means, propose a politics of national and/or world domination; and it is not the domination of politics and the state by the financial interests of a minority but rather a monopoly control over the economy and the state by groups and systems in which the interests of politicians, financiers, and the military are indistinguishable. The masks of Hitler and Stalin are now succeeded by an incorporeal reality we cannot even name and execrate. To name it, we have to know it—and only thus can we defeat it. Another surprise: contemporary bureaucratic regimes reject as false the idea that history is a lineal process analogous to the presentation of a thesis—slavery, feudalism, capitalism, et cetera. But this is not the first time that a historical crisis has given rise to a bureaucratic regime: feudal China was succeeded, not by capitalism, but by the system of the mandarins, a caste of learned men who specialized in politics and who governed that country—in an uneasy alliance with the military, the emperor, and other forces—for some two thousand years. The difference is that our modern bureaucracies are not made up of literati. Basically, this is fortunate: one of the extremely few encouraging aspects of the modern situation is that everywhere culture is critical and anti-authoritarian.

None of us knows the shape of the future. This half-century of disorders teaches us that the future is a secret which is divulged neither in the works of Karl Marx nor in those of his adversaries. But we can say this much to the future which a few impassioned young men are somewhere building: every revolution that stifles criticism, that denies the right to contradict those in power, that prohibits the peaceful substitution of one government for another, is a revolution that defeats itself—is a fraud. My conclusions will irritate many people. No matter: independent thought is almost always unpopular. We must renounce outright the authoritarian tendencies of the revolutionary tradition, especially its Marxist branch. At the same time, we must break up the existing monopolies—whether of the state, of parties, or of private capitalism—and discover forms, new and truly effective forms, of democratic and popular control over political and economic power and over the information media and education. A plural society, without majorities or minorities: not all of us are happy in my political utopia, but at least all of us are responsible. Above all and before all else: we must conceive viable models of development, models less inhuman, costly, and senseless than those we have now. I have said before that this is an urgent task: the truth is, *it is the task of our times.* And there is one more thing: the supreme value is not the future but the present. The future is a deceitful time that always says to us, "Not yet," and thus denies us. The future is not the time of love: what man truly wants he wants *now.* Whoever builds a house for future happiness builds a prison for the present.

Critique
of the Pyramid

The theme of the two Mexicos, one developed, the other underdeveloped, has appeared here and there throughout these pages. It is the central theme of our modern history, the problem on whose solution our very existence as a people depends. The economists and sociologists generally view the differences between the traditional and the modern society as an opposition between development and underdevelopment: the disparities between the two Mexicos are quantitative in nature and the problem is reduced to the question of whether or not the developed half will be able to absorb the underdeveloped. Now although it is normal for statistics to omit a qualitative description of phenomena, it is hardly normal for our sociologists not to perceive that, behind those figures, there are psychic, historical, and cultural realities which cannot be reflected in the broad measurements the census necessarily must take. Furthermore, those statistical schemes have not been designed for Mexico but are crude adaptations of foreign models. It is one more case of "extralogical imitation," with more of slavish thoughtlessness in it than of scientific rigor. For example, wheat and corn have been chosen as two of the indices of development: the eating of wheat bread is among the signs that one has crossed the line between the underdeveloped and the developed; the eating of corn tortillas indicates that one has not. Two reasons are put forward to justify the inclusion of wheat among the signs of development: it has greater nutritive value and it is a product whose consumption reveals that the leap from a traditional to a modern society has been made. This criterion condemns Japan to eternal underdevelopment, for rice is less nutritive than wheat and is no less "traditional" than corn. Besides, wheat is not really "modern" either, since little distinguishes it from rice and corn except its belonging to a different cultural tradition, that of the West (although the Hindu *chapati* is made of wheat!). So actually the intended meaning is that in all ways, including even diet and cuisine, Western civilization is superior to the others and that, within it, the North American version is the most nearly perfect. Another of the signs of underdevelopment, according to the statisticians, is the use of huaraches. If one thinks in terms of comfort and appearance, then huaraches, in our climate, are superior to shoes; but the fact is that, in the context of our society, corn and sandals are characteristic of the other Mexico.

The developed half of Mexico imposes its model on the other, without noticing that the model fails to correspond to our true historical, psychic, and cultural reality and is instead a mere copy (and a degraded copy) of the North American archetype. Again: we have not been able to create viable models of development, models that correspond to what we are. Up to now, development has been the opposite of what the word means: to open out that which is rolled up, to unfold, to grow freely and harmoniously. Indeed, development has been a strait jacket. It is a false liberation: if it has abolished many ancient, senseless prohibitions, it has also oppressed us with exigencies no less frightening and onerous. It is true that when modern progress arrived, our house, built with the rubble of the pre-Columbian world and the old stones of Spanish-Catholic civilization, was falling apart; but what we have built in its place, a lodging for only a minority of Mexicans, has been deserted by the spirit. The spirit has not gone away, however: it has gone into hiding. When referring to the underdeveloped Mexico, some anthropologists use a revealing expression: "the culture of poverty." The phrase is not so much inexact as insufficient: the other Mexico is poor and in misery; it also is really *other*. This otherness eludes the notions of poverty and wealth, development or backwardness: it is a complex of unconscious attitudes and structures which, far from being survivals from an extinct world, are vital, constituent parts of our contemporary culture. The other Mexico, the submerged and repressed, reappears in the modern Mexico: when we talk with ourselves, we talk with it; when we talk with it, we talk with ourselves.

The division of Mexico into two parts, one of them developed, the other underdeveloped, is scientific and corresponds to our country's economic and social realities. At the same time, on a different stratum there is an *other* Mexico. I am in no way referring to an ahistorical, atemporal entelechy, nor to an archetype in the sense meant by Jung or Mercia Eliade. It is possible that the expression "the other Mexico" lacks precision, but the truth is that I have not been able to find a more appropriate one. By it, I mean that gaseous reality formed by the beliefs, fragments of beliefs, images, and concepts which history deposits in the subsoil of the social psyche, that cave or cellar in continuous somnolence and likewise in perpetual fermentation. It is a notion that derives from both Freud's concept of the subconscious (individual) and the ideology (social) of Marx. An ideology that represents what Marx himself called "the absurd consciousness of the world" and that never is entirely conscious. It seems to me, though, that the concepts of Marx and Freud, each for different reasons which I will not analyze here, do not explain the totality of the phenomenon: the existence in each civilization of certain complexes, presuppositions, and mental structures that are generally unconscious and that stubbornly resist the erosions of history and its changes. Duzèmil calls these structures "ideologies," but in his use of the term he is closer to Kant than to Marx: a certain particular disposition of the mind with regard to objective reality. In short, for me the expression "the other Mexico" invokes a reality that is made up of different strata and that alternately folds in on itself and unfolds, hides itself and reveals itself. If man is double or triple, so are civilizations and societies. Each people carries on a dialogue with an invisible colloquist who is, at one and the same time, itself and the other, its double. Its double? Which is the original and which the phantasm? As with the Moebius strip, there is neither inside nor outside, and otherness is not there, beyond, but here, within: otherness is ourselves. Duality is not something added, artificial, or exterior: it is our constituent reality. Without otherness there is no oneness. And what is more, otherness is oneness made manifest, the way in which it reveals itself. Otherness is a projection of oneness: the shadow with which we battle in our nightmares. And, conversely, oneness is a moment of otherness, that moment in which we know ourselves as a body without a shadow—or as a shadow without a body. Neither within nor without, neither before nor after: the past reappears because it is a hidden present. I am speaking of the real past, which is not the same as "what took place": dates, persons, everything we refer to as history. What took place is indeed in the past, yet there is something that does not pass away, something that takes place but does not wholly recede into the past, a constantly returning present. The history of every people contains certain invariable elements, or certain elements whose variations are so slow as to be imperceptible. What do we know of those invariables and the forms in which they join together or separate? By analogy with what occurs in other areas, we can glimpse their mode of operation as the combining of a few elements; as in the case of biological processes, cinematographic montages, or the verbal associations of poets, those combinations produce distinct and unique figures: that is, history. But it is deceptive to speak of elements and invariables as if one were dealing with isolated realities with a life of their own: they always appear in relation to one another and cannot be defined as elements but only as parts of a combining. Hence it would not be licit to confuse these complex systems with what are called historical factors, whether economic or cultural. Although those factors are, say, the motor of history, what seems to me decisive, from this perspective, is to determine how they combine: *their form of producing history*. Perhaps the same system of combinations operates among all peoples and in all civilizations—otherwise both the oneness of the human species and the universality of history would be broken—except that in each culture the mode of association is different.

Otherness is what constitutes us. I am not saying by this that the character of Mexico—or of any other people—is unique; I maintain that those realities we call cultures and civilizations are elusive. It is not that Mexico escapes definitions: we ourselves escape them each time we try to define ourselves, to grasp ourselves. Mexico's character, like that of any other people, is an illusion, a mask; at the same time it is a real face. It is never the same and always the same. It is a perpetual contradiction: each time we affirm one part of us, we deny another. That which occurred on October 2, 1968, was simultaneously a negation of what we have wanted to be since the Revolution and an affirmation of what we have been since the Conquest and even earlier. It could be said that it was a manifestation of the other Mexico, or, more precisely, of

one of its aspects. I hardly need to repeat that
the other Mexico is not outside of but within us:
we could not extirpate it without mutilating ourselves. It is a Mexico which, if we learn to name
and recognize it, we can someday bring to an
end by transfiguring it. Then it will cease to be
that phantasm that glides into reality and turns
it into a blood-drenched nightmare. The double
reality of October 2, 1968: it is a historical fact
and it is also a symbolic acting-out of what could
be called our subterranean or invisible history.
And I am mistaken when I call it an acting-out,
because what unfolded before our eyes was a
ritual: a sacrifice. To live history as a rite is our
way of assuming it: if, for the Spaniards, the
Conquest was a *deed,* for the Indians it was a
rite, a human representation of a cosmic catastrophe. The sensibilities and imagination of the
Mexican people have always oscillated between
those two extremes, the deed and the rite.

All of the histories of all peoples are symbolic. I mean that history and its events and
protagonists allude to another, occult history,
and are visible manifestations of a hidden reality.
That is why we ask ourselves what the true meaning is of the Crusades, the discovery of America,
the sack of Baghdad, the Jacobin Terror, the
North American War of the Secession. We live
history as if it were a performance by masked
actors who trace enigmatic figures on the stage.

Despite the fact that we know our actions mean something, say something, we do not know what they say and therefore the meaning of the piece we perform escapes us. Does anyone know it? No one can know the final outcome of history because its end is also that of mankind. But we cannot linger over these answerless questions because history obliges us to live it: it is the substance of our life and the place of our death. We pass our lives between living history and interpreting it. In interpreting it, we live it: we make history; in living it, we interpret it: each of our acts is a sign. The history we live is a document, and in this document of our visible history we should read the changes and metamorphoses of our invisible history. This reading is a decipherment, a translation of a translation: we shall never read the original. Each version is provisional: the text changes incessantly (though perhaps it always says the same thing), and so, from time to time, certain versions are discarded in favor of others that in turn had been discarded earlier. Each translation is a creation, a new text. What follows here is an attempt to translate October 2 in terms of what I believe is the true, though invisible, history of Mexico. On that afternoon our visible history unfolded our other history, the invisible one, as if it were a pre-Columbian codex. That vision was shocking because the symbols became transparent.

Geographies, too, are symbolic: physical spaces turn into geometric archetypes that are emissive forms of symbols. Plains, valleys, mountains: the accidents of terrain become meaningful as soon as they enter history. Landscape is historical, and thus becomes a document in cipher, a hieroglyphic text. The oppositions between sea and land, plain and mountain, island and continent, symbolize historical oppositions: societies, cultures, civilizations. Each land is a society: a world and a vision of the world and the otherworld. Each history is a geography and each geography is a geometry of symbols. India is an inverted cone, a tree whose roots are fixed in the heavens. China is an immense disc—belly and navel of the cosmos. Mexico rises between two seas like a huge truncated pyramid: its four sides are the four points of the compass, its staircases are the climates of all the zones, and its high plateau is the house of the sun and the constellations. It is hardly necessary to remind ourselves that to the people of antiquity the world was a mountain and that, in Sumer and Egypt, as in Mesoamerica, the geometric and symbolic representation of the cosmic mountain was the pyramid. The geography of Mexico spreads out in a pyramidal form as if there existed a secret but evident relation between natural space and symbolic geometry and between the latter and what I have called our invisible history.

The Mesoamerican pyramid, archaic archetype of the world, geometric metaphor for the cosmos, culminates in a magnetic space: the platform-sanctuary. It is the axis of the universe, the place where the four compass points cross, the center of the quadrangle: the end and the beginning of motion. An immobility in which the dance of the cosmos ends and again begins. The four sides of the pyramid, petrified time, represent the four suns or ages of the world, and its staircases are days, months, years, centuries. At the top, on the platform: the birthplace of the fifth sun, the Nahua and Aztec era. An edifice made of time: what was, what shall be, what is. As space, the platform-sanctuary is the place where the gods appear and the place of the sacrificial altar: the point of convergence of the human world and the divine. As time, it is the center of motion, the end and beginning of the eras: the everlasting present of the gods. The pyramid is an image of the world; in turn, that image of the world is a projection of human society. If it is true that man invents gods in his own image, it is also true that he sees his own image in the images that the sky and the earth offer him. Man makes human history of the inhuman landscape; nature turns history into cosmogony, the dance of the stars.

The pyramid assures the continuity of time (both human and cosmological) through sacri-

fice: it is a life-generating space. The metaphor
of the world as a mountain and the mountain as
the giver of life materializes with ˙astonishing
literalness in the pyramid. Its platform-sanctuary,
quadrangular like the world, is the theater of the
gods and their playing field. And what is the
game of the gods? They play with time, and
their game is the creation and destruction of
the worlds. There is an opposition between human labors and divine play: man labors in order
to eat, the gods play in order to create. Rather,
there is no difference to them between play and
creation: each of their pirouettes is a world that
is born or annihilated. Creation and destruction
are antithetical notions to man, but identical to
the gods: all is play. In their games—which are
wars which are dances—the gods create, destroy,
and, sometimes, destroy themselves. After their
self-immolation they re-create the world. The
game of the gods is a bloody game culminating
in a sacrifice that is the creation of the world.
The creative destruction of the gods is the model
for man's rites, ceremonies, and fiestas: sacrifice
is equal to productive destruction. To the ancient
Mexicans, *dance* was synonymous with *penitence*. It may seem strange, but it is not: dance
is primordially rite, and rite is ceremony—ceremony that reproduces the gods' creation of the
world in a game that is creative destruction.
There is an intimate connection between divine

play and the gods' sacrifice that engenders the universe; this celestial model has a human counterpart: the ritual dance is penitential.

The dance-penitence equation is repeated in the symbolism of the pyramid: the platform at its summit represents the sacred space where the dance of the gods unfolds, a creative game of motion and thus of time itself. The dancing place, for the same reasons of analogy and correspondence, is also the place of sacrifice. Now, to the Aztecs the world of politics was not distinct from the world of religion: the celestial dance, which is creative destruction, is also cosmic war. This series of divine analogies is repeated in another that is terrestial: the ritual war (or "flower war") is a duplicate of the war dance of the gods and culminates in the sacrifice of prisoners of war. Creative destruction and political domination are the double face, the divine and the human, of a single conception. The pyramid—petrified time, place of divine sacrifice—is also an image of the Aztec state and of its mission: to assure the continuity of the solar cult, source of universal life, through the sacrifice of prisoners of war. The Mexicas* identified themselves with the solar cult: their domination is similar to that of the sun, which daily is born, fights, dies, and is reborn. The pyramid is the

---

* The Aztecs.

world and the world is México-Tenochtitlán: deification of the Aztec capital because of its identification with the ancestral image of the cosmos, the pyramid. To those who inherited the Aztec power, the connection between religious rites and acts of political domination disappears, but, as we shall see, the unconscious model of power is still the same: the pyramid and the sacrifice.

If Mexico is a truncated pyramid, the Valley of Anáhuac is the platform of that pyramid. And in the center of that valley stands Mexico City, the ancient México-Tenochtitlán, seat of Aztec power and today the capital of the Republic of Mexico. As far as I know, it has not been commented on, but there is a special significance in the fact that the capital has given its name to the country. This is a strange thing. Almost everywhere else in the world—the exceptions can be counted on one's fingers—the name of the capital is different from that of the nation. The reason for this, I think, is a universal though unformulated rule: the singular reality of a city must be carefully distinguished from the plural and more extensive reality of a nation. The distinction becomes imperative if, as often happens, the capital is an old metropolis with a history of its own, and, above all, if that history has been one of domination over other cities and provinces: Rome/Italy, Paris/France, Tokyo/Japan,

London/England. Not even the centralists of Castile dared to break that rule: Madrid/Spain. The case of Mexico becomes even stranger if one recalls that, for the peoples who made up the pre-Hispanic world, the name of México-Tenochtitlán evoked the idea of Aztec domination—I should say, the terrible reality of that domination. The fact that the whole country was given the name of the city of its oppressors is one of the keys to the history of Mexico, her unwritten, unspoken history. The fascination that the Aztecs have exerted has been such that even their conquerors, the Spaniards, did not escape from it: when Cortés decided that the capital of the new kingdom would be built on the ruins of México-Tenochtitlán, he became the heir and successor of the Aztecs. Although the Conquest destroyed the indigenous world and built another and different one on its remains, there is an invisible thread of continuity between the ancient society and the new Spanish order: the thread of domination. That thread has not been broken: the Spanish viceroys and the Mexican presidents are the successors of the Aztec rulers.

If there has been a secret political continuity since the fourteenth century, is it any wonder that the unconscious basis of that continuity is the religious-political archetype of the ancient Mexicans: the pyramid, the implacable hierarchies, and, over all, the hierarch and the platform of sacrifices? When I speak of the unconscious basis of our idea of history and politics, I am thinking, not of those who govern, but of the governed. It is apparent that the Spanish viceroys were unaware of the mythology of the Mexicans, but their subjects were not, whether Indians, mestizos, or Creoles: all of them, naturally and spontaneously, saw the Spanish state as the continuation of Aztec power. This identification was not explicit and never assumed a rational form: it was something that was in the nature of things. Besides, the continuity between the Spanish viceroy and the Aztec lord, between the Christian capital and the ancient idolatrous city, was only one aspect of the idea that colonial society had of the pre-Columbian past. That continuity could also be seen in the realm of religion. The appearance of the Virgin of Guadalupe on the ruins of a shrine sacred to the goddess Tonantzin is the central example, but not the only one, of this relationship between the two worlds, the indigenous and the colonial. In *The Divine Narcissus,* an *auto sacramental* by Sor Juana Inés de la Cruz, the ancient pre-Columbian religion, despite its bloody rites, is shown as a prefiguration of the arrival of Christianity in Mexico. The Spaniards' historical model was Imperial Rome: México-Tenochtitlán and, later, Mexico City were simply reduced versions of the Roman archetype. Christian Rome prolonged, while rectifying, pagan Rome; in the same way, the new Mexico City prolonged, rectified, and in the end affirmed the Aztec metropolis. Independence did not alter this conception radically: it was decided that the Spanish colonial period had been an *interruption* in Mexico's history and that, by freeing itself from foreign domination, the country had re-established its liberties and resumed its traditions. From this point of view, independence was a kind of restoration. This historical-juridical fiction consecrated the legitimacy. of Aztec domination: México-Tenochtitlán was and is the origin and source of power. After independence the process of sentimental identification with the pre-Hispanic world became so important that following the Revolution it became one of the most notable characteristics of modern Mexico. What has not been said is that the vast majority of Mexicans has made the Aztec point of view its own and has thus, without knowing it, strengthened the myth that is embodied in the pyramid and the sacrifice stone.

As our knowledge of the Mesoamerican world increases, it changes our attitude toward the Aztecs. For a long time it was thought that pre-Columbian civilization had reached its apogee in México-Tenochtitlán. That was what the Spaniards believed, and it is still believed by a great many Mexicans, not excluding various historians,

archaeologists, art critics, and other students of
our past. But we now know for certain that the
great creative period in Mesoamerica occurred
a number of centuries prior to the arrival of the
Aztecs in the Valley of Anáhuac. It is even probable that Teotihuacán was not Nahua, at least
not exclusively. Hence, though there was an unquestionable relationship between the culture of
Tula and that of Teotihuacán—the relationship
of a barbarian who inherits and interprets a civilization—it is a mistake to study the totality of
Mesoamerican civilization from the Nahua point
of view (and, worse, from that of its Aztec version), because that totality is older, richer, and
far more diverse. I have discussed this theme
elsewhere at some length.* In any case, the creative phase of Mesoamerica—which today's archaeologists call, I wonder how accurately, the
"period of the great theocracies"—ended in about
the ninth century. The extraordinary artistic and
intellectual fecundity of this period was due, as
I see it, to the coexistence in different parts of
the country of various original cultures (though
possibly they branched from a common bole):
the Mayas, the Zapotecs, the people of Teotihuacán, the people of El Tajín. Instead of the

---

* "El punto de vista nahua," in *Puertas al campo*
(Mexico City: Universidad Nacional Autónoma de
México, 1966).

hegemony of one state over the others there was diversity and confrontation, that play of influences and reactions on which all creativity finally depends. Mesoamerica was not a pyramid but an assemblage of pyramids. Of course this period was not an epoch of universal peace, as some of our archaeologists have ingenuously called it. Theocracies or not, these city-states were not pacific: the walls of Bonampak commemorate a battle and its ritual corollary, the sacrifice of prisoners, and in Teotihuacán one can see many of the symbols that later figured in the Aztec sun cult, together with the emblems of the military orders of the eagle and the jaguar and various indications of ritual cannibalism. Many scholars minimize these traits of Mesoamerican civilization—a tendency no less harmful than that of those who exaggerate them. Both sides forget that the object of scientific investigation is not to judge but to understand. Besides, Mesoamerica needs neither apologists nor detractors.

The second epoch, which has been called the "historic period," was the epoch of the great hegemonies. It was predominantly Nahua, and began with Tula and its domination over other areas. The Toltecs reached as far as Yucatan, and there the Mayas looked on them with the same wonder and the same horror they later felt in the presence of the Aztecs. To understand the significance of this domination of one people over another, it is necessary to have seen the Nahua stone serpent across the front wall of the temple to the Maya god Chac in Uxmal: it crosses it and disfigures it like the brand on the forehead of a slave. Then, after a period of confusion and struggle, Tula's hegemony gave way to that of México-Tenochtitlán. The new lords, only recently nomads, had skulked for many years around the gates of the cities they later conquered. The Aztec version of Mesoamerican civilization was grandiose and somber. The military and religious groups, and also the common people, were possessed by a heroic and inordinate belief: that they were the instruments of a sacred task that consisted in serving, maintaining, and extending the solar cult and thus helping to preserve the order of the cosmos. The cult demanded that the gods be fed human blood in order to keep the universe operating. A sublime and frightening idea: blood as the animating substance of the motion of the worlds, a motion analogous to that of the dance and to that of war. The war dance of the stars and planets, a dance of creative destruction. A chain of equations and transformations: rite→ dance→ ritual war→ sacrifice. In this cosmology the Nahua age and that of its inheritors, the Aztecs, was the fifth age of the world, that of the fifth sun: the sun of motion, the warrior sun that drank blood and each day saved the world from ultimate destruction. Polemical sun, sun of mo-

tion: wars, earthquakes, eclipses, the dance of
the cosmos. If the Aztecs were the people of the
fifth sun, the end of the world was related to the
end of Aztec supremacy; hence the avoiding of
both, through wars, the enslavement of other nations, and sacrifices, would be a sacred task as
well as a political-military enterprise. That identification of a cosmic era with their own national
destiny is the most notable aspect of the over-
lapping of the Aztecs' religious and philosophical
ideas and their political interests. One of Sahagún's native informants explained in a mem-
orable way the true religious significance of
Huitzilopochtli, national god of the Mexicas: *The
god is us.* Not "the people is god," as with Western democrats, but *the god is the people·* divinity
is incarnate in society and imposes on it inhuman
tasks, those of sacrificing and being sacrificed.
The "Aztec peace," as the Mexicas' hegemony
has been called by one of its erudite contemporary idolaters, made ritual warfare a permanent
institution: the vassal peoples, such as those of
Tlaxcala, were periodically obliged to celebrate
pitched battles with the Aztecs and their allies
so as to provide them (and themselves) with
prisoners to be sacrificed. The subject nations
constituted a reserve of sacred sustenance. The
"flower war" combined the hunt and the tourney
with a modern philanthropic institution: the blood
bank.

The Aztecs modified their national religious tradition in order to adapt it to an earlier cosmology created by the Toltecs or, perhaps, by the people of Teotihuacán itself. The tribal god, Huitzilopochtli, "the Warrior of the South," was at the center of the cult; at his side were the great gods of the cultures that had preceded the Aztecs in the Valley of Anáhuac: Tláloc, Quetzalcóatl. Thus they confiscated a singularly profound and complex vision of the universe to convert it into an instrument of domination.* Solar religion and expansionist ideology, superhuman heroism and inhuman political realism, sacred madness and cold astuteness—such were the extremes between which the Aztec ethos moved. This psychic and moral duality was in correlation with the dualism of their social organization and with that of their religious and cosmological thought. Upon this dualism—a distinctive trait of the Nahuas and perhaps a characteristic of all American Indians—there was superimposed another of a historical nature: an amalgamation of the beliefs of the sedentary peoples of the Central Plateau with those of the nomads which the Aztecs had been. A solar religion and an agricultural religion, Jacques Soutelle has remarked. This religious

---

* Various authors have written studies on this topic; among the most recent and perceptive are those by Laurette Séjourné.

and cosmological syncretism corresponded, on the one hand, to the moral duplicity I mentioned earlier and, on the other, to a hybrid art that varied between the sublime and the grotesque, between the monotony of the official style and an art that combined fierce life with intellectual rigor, passion, and geometry. Our art critics wax ecstatic about the statue of Coatlicue, an enormous block of petrified theology. Have they ever *looked* at it? Pedantry and heroism, sexual puritanism and ferocity, calculation and delirium: a peopie made up of warriors and priests, astrologers and immolators. And of poets, too: that world of brilliant colors and somber passions was crisscrossed with lightning flashes of poetry. And in all the manifestations of that extraordinary and horrifying nation, from the astronomical myths to the poets' metaphors, from the daily rites to the priests' meditations, there is always the smell of blood, the obsessive reek of it. The Aztec year, like those wheels-of-torture circles that appear in the novels of Sade, was a circle of eighteen blood-soaked months, eighteen ceremonies, eighteen ways of dying: by arrows, by drowning, by beheading, by flaying . . . Dance and penitence.

What religious and social aberration caused a city as beautiful as Mexico-Tenochtitlán— water, stone, and sky—to be the scene of a hallucinatory and funereal ballet? And what obfuscation of the spirit is responsible for that fact that no one among us—I am speaking, not of our outdated nationalists, but of our philosophers. historians, artists, poets—wishes to see and to admit that the Aztec world was one of history's aberrations? The case of the Aztecs is unique because their cruelty was the result of a system impeccably and implacably coherent, an irrefutable syllogism-dagger. That violence can be explained as the result of sexual puritanism, repression of the senses, and the crushing weight of religion; but what stuns and paralyzes the mind is the use of realistic means in the service of a metaphysic both rigorously rational and delirious, the insensate offering up of lives to a petrified concept. It was not the homicidal rage of Genghis Khan and Tamerlane nor the White Huns' intoxicated delight in killing and burning. Instead, the Mexicas are reminiscent of the Assyrians, and not only because of the splendor of their capital and the grandiose and liturgical nature of their slaughters: the Assyrians, too, were inheritors of a high culture and were equally partial to the truncated pyramid (the ziggurat). But the Assyrians were not theologues. In fact, the real rivals of the Aztecs are not to be found in the East at all but rather in the West, for only among ourselves has the alliance between politics and metaphysics been so intimate, so exacerbated, and so deadly: the inquisitions, the religious wars, and, above all, the totalitarian societies of the twentieth century. I do not presume, of course, to judge the Aztec world, and still less to condemn it. México-Tenochtitlán has disappeared, and what concerns me, as I gaze upon its fallen body, is not the problem of historical interpretation but the fact that we cannot contemplate the cadavar face to face: its phantasm inhabits us. For this reason I believe that a critique of Mexico and its history—a critique resembling the therapeutics of the psychoanalysts—should begin by examining what the Aztec world view meant and still means. The image of Mexico as a pyramid is one viewpoint among many others equally possible: the viewpoint of what is on the platform at its top. It is the viewpoint of the ancient gods and of those who served them, the Aztec lords and priests. It is also that of their heirs and successors: the viceroys, the generals, the presidents. And, furthermore, it is the viewpoint of the vast majority, of the victims crushed by the pyramid or sacrificed on its platform-sanctuary. The critique of Mexico begins with the critique of the pyramid.

Mesoamerica's second epoch, as I have said, was that of Tula and México-Tenochtitlán. Both states weighed down upon the other peoples like those gigantic stone warriors the archaeologists have excavated in the first of those cities. Repe-

titions, amplifications, immense works, inhuman
grandeur—but nothing comparable to the great
creative period. What I want to emphasize, however, is the relationship of the Aztecs with the
Mesoamerican tradition. It is known that they
were wholly or almost wholly ignorant about the
"great theocracies" that had preceded Tula. I
must confess that their ignorance makes me shudder: it was the same as that of the Dark Ages regarding Greco-Roman civilization, the same as
that of our descendants someday regarding Paris,
London, New York. If the Aztecs' notions about
Teotihuacán and its builders were rudimentary
and grotesque, their notions about Tula were top-
lofty. They always claimed, with enormous pride,
that they were the direct and legitimate heirs of
the Toltecs, that is, of Tula and Culhuacán. To
understand the reason for their pretension one
must remember that for the Aztecs the universal
dichotomy *civilized/barbarian* was expressed by
the terms *Toltec/Chichimec.* The Aztecs wanted
to forget their Chichimec (barbarian) past. This
pretension had little basis: before the founding
of México-Tenochtitlán they had been a band
of fugitives beyond the pale. The feeling of illegitimacy, common to all barbarians and new-
comers, was like a wound in the Aztecs' psyche;
it was also a defect in their credentials as rulers
of the world by the will of Huitzilopochtli. In
fact, Huitzilopochtli, supposed center of the fifth-

sun cosmology and support of the solar cult, was only a tribal god, an upstart among the ancient divinities of Mesoamerica. That is why the Aztec ruler Itzcóatl, with the counsel of the celebrated Tlacaélel, architect of Mexica grandeur, ordered that the ancient codices and documents be burned and that new ones be fabricated, the purpose of the latter being to "prove" that the Aztecs were the descendants of the lords of Anáhuac. By affirming their direct relationship with the Toltec world, the Aztecs also affirmed the legitimacy of their hegemony over the other nations of Mesoamerica. This makes clearer the correlation between their falsifying of history and their religious syncretism.

The subject nations looked on these doctrines skeptically. The Aztecs themselves knew that a fraud had been perpetrated, but none of them dared to admit it, even to himself. All this explains why Montezuma II, receiving Cortés, greeted him as the envoy of someone who was claiming his inheritance. I want to make it clear that he did *not* receive him as an emissary of the Emperor Charles, but rather as a god (or semi-god or warlock-warrior—the Aztecs never succeeded in formulating definite ideas about the nature of the Spaniards) who had been sent to re-establish the sacred order of the fifth sun, which had been interrupted by the fall of Tula. The Spaniards' arrival coincided with an inter-

regnum in Mesoamerica. The destruction of Tula
and the flight of Quetzalcóatl (god-chieftain-
priest), who prophesied that one day he would
come back, had been followed by the hegemony
of México-Tenochtitlán; but the Aztecs, because
of their barbarian origins, were perpetually
threatened by the return of those who truly embodied the principle of the fifth sun, that is, the
legendary Toltecs. The attitude of the Mesoamerican world toward the Spaniards is still more
understandable when one recalls that, according
to legend, the priest-king Topiltzin Quetzalcóatl
was born in the year 1-Ácatl (cane) and that his
flight and disappearance took place fifty-two
years later, again in the year 1-Ácatl. It was
generally believed that Quetzalcóatl would return in another 1-Ácatl year—and Cortés arrived
in Mexico in 1519, again 1-Ácatl! The speech
with which Montezuma greeted Cortés is remarkable: "My lord, you are tired, you are weary;
you have now come back to your land. You have
arrived in your city, Mexico. You have come to
sit on your throne, under its canopy. Oh, brief
was the while they held it for you, preserved it
for you, those who have gone before, your substitutes." The Aztec sovereign did not question the
Spaniard's divine credentials; Mexico belonged
to Cortés, not by right of conquest but because
of his original property rights: he had come to
recover his inheritance. And Montezuma specifi-

cally said that "those who have gone before"—
by which he meant his predecessors, the former
rulers of Mexico: Itzcóatl, Montezuma I, Tizoc,
Axayácatl, Ahuítzotl—governed only as *substi-*
tutes, as regents. Like Montezuma himself, they
were nothing more than the guardians, the custodians, of the Toltec legacy. Montezuma pointed
out—I am not sure whether in sadness or in an
attempt to win favor with Cortés—that the regency lasted for only a short spell: "Oh, brief was
the while they held it for you . . ." And there
is pathos in his insistence: "I was in agony for
five days, for ten days, with my eyes fixed on the
Region of Mysteries. And you have come, among
clouds, among mists. For that is what our kings
had foretold, those who reigned, those who governed your city: that you would assume your
throne, that you would come here." * But I cannot give more time to an analysis of this theme.
One could spend a whole lifetime studying and
explaining the Conquest.

This attitude of Montezuma and the ruling
class of México-Tenochtitlán is not so fantastiç
as it seems at first glance: the return of Tula and
Quetzalcóatl fitted naturally into a circular conception of time. The idea disturbs us because we

---

* Miguel León-Portilla, ed., *Visión de los vencidos*
(Mexico City: Universidad Nacional Autónoma de
México).

are moderns, at once the devotees and victims of the different conception that progress imposes on us: we think of time as being rectilinear and unrepeatable, and cannot accept the idea of cyclical time and its many consequences. In the case of the Aztecs, the idea of time returning was rooted in a feeling of guilt: earlier time, on returning, assumed the form of a *reparation*. This would not have been possible if the Aztecs had not felt guilty about Tula's mythic past and their own domination over other peoples. The proof of this is the strange episode of the god Tezcatlipoca's appearance. We know that this god played a decisive role in the fall of Tula. Like Satan with Christ and Mara with Buddha, Tezcatlipoca was Quetzalcóatl's tempter—except that, being luckier and cleverer, he succeeded through sorcery in inducing that ascetic god to get drunk and then to commit incest with his sister. The ruination of both Quetzalcóatl and his city was the result.

Tezcatlipoca was especially venerated by the Mexicas. Therefore, when Montezuma II learned that Cortés and his soldiers—deaf to pleas, deaf to veiled threats—had refused to turn back and were continuing to march toward México-Tenochtitlán, the Aztec ruler decided to oppose them with the one infallible weapon: sorcery. He sent out a group of warlocks and magicians, but just as they were about to reach the

Spaniards they ran across a young man "who
spoke as if he were drunk" (possessed by divine
madness?) and who halted them to say: "What
is it you want? What is Montezuma trying to do?
. . . He has committed errors . . . he has destroyed people." The warlocks listened intently
to the confused and muttered words of the young
"drunkard." When they tried to touch him, he
vanished. Yet they still heard his voice, which
told them to look behind, toward the valley
where the capital stood. "The temples were on
fire, and so were the communal halls and the religious schools and all the houses of the city. And
it was as if a great battle were raging. And when
the warlocks saw this, their hearts fled away
from them. Now they could not speak clearly
. . . They said, 'He was not an anybody, he
was the young Tezcatlipoca!' " The magicians
returned without having accomplished their mission and told Montezuma what they had seen
and heard. At first he was so dejected that he said
nothing, but at last he murmured: "What help
is there now, my stalwarts? . . . With this they
have given us fit punishment!" * To Montezuma
the arrival of the Spaniards meant, in a way, the
paying of an old debt, incurred by the Aztecs'
sacrilegious usurpation. Their mingling of religion and politics had served the Aztecs well as

---

* Cf. *Visión de los vencidos.*

a justification of their hegemony, but it became a liability once the Spaniards arrived: the divinity of the latter had the same origin as the purported cosmic mission of the Aztec people. Both were agents of the divine order, representatives and instruments of the fifth sun. The strangest aspect of the situation is that the Spaniards had no inkling of how complex the Indians' attitudes toward them really were. And there was another element that further increased the tragic confusions these errors created: the Spaniards' Indian allies hoped that the fall of México-Tenochtitlán would put an end to the interregnum, the usurpation, and their own vassalage. Perhaps their horrible disillusionment was the cause of their centuries-long passivity: the Spaniards, on making themselves the successors of the Aztecs' rule, also perpetuated their usurpation.

As the heirs of México-Tenochtitlán, the Spaniards became the transmitters of the Aztec archetype of political power: the *tlatoani,* or ruler, and the pyramid. The transmission was involuntary and, for that reason, incontrovertible: an unconscious transmission, exempt from rational examination and criticism. During the course of our history the Aztec archetype has sometimes opposed, sometimes become fused with, the Hispanic-Arabic archetype, which is the *caudillo.* This oscillation between the *tlatoani* and the *caudillo* is one of the traits that differentiate us from Spain, Portugal, and most of the other Latin-American countries,* where *caudillismo* reigns without a rival. The *tlatoani* is impersonal, priestly, and institutional—hence the abstract figure of the president corresponds to a bureaucratic and hierarchic corporation like the Institutional Revolutionary Party. The *caudillo* is personal, epic, and exceptional—hence he makes his appearance when the normal order of affairs is upset. The *tlatoani* represents an impersonal continuation of the rule, while a caste of priests and hierarchs exercises power during its successive incarnations. The president *is* the Party during his six-year term; but, when it ends, another president appears, and is only another incarnation of the Party. Different and the same: the double exigency of Mexico's presidential institution. The power concentrated in the president's hands is enormous, but it never is personal power, it is instead a consequence of his impersonal investiture. The *caudillo* belongs to no caste and is not selected by any governing body, sacred or profane: he is an unexpected presence who appears in times of crisis and confusion, rules until the storm blows itself out, and then vanishes as suddenly as he appeared. The *caudillo* governs behind the back of the law: he

---

* The exceptions are Chile, Uruguay, and Costa Rica.

makes the law. The *tlatoani*—whether his power
derives from the Aztecs' usurpation or the Party's
monopoly—always takes refuge in legality: whatever he does is done in the name of the law.

We have had many a *tlatoani* and many a
caudillo in our history: Juárez and Santa Ana,
Carranza and Villa. None of them has been completely the one or the other, of course, but there
is a clue that reveals the secret supremacy of
the Aztec model: all of the leaders we have had,
even the most arbitrary and *caudillo*-like, have
aspired to the category of *tlatoani*. There is a
Mexican nostalgia for legality that other Spanish-
American *caudillos* do not feel; all of them—
whether one considers Bolívar and Fidel Castro
or Rosas and Juan Perón—have believed and
believe that an act is a deed, whereas Mexicans
affirm that the same act is a rite. In the one
case, violence is transgression; in the other, expiation. The founding of the National Revolutionary Party initiated the decline of Mexican
caudillismo; at the same time, the Aztec archetype became more and more solidly consolidated.
It could not have been otherwise: that archetype
is the very model of stability, and, after some
twenty years of civil war and of violent quarrels
among the revolutionary *caudillos*, stability is the
political value that Mexico most desires and ap-
preciates. But the partisans of stability *à outrance*
forget a circumstance that upsets the whole pyra-

midal edifice, however solid it may appear: the
Institutional Revolutionary Party was conceived
as a solution to the problems of exception and
transition, so that the continuation of its political monopoly has a certain analogy with the
usurpation committed by México-Tenochtitlán
and with that city's pretension that it was the
axis of the fifth sun. The translation ·of pre-
Hispanic mythical concepts into contemporary
political terms does not end, however, with the
equivalence between the Party's usurpation of
the revolutionary heritage and the Aztecs' usurpation of the Toltec heritage. The fifth sun—
the era of motion, of earthquakes, of the collapse of the great pyramid—corresponds to the
historical period in which the whole world now
lives: revolts, rebellions, and other social upheavals. We will not be rescued from the agi-
tations and convulsions of the fifth sun by the
stability, solidity, and hardness of stone but rather
by lightness, flexibility, and capacity for change.
Stability leads to petrification, to the stone mass
of the pyramid, which the sun of motion shatters
and grinds to dust.

The plaza of Tlatelolco is magnetic with
history. Tlatelolco itself, an expression of Mesoamerican dualism, was actually a twin center with
México-Tenochtitlán. Although it never lost its
autonomy entirely, it lived in strict dependence

on the dominant power after an attempt at rebellion had been harshly put down by the *tlatoani*
Axayácatl. It was the seat of the merchant class,
and its great plaza contained not only temples
but also a celebrated market that Bernal Díaz
and Cortés have described with detailed and enchanted exaltation, as if they were recounting a
legend. During the siege, Tlatelolco resisted the
Spaniards tenaciously and was the last Aztec
stronghold to surrender. Then, in the midst of
that immense stone esplanade, the evangelizers
—as if laying a risky bet—planted (it is the only
word) a minuscule church. It is still standing.
Tlatelolco is one of Mexico's roots: there the
missionaries taught classical literature, Spanish
literature, rhetoric, philosophy, and theology to
the Aztec nobles; there Sahagún founded the
study of pre-Hispanic history. The crown and
the church brutally interrupted these studies, and
both Mexicans and Spaniards are still paying the
consequences of that deadly interruption: Spain
isolated us from our Indian past and thus isolated herself from us. Afterward, Tlatelolco lived
an obscure life: military prison, railroad yards,
dusty suburb. A few years ago the regime transformed the area into a complex of huge low-rent
apartment buildings, and in doing so wanted to
rescue the venerable plaza: it discovered part of
the pyramid and, in front of it and the minuscule
church, built an anonymous skyscraper: the Min-

istry of Foreign Affairs. The conjunction is not a happy one: three excesses in an urban desolation. The name chosen for the plaza was that platitude of Columbus Day speakers: Plaza of the Three Cultures. But nobody uses the official name; everybody calls it Tlatelolco. This preference for the ancient Mexican name is not accidental: October 2, Tlatelolco, inserts itself with terrifying logic in our history, both the real and the symbolic.

Tlatelolco is the counterpart, in terms of blood and sacrifice, of the petrification of the Institutional Revolutionary Party. Both are projections of the same archetype, although with different functions within the implacable dialectic of the pyramid. It is as if contemporary facts were a metaphor for that past which is a buried present: the relation between the ancient plaza of Tlatelolco and the main plaza of México-Tenochtitlán is now repeated in the connection between the new Plaza of the Three Cultures and the Zócalo.* The relation between these two places is explicit if one considers our visible history, but it also becomes symbolic when one recognizes that it alludes to what I have called the invisible history of Mexico. True, we can

---

* The main plaza of Mexico City, built on the ruins of that of México-Tenochtitlán. It contains both the Cathedral of Mexico and the National Palace.

shrug our shoulders and reject any interpretation that goes beyond what the newspapers and the statistics tell us. But to reduce the significance of a fact to our visible history is to deny oneself real comprehension and, indeed, to submit to a kind of spiritual mutilation. To make clear the true character of the relation between the Zócalo and Tlatelolco we must turn to a third landmark and question another place no less magnetic with history: Chapultepec Park. The regime has constructed a proud monument there, the National Museum of Anthropology. If Mexico's visible history is the symbolic script of its invisible history and if both are the expression, reiteration, and metaphor—on different levels of reality—of certain repressed and submerged moments, it is evident that in this museum we can find, even though in dispersed fragments, the elements that can serve us to reconstruct the figure we seek. But the museum offers us something more—and something more immediate, tangible, and obvious—than the broken symbols and excavated stones its halls contain: in both the museum itself and in the spirit that animates it the archetype is at last completely unveiled. In fact, the image it presents us of Mexico's past obeys not so much the exigencies of science as the aesthetics of the paradigm. It is not a museum, it is a mirror—except that in its symbol-crammed surface we do not reflect ourselves but instead contemplate the giganticized myth of México Tenochtitlán with its Huitzilopochtli ánd his mother Coatlicue, its *tlatoani* and Serpent-Woman, its prisoners of war and hearts-as-fruits. In that mirror we do not see deep into our own image: we adore the image that is crushing us.

To enter the Museum of Anthropology is to penetrate an architecture built of the solemn matter of myth. There is an enormous rectangular patio, and in that patio there is a great parasol from which light and water fall with a sound of broken calendars—a rain of years and centuries splashing on the gray-green stones. The parasol is supported by a stone column that would be impressive if it were not covered with reliefs that repeat the themes of the official rhetoric. But it is ethics, not aesthetics, that prompts me to speak of the museum: in it, anthropology and history have been made to serve an idea about Mexico's history, and that idea is the foundation, the buried and immovable base, that sustains our conceptions of the state, of political power, and of social order. The visitor strolls enchanted through hall after hall: the smiling Neolithic world with its little nude figures; the Mayas, miners of time and the heavens; the Huastecos with their great stones whose carving has the simplicity of line drawings; the culture of El Tajín, an art that escapes both "Olmec" heaviness and the hierarchism of Teotihuacán without falling into Mayan baroque, being instead a wonder of feline grace; and the Toltecs with their tons and tons of sculpture—all the diversity and complexity of two thousand years of Mesoamerican history presented as a prologue to the last act, the apotheosis-apocalypse of México-Tenochtitlán. I hardly need to point out that, from the viewpoint of science and history, the image of the pre-Columbian past which the Museum of Anthropology offers us is false. In no way do the Aztecs represent the culmination of the diverse cultures that preceded theirs. Indeed, the contrary is true: their version of Mesoamerican civilization simplifies it on the one hand and exaggerates it on the other, and in both ways it impoverishes it. This exaltation and glorification of México-Tenochtitlán transforms the Museum of Anthropology into a temple. The cult propagated within its walls is the same one that inspires our schoolbooks on Mexican history and the speeches of our leaders: the stepped pyramid and the sacrificial platform.

Why have we sought Mexico's archetype among those pre-Hispanic ruins? And why must that archetype be only Aztec and not Mayan or Zapotec or Tarascan or Otomí? My answer to these questions will not please a lot of people: the true heirs of the pre-Columbian world are not the peninsular Spaniards but ourselves, we Mexicans who speak Spanish, whether we are

Creoles, mestizos, or Indians. Thus the museum expresses a feeling of guilt—except that, by a process of transference and unburdening which psychoanalysis has often studied and described, the guilt is transfigured into a glorification of the victim. At the same time—and this is what seems to me decisive—its ultimate exaltation of the Aztec period confirms and justifies what in appearance condemns the museum: the survival, the continuing strength, of the Aztec model of domination in our contemporary history. I have already said that the relationship between the Aztecs and the Spaniards was not only one of opposition: Spanish power took the place of Aztec power and thus continued it. Independent Mexico, in its turn, explicitly and implicitly prolonged the centralist, authoritarian, Aztec-Spanish tradition. I repeat: there is a bridge that reaches from *tlatoani* to viceroy, viceroy to president. The glorification of México-Tenochtitlán in the Museum of Anthropology is an exaltation of the image of the Aztec pyramid, now guaranteed, so to speak, by science. The regime sees itself, transfigured, in the world of the Aztecs. And in contemplating itself it affirms itself. Therefore a critique of Tlatelolco, the Zócalo, and the National Palace—a political, social, and moral critique—includes the Museum of Anthropology and is also a historical critique. If politics is a dimension of history, a critique of history is like-

wise political and moral criticism. We must oppose the Mexico of the Zócalo, Tlatelolco, and
the Museum of Anthropology, not with another
image—all images have a fatal tendency to become petrified—but with criticism, the acid that
dissolves images. In this case (and perhaps in
others), criticism is but one of the imagination's
ways of working, one of its manifestations. In our
age the imagination operates critically. True, criticism is not what we dream of, but it teaches us
to distinguish between the specters out of our
nightmares and our true visions. Criticism is the
imagination's apprenticeship in its second turn,
the imagination cured of fantasies and determined
to face the world's realities. Criticism tells us that
we should learn to dissolve the idols, should learn
to dissolve them within our own selves. We must
learn to be like the air, a liberated dream.

Return
to
the
Labyrinth
of
Solitude

TRANSLATED BY YARA MILOS

(CONVERSATION WITH CLAUDE FELL)*

At this time, which is something like an anniversary, twenty-five years after the first publication of The Labyrinth of Solitude, *we could set up a balance sheet of the problems raised in that book. In 1970, after the 1968 events in Mexico and elsewhere in the world, you yourself felt the need to revert to this book and give it an "extension." My first question will be somewhat technical: what are the essential differences between the first edition of* Labyrinth, *published in 1950, and the second, in 1959?*

I don't think that there is any essential difference between the two editions. The main revisions tend to bring the book up to date. Besides, there are secondary alterations, an attempt at greater precision, at more conciseness. In the first edition some things were a little naïve and I tried to correct them. . . . But it is fundamentally the same book.

What had changed in Mexico's internal situation between the two versions of the book?

I think it was visible already, when I wrote the second version, that we were past the active period of the Mexican Revolution. We were in the midst of an institutionalist regime, of this paradox of a petrified or institutionalized revolution.

Regarding the international situation, had the opposition between developed and underdeveloped countries fully asserted itself?

This was something that impressed me very much during

---

*Claude Fell is a University Professor in France and the author of several studies on Mexico and Latin America.

those years. The opposition between poor countries and rich countries, from the viewpoint of history and culture, means: central or imperial countries and peripheral or marginal countries, subject countries and object countries. The book is part of the attempt of literally marginal countries to regain consciousness: to become subjects again. Another theme did not appear in the first edition: criticism of the one-party system. It is a book written after the terrible experience of Stalinism. Yet, one is dealing with a universal phenomenon: one-party systems appeared the same in Fascist countries (Italy and Germany) as in those where revolutions were in power, like the Soviet Union, or like Mexico. And now the phenomenon, far from having subsided, is spreading to the entire Third World. A concomitant fact has been the appearance of ideological dogmatisms. Orthodoxy is the natural complement of political and ecclesiastical bureaucracies. Toward modern orthodoxies and their bishops I feel the same repulsion as did the pagan Celsus in front of primitive Christians and their belief in an only truth. Fortunately, the Mexican party is not an ideological party; like India's Congress party, it is a coalition of interests. This explains the fact that in Mexico there has been no *terror*, in the modern meaning of the word. Nor has there been an inquisition. There have been state violence and popular violence but nothing resembling the ideological terrorism of Nazism and Bolshevism.

How was the book received when it was published?

Rather negatively. Many people were indignant: some thought it was a book against Mexico. A poet told me something quite amusing: that I had written an elegant insult against Mexican mothers.

What was the position of the book in relation to the work of Samuel Ramos and to the production of what could be called the school of José Gaos?

Such reflections on countries are as old as modern culture. In France, during the last century, there were some important essays of this kind. In our own tongue, the Spanish generation of 1898 initiated the genre. In Argentina, there was the essay of Ezequiel Martínez Estrada. I had not yet read it when I wrote *The Labyrinth of Solitude*; on the other hand, I had read two or three brief essays by Borges that treat aspects of the Argentinian character and language with grace and keenness. In Mexico, the reflection on these subjects began with Samuel Ramos. His remarks were, above all, of a psychological nature and he was greatly influenced by Adler, the German psychologist and more or less heterodox disciple of Freud. Ramos centered his description around the so-called "inferiority complex" and what compensated for it: machismo. Although not entirely wrong, his explanation was limited and terribly dependent on Adler's psychological models.

After Ramos, under the influence of Gaos, the Spanish philosopher, there was much insistence on the history of ideas. Several books came out, one of them by Leopoldo Zea on positivism in Mexico. When that book appeared, I published an article in *Sur*, in Buenos Aires, making certain critical reservations. The book is an excellent examination of the historical function of positivism in Mexico and it explains how that philosophy was adopted by the dominant classes. In Europe, as among ourselves, positivism was a philosophy destined to justify the prevailing social order. But—and in this resides my criticism—when positivism crossed the ocean, its nature changed. Over there, the social order was that of bourgeois society: democracy, free discussion, technology, science, industry, and progress. In Mexico, with the same verbal and intellectual schemata, there was the mask of an order founded on the system of the great landed estates. Mexican positivism introduced a certain kind of bad faith in the relations with ideas; an ambiguity not only between social reality and the ideas that pretended to justify it, but also the appearance of a particular type of bad faith, since it was introduced into the very consciousness of Mexican positivists. A psychic scission occurred: those gentlemen who swore by Comte and Spencer were not the enlightened and democratic bourgeois but the ideologists of a landowner's oligarchy.

As for my book, it is a book of social, political and psychological criticism. It is a book in the French tradition of "moralism." It is a description on the one hand of certain attitudes and an essay, on the other, on historical interpretation. It has no bearing on Ramos's examination: he dwells on psychology; in my case psychology is but a way of reaching moral and historical criticism.

And, in The Labyrinth, *you say that the typology as established by Ramos would have to be psychoanalysis.*

Yes. One of the pivotal ideas of the book is that there is an interred but living Mexico. Better still: there is among Mexicans, men and women, a universe of buried images, desires and impulses. I attempted a description (of course insufficient—a mere glimpse) of the world of repressions, inhibitions, memories, appetites and dreams which Mexico has been and is. I was much impressed by Freud's study of Judaic monotheism. I was speaking of morality before; I should now add another word: therapeutics. Moral criticism is a self-revelation of what we conceal and, as Freud teaches, a . . . relative cure. In this sense my book tried to be an essay on moral criticism: the description of a hidden reality that hurts. Critical thinking during these times was inseparable from Marxism and I was under the influence of Marxism. Those years I read Caillois's studies and, a little later, those of Bataille and of the master of both of them, Mauss, on the feast, the sacrifice, the gift, and sacred and profane time. I immediately found certain analogies between those descriptions and my everyday experiences as a Mexican. I also learned a lot from the German philosophers whom Ortega y Gasset had made known a few years before in our tongue: phenomenology, the philosophy of culture, and the work of historians and essayists such as Dilthey and Simmel.

I already thought at that time what I think now: history is knowledge situated between science properly so-called and poetry. Historical learning is not quantitative, nor can a historian discover historical laws. A historian describes like a scientist and has visions like a poet. This is why Marx is a great historian (that was his true vocation). So is Machiavelli. History gives us an understanding of the past and, sometimes, of the present. It is wisdom rather than learning. So my aim was to view the Mexican character through the history of Mexico.

With this, we come to a key to The Labyrinth of Solitude, *that is to say, to the conception of history which may be inferred from the book. It is an antianecdotic book. You reject any factual history, any historical determinism, and try to determine what some present-day French historians call "intrahistory." This orientation can be confirmed by quoting one of the first phrases in* The Other Mexico: *"The Mexican is not in history, he is history."*

Could you explain this point?

Spanish has an advantage over French and English: we have *estar* and *ser*. "*Estar* in history" means to be surrounded by historical circumstances; "*ser* in history" means that one is, oneself, historical circumstances; that one is, oneself, changing. That is to say, man is not only an object or subject of history; he himself is history, he is the changes. One of the so-called historical factors that govern him is . . . he himself. There is continuous interaction. It seems to me that the expression "intra-history" (weren't the Spaniards—either Un-

334 / The Labyrinth of Solitude

amuno or Américo Castro—the first to use it?) is more adequate than another expression: "history of mentalities." Because mentalities, at least for a Spanish-speaking person, are something external: they concern the mind and ideas. I believe that the authentic history of a society concerns not only explicit ideas but, above all, implicit beliefs. Ortega y Gasset distinguished (rightly enough, I think) two domains: that of ideas and that of beliefs. Beliefs live in the innermost soul and, for this reason, change much less than ideas. For example, we all know that the Middle Ages were Thomist, that the seventeenth century was Cartesian and that now many people are Marxist. Yet, in London, Moscow and Paris, people are still reading astrological treatises whose origins are Babylonian, or pursuing magical practices of neolithic times. What interested me in the case of Mexico was the tracing of certain buried beliefs.

All this brings us to another essential notion: myth. Can The Labyrinth of Solitude *be conceived as a decryptment of Mexican myths?*

Yes, that was my intention. Here one must remember what Lévi-Strauss has said: any deciphering of a myth is another myth. The four volumes of *Le cru et le cuit* are a treatise on South American mythology and, moreover, another myth. A myth in another language. I think that *The Labyrinth of Solitude* was an attempt to describe and understand certain myths; at the same time, insofar as it is a literary work, it has in turn become another myth.

In an article in the review Esprit, *Lévi-Strauss wrote that myth "exhausts itself but does not, despite this, disappear. Two roads still remain open: that of romanesque elaboration and that of re-employment for the purposes of historical legitimation." Do you think, like Lévi-Strauss, that myths degenerate and die? Haven't Mexican myths become parts of political programs or intellectual works?*

I believe that myths, like every living thing, are born, degenerate and die. I also believe that myths come back to life. But, on one point, I don't agree with Lévi-Strauss. I have developed this divergence in the essay which I wrote on him. For Lévi-Strauss there is an essential difference between poetry and myth: myth can be translated and poetry is untranslatable. I believe the opposite: I believe that myth and poetry are translatable, though translation implies transmutation or resurrection. A poem by Baudelaire, translated into Spanish, is another poem and it is the same poem. This holds true of myths, too: the old pre-Columbian goddesses are born again with the Virgin of Guadalupe, which translates them into the Christianity of New Spain. The Creoles* translate the Virgin of Guadalupe—a Spanish virgin—into the Mexican context, a double translation of Hispanic and Indian mythology. The Virgin of Guadalupe is one of the few living myths of Mexico. We witness its resurrection every day in popular sensitivity. The case of Quetzalcóatl is very different. Yes, there the myth, as Lévi-Strauss thinks, has been transformed into politics and literature. The Quetzalcóatl literary myth—the novel, the poem, the play—has been rather unfortunate. The best was Lawrence's *The Plumed Serpent*, a brilliant, uneven and disjointed book. As a political myth, Quetzalcóatl has been luckier: in the popular imagination, many of our heros are only translations of Quetzalcóatl. They are, in fact, unconscious translations. This is significant because the theme of the Quetzalcóatl myth is the legitimation of power. This was the obsession of the Aztecs and of New Spain's Creoles; it still is the PRI's (Partido Revolucionario Institucional).

In the depths of the Mexican psyche, there are realities covered up by history and by modern life. Hidden but present

---

*I wanted to note again here—even though it was mentioned in *The Labyrinth*—that Creoles are Spaniards born in Mexico.

realities. One example is our image of political authority. In it are evidently pre-Columbian elements and also the remains of Hispanic, Mediterranean and Moslem beliefs. Behind the respect for Señor Presidente there is the traditional image of the Father. The family is a very powerful reality. It is the home in the original meaning of the word: center and reunion of the living and the dead, at once the altar, the bed in which one makes love, the hearth on which one cooks, the ash that buries one's forebears. The Mexican family has lived harmlessly through various centuries of calamities and is only now starting to disintegrate in the cities. The family has given Mexicans their beliefs, values and concepts on life and death, the good and the bad, masculine and feminine, prettiness and ugliness, what must be done and what is not right. In the center of the family: the father. The father figure is two-pronged, the duality of patriarch and *macho*. The patriarch protects, is good, powerful, wise. The macho is the terrible man, the *chingón*, the father who has left, who has abandoned a wife and children. The image of Mexican authority is inspired by these two extremes: Señor Presidente and Caudillo.

The caudillo image is not only Mexican but also Spanish and Hispanic American. Perhaps it is of Arab origin. The Islamic world has been characterized by its inability to create stable systems of government; that is, it has not instituted a supra-personal legitimacy. The remedy against instability has been, and is, the chiefs, the caudillos. In Latin America, an unstable continent, the caudillos came into being with Independence; in our times they are called Perón, Castro and, in Mexico, Díaz, Carranza, Obregón, Calles. The caudillo is heroic, epic: he is the man beyond the law, the one who creates the law. The President is the man of the law: his power is institutional. Mexican presidents are constitutional dictators, not caudillos. They have power while they are presidents; and their power is almost absolute, almost sacred. But they owe their power to the *investiture*. In the case of Hispanic American caudillos, they do not get power with the investiture but rather they give power to the investiture.

The rotation principle, one of the characteristics of the Mexican system, does not exist in the caudillesque regimes of Latin America. There appears here, next to the theme of the terrible father, once more the legitimacy theme. It is the mystery or enigma of the origin, something particularly grave for Latin America, since Independence. The caudillo system, which has been and is Latin America's true system of government, has not succeeded in solving it. In the caudillesque regime, succession takes place through a coup overthrowing the government or upon the caudillo's death. The caudillo system, conceived as a heroic remedy against instability, is the great producer of instability in the continent. Instability is the consequence of illegitimacy. After almost two centuries of independence from the Spanish monarchy, our peoples have not yet found a form of legitimacy. In this sense, the Mexican compromise—the combination of presidentialism and a single party's bureaucratic domination—was a solution. It is less and less so.

Perhaps we should now stop to consider the historical process analyzed in The Labyrinth of Solitude. *In your presentation of the 1910 Mexican Revolution, you focused attention on Zapatism. When the book was written this was something new and exceptional, insofar as there was almost no talk of Emiliano Zapata at the time. When mentioned in newspapers or some writings, he was invariably described as the "Attila of the South," or as a bloodthirsty bandit. How can the prominent position of Zapatism in your book be explained?*

There are two reasons. The first is kind of anecdotic and is because my father, though he came from a middle-class family, was a friend and companion of the great revolutionary, Antonio Díaz Soto y Gama, one of the founders of the Casa del Obroro Mundial (World Worker's House). My father belonged to a group of youths more or less influenced by the anarchism of Soto y Gama. These youths, at the time of Victoriano Huerta's dictatorship, wanted to go north, where were located the most disciplined armies, those which, from a military viewpoint, made the Revolution triumph. In the North, the ranchers and middle class dominated; in the South, it was the landless peasants, in gangs which the newspapers called "barbarians," Huns. It happened that those youths could not join the northern forces and went south, where they met Zapata and were conquered by Zapatism. After that, my father thought that Zapatism was Mexico's truth. I believe he was right. Later on, my friendship with Soto y Gama and others who had fought in the South with the peasant armies confirmed my beliefs and feelings. The South was, and is at the present time, Indian; there the traditional culture is still alive. When I was a child, many aged Zapatist leaders visited my home and so did many peasants whom my father, as a lawyer, defended in their lawsuits and land demands.

The idea of Zapatism given in the official propaganda is quite false and conventional. As I tried to explain in *The Labyrinth of Solitude*, what distinguished Zapatism from the other factions was its attempt to return to the origins. There is, in all revolutions, this impulse to regress to a past that is confused with society's origins. It is a past in which there reigned harmony and justice, violated by the powerful and the violent. Revolutions are the modern incarnations of the myth of the return to the golden age. Hence their immense power of contagion. In Zapatism this longing was expressed as a return to communal land ownership, to the *ejido*. This form of ownership had actually existed during the pre-Columbian epoch and, what is more noteworthy, had been recognized by the Spanish monarchy. Though painfully and with difficulty, the ejido coexisted with the large colonial estate and the Church's enormous land holdings. The first demand of the Zapatists was *return* of the land; the second, a subsidiary demand, was for *distribution. Return*: back to the origin.

The paradox of Zapatism lies in that it was a deeply traditionalist movement; and precisely in this traditionalism resides its revolutionary power. Better still: because of its traditionalism Zapatism was radically subversive. From the beginning it was this at once traditional and revolutionary element that excited my passion. Zapatism means the revelation, the setting afloat, of certain hidden and repressed realities. It is revolution not as an ideology but as an instinctive movement, a burst that is the revelation of a reality prior to hierarchies, classes and property.

Precisely, you greatly insist that the Mexican Revolution had no ideological bases.

This is how it differs so much from the last century's liberalism. To call *revolution* the changes and upheavals that started toward 1910 is to yield, perhaps, to a linguistic expediency. Years later, as I reconsidered the subject of the twentieth century's great upheavals and commotions, I reached the conclusion that one must distinguish among revolution, revolt and rebellion. I have devoted some pages of *Alternating Current, Conjunctions and Disjunctions* and *The Other Mexico: Critique of the Pyramid* to this. Revolutions, daughters of linear and progressive time concept, mean the violent and definite change of one system by another. Revolutions are the consequence of development, as Marx and Engels never tired of saying. Rebellions are acts of marginal groups and individuals: the rebel does not want to change order, as does the revolutionary, but would dethrone the tyrant. Revolts are the daughters of cyclic time: they are popular uprisings against a reputedly unfair system and they aim at restoring original time, the inaugural moment of the pact among equals.

Among Mexico's upheavals between 1910 and 1929, we should distinguish various phenomena. First, a bourgeois and middle class revolution to modernize the country; it is the one that has triumphed and to it we owe many of the good things and many of the bad things existing today—for example, this horror of Mexico City. Against this progressive revolution prolonging liberalism and Porfirism, there is its negation, the *revolt* of the Mexican peasants in the South. This revolt was vanquished militarily and its chieftain, Zapata, was assassinated. Afterward, ideologically, it was expropriated and disfigured by the victors. The triumphant faction conceived the ejido in predominantly economic terms. Now, as a system of production the ejido is inferior to capitalist agriculture. But the ejido does not serve to produce more but rather to live better—to live differently, with more fairness, harmony and freedom than at present. Its function consists in being the economic basis of a type of society that is equally far from the capitalist model and the one called, not very accurately, socialist.

The Zapatist movement was a true revolt, a turning backward of things, a returning to the beginning. Its foundation was historical because the peasants wanted to return to the communal ownership of land; at the same time they were inspired by a myth: the golden age of the beginning. The revolt had intense utopian coloring: they wanted to create a community in which the hierarchies would not be of an economic, but instead of a traditional and spiritual, nature. A society wrought in the image and likeness of neolithic villages: economically self-sufficient, egalitarian—except for "natural" hierarchies: fathers and sons, men and women, old and young, married and single—and in which the political and religious authority was reduced to a minimum, that is, with elimination of both bureaucracies, state and ecclesiastic. One significant fact: The Zapatists wore standards and insignia of the Virgin of Guadalupe; they were religious but not clerical. Nor were they Nationalists: the reality that they defended was the village, the small community of farmers and artisans, not such cruel abstractions as the nation and the state. Had he been able to, Zapata would have burned the president's chair. Soto y Gama, in his famous speech at the Covention, crumpled the national flag and called it "this rag."

This concept of utopia reappears periodically in Mexican history: at the time of the Conquest, with the missionaries; in the nineteenth century, with liberalism; at the start of the twentieth century, with Zapatism.

Yes, this utopian, communitarian concept, I find it among missionaries and also in Zapatism. I do not find it in liberalism, which is utopianism in the rationalistic sense of the word. Most revolutions in the twentieth century have been like the liberal Mexican revolution in the nineteenth century: attempts to impose geometric patterns upon living realities. They have engendered monsters. In Mexico, the victorious faction in the revolutionary struggles continues the "modernization" process begun in the nineteenth century. Between Juárez and Carranza there is a very clear connection; there is no such connection between Juárez and Zapata. Because of his blind hatred of Juárez, Vasconcelos did not realize that Zapata was the anti-Juárez, the negation of all Jacobinism and all progressivism. The attempt to "modernize" Mexico has really been a desire to efface, as it were, the stigma, the original sin, of Mexico: her birth during the Counter-Reformation, facing and against the modern world. Zapata is the negation of this progressivism. Zapata is beyond the controversy between liberals and conservatives, Marxists and neocapitalists: Zapata is *before*—and perhaps, if Mexico is not extinguished, he will be *after*.

One last question on this revolutionary period. Regarding Cárdenism, your position seems, at least, very qualified.

I witnessed Cárdenism, I lived through it, whereas I read, studied, breathed, suckled but did not live through Zapatism. In many aspects I think that General Cárdenas's policies were admirable. For example, in the field of international politics, in his attitude against Fascism, Hitler, Mussolini, the invasion of Ethiopia, and Spain. All this was irreproachable. Nor should we forget that he was the only chief of state who gave asylum to Leon Trotsky. Cárdenas was the man who first opened the doors to Spanish, then to other European, refugees. Cárdenas's international action was possible not only because the internal conditions existed to carry it out—that is, because it corresponded to a national reality and expressed Mexico's necessities and aspirations at that time—but also because the international situation was favorable then. The world had not yet been petrified into two blocks and the rivalries of the major powers gave medium-size and even small nations some latitude to maneuver. After the Second World War we have witnessed the progressive freezing of international life. The Cuban example shows that it is almost impossible to free oneself from the clutches of either superpower without falling into the other's nets.

In the Mexico of the war decade, the presence of European intellectuals, especially Spaniards, was very beneficial. We are indebted to them in great measure for the renewal of Mexican culture. But Cárdenas's policies in cultural matters suffered from serious limitations. He was not at all attracted to the University or the higher aspects of culture, I mean to sci-

ence and disinterested learning and to free art and free literature. His artistic tastes—or those of his close collaborators—
tended toward pseudorevolutionary didactism and nationalism. This has been, furthermore, the policy of Mexican governments in matters of art and literature. Mexico's public art
is state art, swollen like a circus athlete. Its only major rival is
Soviet art. Our speciality is the glorification of official figures
painted or sculptured with the well-known method of ampli-
fication. The mass production of cement giants. Our parks and
squares smother under a vegetation of heavy civic monoliths.
Cárdenas did allow the ouster from the government and the
disparagement of poets and writers in the *Contemporáneos*
group—the best of Mexican literature at that time—under
the odious accusation that they were homosexuals and reac-
tionaries. Most extravagant of the Cárdenas period was the
matter of socialist education in a country that was not socialist.
It was ideological alienation once again.

The work of Cárdenas was important and, in general, positive in economic and social aspects. But neither Cárdenas nor
his successors suspected what the future held in store for us
and they were unable to foresee the disastrous consequences
of the thoughtless cult of out-and-out development and industrialization. The conservative policy of his successors—short-
term adoption of North America's model for development—
only precipitated what is now in sight: failure. The course that
was chosen to solve Mexico's old problems was not a course
but rather a wall against which we have crashed. As they were
intent on "modernizing" the country, none of our rulers—all
of them surrounded by "expert" counselors and ideologists—
realized in time the perils of the population's excessive and
uncontrolled growth. The "other," the undeveloped Mexico,
grows more rapidly than developed Mexico and will in the
end stifle it. Nor did they take measures against the demo-

graphic, political, economic and cultural centralization that has converted Mexico City into a monstrous inflated head, crushing the frail body that holds it up. All they would have had to do was to venture over the frontier so as to know that in the large American cities to the north the air was already unbreathable—not to speak of the other physical and moral horrors of industrial societies—but they did nothing against atmospheric pollution. Nor did they foresee the gigantic failure of educational plans and the collapse of higher education. . . . Shall I go on?

As regards politics *per se*, there was great freedom of expression under Cárdenas. An immense merit. Another one, no less great: Cárdenas was the first president to relinquish power voluntarily and he did not want to govern from behind the throne, like Calles. Cárdenas's governing *style*, too, was admirable. The temptatior to convert themselves into idols is very great for Mexican presidents; Cárdenas resisted it. While he was in power, we had the most strange sensation that a man, a being like ourselves, was governing us. However, Cardenism did not try the democratic experiment but rather it strengthened the single party. General Cárdenas followed the former heads of the revolution who had founded the *Partido Nacional Revolucionario*, which he transformed into the *Partido de la Revolución Mexicana*, now called *Partido Revolucionario Institucional*. In these three names—Institutional Revolutionary Party—is concentrated the history of the political bureaucracy that has dominated the country for half a century.

No one can understand Mexico if he overlooks the PRI. Marxist descriptions are insufficient. The PRI is not a "bourgeois party" in the proverbial and hackneyed sense of this expression. Imbricated in state structures, like a political caste with its own characteristics, a grand canal for social mobility, since it spans from the village municipality to the highest spheres of national politics, the single party is a phenomenon that does not appear in the rest of Latin America (except Cuba, recently and with very different features). Most certainly, power is more coveted in Mexico than riches. If you are a millionaire, it will be very difficult—almost impossible—for you to switch from business to politics. The enormous prestige of power—as opposed to money—is an antimodern feature of Mexico. Another example of how premodern, precapitalist modes of thinking and feeling appear in our daily life.

Coming back to the historical evocations of The Labyrinth of Solitude, *we should pause in the colonial period. You have written that, by some kind of dialectical balance, the Catholic religion served as a "refuge" for the Indian populations. And you add, a few lines below, that it was in actuality a "petrified" religion. How does one reconcile these two aspects?*

One has to infer from a fact: syncretism. When the Spaniards reached Mexico, they encountered the Aztec society. In Mexico's major temple stood the images of Huitzilopochtli, the Aztec tribal god, and of Tlaloc, the rain god. The first to describe the syncretism of the Aztec state was Jacques Soustelle, in *La Pensée cosmologique des anciens Méxicains*. The version of Western civilization that reached Mexico was also syncretist. On the one hand, there was Catholic syncretism that had assimilated Greco-Latin antiquity and the gods of Orientals and barbarians; on the other hand, was Spanish syncretism. Centuries of struggle with Islam had permeated the religious conscience of Spaniards: the notion of crusade and holy war is Christian but also deeply Moslem. One must compare the attitude of Spaniards with that of the English, Dutch and French, none of whom has the Spanish idea of a "mission," with medieval and Moslem roots. When Bernal Díaz del Castillo saw the temples of Tenochtitlán, he spoke of "mosques." For him, as for Cortes, the Indians were "the others" and the others were preeminently Moslems.

The Spaniards knocked down the statues of the gods, destroyed the temples, burned the codices and annihilated the priestly caste. It was as though they had removed the eyes, ears, soul and memory of the indigenous people. At the same time, Catholicism imparts to them a vision of the world and of beyond; it gives them a statute and offers them a heaven; it christens them; that is, it opens for them the doors to a different order. Catholicism was a refuge because it was a syncretist relgion: by christening the Indians it christened their beliefs and gods. But aside from that, Catholicism was a religion on the defensive. The Catholicism that came to Mexico was the Catholicism of the Counter-Reformation. At the University of Mexico, the oldest in America, Neo-Thomism was taught; that is to say, Mexican culture sprung from the philosophy that the West was then giving up. The meaning of traditional Mexico's opposition to the modern world, above all to the United States, cannot be understood if one forgets that Mexico came into being during the Counter-Reformation. It is an essential difference: the Americans were born with the Reformation; we, with the Counter-Reformation. In this sense, I am speaking of a "petrified" religion. Perhaps the adjective "petrified" is too strong: Mexican Catholicism is alive and is not an ideology.

Don't you think that over the course of years the form of Catholicism has changed, as Mariano Pincón Salas, for example, has pointed out in his essay De la Conquista a la Independencia, *where he maintains that, although Catholicism was in early times essentially militant, missionary, itinerant, open, later it confined itself to the cities under the influence of the Jesuits?*

Catholicism changed but not the way Picón Salas said it did. There was no reason for the Jesuits to go out into the country: it had already been converted. But the conversion of California was for the most part the work of the Jesuits. So was the evangelization of the nomads in northern Mexico and the southern United States. According to Robert Ricard, the *tabula rasa* of indigenous beliefs was the policy of the Franciscans and the first missionaries—influenced by the millenarianism of Joaquín de Flora. They were followed by the Jesuits, the richest, most powerful and influential religious order of New Spain in the seventeenth and eighteenth centuries. They were the main authors of the "translation" into Christianity of the indigenous myths. They were fervent Guadalupians and those who tried to justify the fantastic hypothesis that Quetzalcóatl was the Apostle Saint Thomas. That was the decisive change in the Church: the Jesuits Mexicanized Catholicism while the Franciscans tried to Christianize the Indians. I say all this despite my little fondness for the Company of Jesus. The Jesuits are Catholicism's Bolsheviks.

Of course, on the other hand, little by little the Church became Mexico's most important landowner and Catholicism spread over the country—at least on the level of the Indian and peon—an oppressive structure.

Yes, but to call the Church a landowner is perhaps too simplistic. At least two distinctions must be drawn. In the first place, one ought to speak in the plural and say the *ecclesiastic properties*; there were many: those of the secular Church, those of the religious orders, those of the convents, and so forth. Second, these properties were not privately owned but belonged to different collectives. In this sense, they seemed instead the communal property of villages. They were thus viewed by Juárez and the liberals, who decreed at the same time the disappearance of both forms. The latifundism of the

Porfirist regime was one consequence of the liberal reform. Church property, if you wish, could also resemble that of modern stock companies and associations. In these companies what counts is not so much the will of the individual stockholders as what the technical bureaucracy that runs them wants. Something similar happened with the properties of convents, orders and bishoprics. But it would be an exaggeration to compare modern capitalist companies with the Church of New Spain. After all, profit is the visible aim of these corporations, whereas not even the most primary anticlericalism can reduce the function of the Church during those centuries to mere gain. The social and historical nature of New Spain has to be reexamined. It is one of the omissions of *The Labyrinth of Solitude* and I would like to write about this. I insinuated something in my prologue to the book by Lafaye on Guadalupe and Quetzalcóatl.* Lafaye makes inferences based on the idea that Mexico's history is a continuous span from the pre-Columbian world to our times; I think that it is not so, that there is a break and various interruptions. Actually, we are viewing three different societies. First, the pre-Columbian society, itself divided during that civilization's highest period, so-called of great theocracies (Teotihuacán Palenque, Monte Albán), and afterward the period of the militarist city-states that began at Tula and reached its apogee in Tenochtitlán. The great split of the Conquest occurred here. It is the dividing line. The new society arises in the seventeenth century: the Creole society, dependent upon Spain but increasingly autonomous. New Spain is an original creator in architecture, the art of governing, poetry, urban development, cooking, beliefs. At the end of the seventeenth century a national project, Mexico's first, is brought forth: to make

---

*Jacques Lafaye, *Quetzalcoatl and Guadalupe: The Formation of Mexican National Consciousness, 1531–1813* (Chicago: University of Chicago Press 1976).

New Spain into *another* Spain, the Empire of North America. It is a double reflection of Rome and Mexico-Tenochtitlán: the Latin and the indigenous heritages. The Jesuits had a cardinal participation in that project. But Independence—which was simultaneously the dismemberment of the Spanish Empire and the birth of another society—meant the end of the Creole society. New Spain's agony was protracted, consummated only toward the second half of the nineteenth century, with the victory over Maximilian. Thus, the imperial project of the eighteenth century miscarried in the nineteenth century. From the ruins of this project there issued a third society, the one in which we are living now, a still unfinished society. The New-Spanish society of the seventeenth and eighteenth centuries was on the whole much closer to perfection and harmony than the Mexican society of the first half of the twentieth century. For me, architecture is a society's unbribable witness. Let us, in its works, compare the three societies: the Mesoamerican pyramids and temples; New Spain's churches, convents and palaces; the vulgar and heavy architecture—state megalomania and profit-mindedness of the Mexican middle class—of the twentieth century.

In The Labyrinth of Solitude, *you state that this "refuge Catholicism" implanted by the Spaniards has also enabled the pre-Cortesian fund to survive. What does this survival amount to?*

The word syncretism says everything. Or the expression of the American journalist, Anita Bremen, "idols behind the altars." Mexican Catholicism, instead of a theology or mystique, has created many images combining those of the West with those of the pre-Columbian world. Woe to the religion or society without images! A society without images is a Puritan society. A society that oppresses the body and the imagination.

Changing the subject again, we might go on to another im-

portant aspect of the book: Mexican cultural life. You define it through two antagonistic terms: "commitment" and "criticism." Moreover, you stress again the necessity of a "critical" attitude in the Other Mexico. Could you give us your feelings on this point?

I think that the term "commitment," which originated with Sartre, is equivocal. One is not quite certain what a commitment means. If by commitment one understands the relation between a writer and his reality and the society in which he lives, we are all committed writers, even those of us who do not want to be committed. What seems unacceptable to me is that a writer or intellectual should submit to a party or church. In the twentieth century, we have seen many writers, great writers, yield to the demands of parties and churches. I am thinking of Claudel and his odes to Franco and Pétain; I am thinking of the hymns to Stalin of Aragon and Neruda. Ours, Benjamin Péret said, has been the century "of the dishonor of poets." Of their honor, too: Mandelstam's satire against Stalin, which cost him his life, or the sacrifice of Lorca.

Criticism is, for me, the *free* form of commitment. A writer should be a guerrilla fighter, should bear solitude and know that he is a marginal being. That we writers should be marginal is a condemnation which is a blessing. For us to be marginal can give validity to our writing. And there is something else which I ought to say about criticism: for me criticism is creative. The significant difference between France and England on the one hand and Spain and Hispanic America on the other is that we had no eighteenth century. We had no Kant, Voltaire, Diderot, or Hume. Criticism made the modern world.

In The Labyrinth *also arise the problems that you stress extensively in later works, for example as in* Rotating Signs: *the problems of language. Language conceived as a mask. . . .*

Well, we've talked about my debts: Freud, Marx. . . . We haven't spoken of an essential influence without which I could not have written *The Labyrinth*: Nietzsche. Especially the book called *The Genealogy of Morals*. Nietzsche taught me to see what was behind words like virtue, goodness, evil. He guided me in exploring the Mexican idiom: If words are masks, what is behind them?

In this quest for an authentic idiom, you have stressed the importance of the work of Alfonso Reyes.

Reyes was true to language, and in this aspect he was admirable. Of course, the man had moral weaknesses. Perhaps he was too obsequious with the powerful. One must forget all this and remember that he was a writer who achieved transparency in Spanish at certain times. Bioy Casares would tell that, when he and Borges wanted to know if a paragraph was well written, they would say: "Let's read it in the tone in which Alfonso Reyes would read it."

What should the creator's attitude be toward language?

I think the creator's attitude toward language should be the lover's attitude. An attitude of fidelity and, at the same time, of lack of respect toward the loved object. Veneration and transgression. The writer should love language but ought to have the courage to transgress it.

In the chapter of The Labyrinth of Solitude *that is entitled "Our Times," you tackle the problem of the confrontation of poor countries against rich countries. Regarding this matter, what do you think of the "poverty culture" concept that Oscar Lewis, the anthropologist, has developed from the Mexican example?*

I don't agree with that. In the first place, this concept is hardly scientific, hardly accurate. What does "poverty" mean? Poverty is a very relative category. Poverty in regard to what? Lewis's merit lies elsewhere. His subject was the peasants who live in a traditional culture and, on account of rural overpopulation and unemployment, are attracted and fascinated by a large city, and leave their villages. This is a phenomenon that Europe experienced in the nineteenth century and that Latin America is living much more tragically in the twentieth century: the perversion and destruction of traditional culture. Peasants are cultured even though they are illiterate. They have a past, a tradition, images. They arrive in Mexico City or Guadalajara and forget everything. And then what do their children and the children of their children have? The culture of modern industrial society. But by the time forms of industrial culture have reached Mexico, they are inferior to those of the United States or Europe. What in turn reaches the members of the *lumpenproletariat* is the remains, the detritus of those forms and ideas. This has nothing to do with poverty in the strict sense but rather with the phenomenon of the co-existence of two societies: industrial societies and traditional societies.

Man, by nature, is alienated. Marx thought that if man controlled his products he would control his destiny: he would recover his natural being and alienation would cease. But I think that alienation consists fundamentally in being another within oneself. That alienation is the basis of human nature and not of class society. I am closer to Nietzsche and Freud than to Marx and Rousseau. All civilizations are civilizations of alienation and all civilized beings rebel against alienation.

Could you answer the question that you have raised in The Labyrinth: *"What is it that gives meaning to our presence on earth?" On the other hand, has Mexico found that "form" which for centuries it has been at once seeking and combating?*

I shall begin with the second question: Mexico has not found that "form." The germ of the answer was probably in Zapatism. But, once again, forms outside our reality were superimposed and the salutary germs inside the Zapatist revolt were crushed. Evidently, in the field of poetic and literary creation, there are indeed expressions that restitute my faith in Mexico's originality. As for knowing "what gives meaning to our presence on earth," I recognize that I am a man not by the answer I could now give to this question but in the question itself. This question, which has been repeated from the beginning, since and even before Babylon, is what gives meaning to our earthly labors. There is no meaning, there is a search for meaning.

In the last chapter of the book, you state that, in our world, love and poetry are forced to be marginal. Do you still think that there is an opposition between "history" and "poetry"?

Yes. I think that there is a fundamental opposition between what I call real reality and the other reality. There is a phrase by Marx (it is in the *Communist Manifesto*) which Luis Buñel thought of using (as a subtitle) for his film *The Golden Age*. You know that the theme of the film is the fate of love in the modern world. Marx's phrase, in Spanish, is a perfect alexandrine: *En las aguas heladas del cálculo egoísta.** That is society. For this reason love and poetry are marginal.

---

*In the icy waters of selfish calculation. —*Tr.*

Mexico and the United States*

TRANSLATED BY RACHEL PHILLIPS BELASH

*First published in *The New Yorker* magazine (September 17, 1979).

When I was in India, witnessing the never-ending quarrels between Hindus and Muslims, I asked myself more than once this question: What accident or misfortune of history caused two religions so obviously irreconcilable as Hinduism and Muhammadanism to coexist in the same society? The presence of the purest and most intransigent form of monotheism in the bosom of a civilization that has elaborated the most complex polytheism seemed to me a verification of the indifference with which history perpetrates its paradoxes. And yet I could hardly be surprised at the contradictory presence in India of Hinduism and Muhammadanism. How could I forget that I myself, as a Mexican, was (and am) part of a no less singular paradox—that of Mexico and the United States.

Our countries are neighbors, condemned to live alongside each other; they are separated, however, more by profound social, economic, and psychic differences than by physical and political frontiers. These differences are self-evident, and a superficial glance might reduce them to the well-known opposition between development and underdevelopment, wealth and poverty, power and weakness, domination and dependence. But the really fundamental difference is an invisible one, and in addition it is perhaps insuperable. To prove that it has nothing to do with economics or political power, we have only to imagine a Mexico suddenly turned into a prosperous, mighty country, a superpower like the United States. Far from disappearing, the difference would become more acute and more clear-cut. The reason is obvious: We are two distinct versions of Western civilization.

Ever since we Mexicans began to be aware of national identity—in about the middle of the eighteenth century—we have been interested in our northern neighbors. First with a mixture of curiosity and disdain; later on with an admiration and enthusiasm that were soon tinged with fear and envy. The idea the Mexican people have of the United States is contradictory, emotional, and impervious to criticism; it is a mythic image. The same can be said of the vision of our intellectuals and writers.

Something similar happens with Americans, be they writers or politicians, businessmen or only travellers. I am not forgetting the existence of a small number of remarkable studies by various American specialists, especially in the fields of archeology and ancient and modern Mexican history. The perceptions of the American novelists and poets who have written on Mexican themes have often been brilliant, but they have also been fragmentary. Moreover, as a critic who has devoted a book to this theme (Drewey Wayne Gunn: *American and British Writers in Mexico*) has said, they reveal less of the Mexican reality than of the authors' personalities. In general, Americans have not looked for Mexico in Mexico; they have looked for their obsessions, enthusiasms, phobias, hopes, interests—and these are what they have found. In short, the history of our relationship is the history of a mutual and stubborn deceit, usually involuntary though not always so.

Of course, the differences between Mexico and the United States are not imaginary projections but objective realities. Some are quantitative, and can be explained by the social, economic, and historical development of the two countries. The more permanent ones, though also the result of history, are not easily definable or measurable. I have pointed out that they belong to the realm of civilization, that fluid zone of imprecise contours in which are fused and confused ideas and beliefs, institutions and technologies, styles and morals, fashions and churches, the material culture and that evasive reality which we rather inaccurately call *le génie des peuples*. The reality to which we give the name of civilization does not allow of easy definition. It is each society's vision of the world and also its feeling about time; there are nations that are hurrying toward the future, and others whose eyes are fixed on the past. Civilization is a society's style, its way of living and dying. It embraces the erotic and the culinary arts; dancing and burial; courtesy and curses; work and leisure; rituals and festivals; punishments and rewards; dealings with the dead and with the ghosts who people our dreams; attitudes toward women and children, old people and strangers, enemies and allies; eternity and the present; the here and now and the beyond. A civilization is not only a system of values but a world of forms and codes of behavior, rules and exceptions. It is society's visible side—institutions, monuments, works, things—but it is especially its submerged, invisible side: beliefs, desires, fears, repressions, dreams.

The points of the compass have served to locate us in history as well as in space. The East-West duality soon acquired a more symbolic than geographical significance, and became an emblem of the opposition between civilizations. The East-West opposition has always been considered basic and primordial; it alludes to the movement of the sun, and is therefore an image of the direction and meaning of our living and dying. The East-West relationship symbolizes two directions, two attitudes, two civilizations. The North-South duality refers more to the opposition between different ways of life and different sensibilities. The contrasts between North and South can be oppositions within the same civilization.

Clearly, the opposition between Mexico and the United States belongs to the North-South duality as much from the geographical as the symbolic point of view. It is an ancient opposition which was already unfolding in pre-Columbian America, so that it antedates the very existence of the United States and Mexico. The northern part of the continent was settled by nomadic, warrior nations; Mesoamerica, on the other hand, was the home of an agricultural civilization, with complex social and political institutions, dominated by warlike theocracies that invented refined and cruel rituals, great art, and vast cosmogonies inspired by a very original vision of time. The great opposition of pre-Columbian America—all that now includes the United States and Mexico—was between different ways of life: nomads and settled peoples, hunters and farmers. This division greatly influenced the later development of the United States and Mexico. The policies of the English and the Spanish toward the Indians were in large part determined by this division; it was not insignificant that the former established themselves in the territory of the nomads and the latter in that of the settled peoples.

The differences between the English and the Spaniards who founded New England and New Spain were no less decisive than those that separated the nomadic from the settled Indians. Again, it was an opposition within the same civilization. Just as the American Indians' world view and beliefs sprang from a common source, irrespective of their ways of life, so Spanish and English shared the same intellectual and technical culture. And the opposition between them, though of a different sort, was as deep as that dividing an Aztec from an Iroquois. And so the new opposition between English and Spaniards was grafted onto the old opposition between nomadic and settled peoples. The distinct and divergent attitudes of Spaniards and English have often been described before. All of them can be summed up in one fundamental difference, in which perhaps the dissimilar evolution of Mexico and the United States originated: in England the Reformation triumphed, whereas Spain was the champion of the Counter-Reformation.

As we all know, the reformist movement in England had political consequences that were decisive in the development of Anglo-Saxon democracy. In Spain, evolution went in the opposite direction. Once the resistance of the last Muslim was crushed, Spain achieved a precarious political—but not national—unity by means of dynastic alliances. At the same time, the monarchy suppressed regional autonomies and municipal freedoms, closing off the possibility of eventual evolution into a modern democracy. Lastly, Spain was deeply marked by Arab domination, and kept alive the notion of crusade and holy war, which it had inherited from Christian and Muslim alike. In Spain, the traits of the modern era, which was just beginning, and of the old society coexisted but never blended completely. The contrast with England could not be sharper. The history of Spain and of her former colonies, from the sixteenth century onward, is the history of an ambiguous approach—attraction and repulsion—to the modern era.

The discovery and conquest of America are events that inaugurated modern world history, but Spain and Portugal carried them out with the sensibility and tenor of the Reconquest. Nothing more original occurred to Cortes's soldiers, amazed by the pyramids and temples of the Mayans and Aztecs, than to compare them with the mosques of Islam. Conquest and evangelization: these two words, deeply Spanish and Catholic, are also deeply Muslim. Conquest means not only the occupation of foreign territories and the subjugation of their inhabitants but also the conversion of the conquered. The conversion legitimized the conquest. This politico-religious philosophy was diametrically opposed to that of English colonizing; the idea of evangelization occupied a secondary place in England's colonial expansion.

The Christianity brought to Mexico by the Spaniards was the syncretic Catholicism of Rome, which had assimilated the pagan gods, turning them into saints and devils. The phenomenon was repeated in Mexico: the idols were baptized, and in popular Mexican Catholicism the old beliefs and divinities are still present, barely hidden under a veneer of Christianity. Not only the popular religion of Mexico but the Mexicans' entire life is steeped in Indian culture—the family, love, friendship, attitudes toward one's father and mother, popular legends, the forms of civility and life in common, the image of authority and political power, the vision of death and sex, work and festivity. Mexico is the most Spanish country in Latin America; at the same time it is the most Indian. Mesoamerican civilization died a violent death, but Mexico is Mexico thanks to the Indian presence. Though the language and religion, the political institutions and the culture of the country are Western, there is one aspect of Mexico that faces in another direction—the Indian direction. Mexico is a nation between two civilizations and two pasts.

In the United States, the Indian element does not appear. This, in my opinion, is the major difference between our two countries. The Indians who were not exterminated were corralled in "reservations." The Christian horror of "fallen nature" extended to the natives of America: the United States was founded on a land without a past. The historical memory of Americans is European, not American. For this reason, one of the most powerful and persistent themes in American literature, from Whitman to William Carlos Williams and from Melville to Faulkner, has been the search for (or invention of) American roots. We owe some of the major works of the modern era to this desire for incarnation, this obsessive need to be rooted in American soil.

Exactly the opposite is true of Mexico, land of superimposed pasts. Mexico City was built on the ruins of Tenochtitlán, the Aztec city that was built in the likeness of Tula, the Toltec city that was built in the likeness of Teotihuacán, the first great city on the American continent. Every Mexican bears within him this continuity, which goes back two thousand years. It doesn't matter that this presence is almost always unconscious and assumes the naïve forms of legend and even superstition. It is not something known but something lived. The Indian presence means that one of the facets of Mexican culture is not Western. Is there anything like this in the United States? Each of the ethnic groups making up the multiracial democracy that is the United States has its own culture and tradition, and some of them—the Chinese and Japanese, for example—are not Western. These traditions exist alongside the dominant American tradition without becoming one with it. They are foreign bodies within American culture. In some cases, the most notable being that of the Chicanos, the minorities defend their traditions against or in the face of the American tradition. The Chicanos' resistance is cultural as well as political and social.

If the different attitudes of Hispanic Catholicism and English Protestantism could be summed up in two words, I would say that the Spanish attitude is inclusive and the English exclusive. In the former, the notions of conquest and domination are bound up with ideas of conversion and assimilation; in the latter, conquest and domination imply not the conversion of the conquered but their segregation. An inclusive society, founded on the double principle of domination and conversion, is bound to be hierarchical, centralist, and respectful of the individual characteristics of each group. It believes in the strict division of classes and groups, each one governed by special laws and statutes, but all embracing the same faith and obeying the same lord. An exclusive society is bound to cut itself off from the natives, either by physical exclusion or by extermination; at the same time, since each community of pure-minded men is isolated from other communities, it tends to treat its members as equals and to assure the autonomy and freedom of each group of believers. The origins of American democracy are religious, and in the early communities of New England that dual, contradictory tension between freedom and equality which has been the leitmotiv of the history of the United States was already present.

The opposition that I have just outlined is expressed with great clarity in two religious terms: "communion" and "purity." This opposition profoundly affects attitudes toward work, festivity, the body, and death. For the society of New Spain, work did not redeem, and had no value in itself. Manual work was servile. The superior man neither worked nor traded. He made war, he commanded, he legislated. He also thought, contemplated, wooed, loved, and enjoyed himself. Leisure was noble. Work was good because it produced wealth, but wealth was good because it was intended to be spent—to be consumed in those holocausts called war, in the construction of temples and palaces, in pomp and festivity. The dissipation of wealth took different forms: gold shone on the altars or was poured out in celebrations. Even today in Mexico, at least in the small cities and towns, work is the precursor of the fiesta. The year revolves on the double axis of work and festival, saving and spending. The fiesta is sumptuous and intense, lively and funereal; it is a vital, multicolored frenzy that evaporates in smoke, ashes, nothingness. In the aesthetics of perdition, the fiesta is the lodging place of death.

The United States has not really known the art of the festival, except in the last few years, with the triumph of hedonism over the old Protestant ethic. This is natural. A society that so energetically affirmed the redemptive value of work could not help chastising as depraved the cult of the festival and the passion for spending. The Protestant rejection was inspired by religion rather than economics. The Puritan conscience could not see that the value of the festival was actually a religious value: communion. In the festival, the orgiastic element is central; it marks a return to the beginning, to the primordial state in which each one is united with the great all. Every true festival is religious because every true festival is communion. Here the opposition between communion and purity is clear. For the Puritans and their heirs, work is redemptive because it frees man, and this liberation is a sign of God's choice. Work is purification, which is also a separation: the chosen one ascends, breaks the bonds binding him to earth, which are the laws of his fallen nature. For the Mexicans, communion represents exactly the opposite: not separation but participation, not breaking away but joining together; the great universal commixture, the great bathing in the waters of the beginning, a state beyond purity and impurity.

In Christianity, the body's status is inferior. But the body is an always active force, and its explosions can destroy a civilization. Doubtless for this reason, the Church from the start made a pact with the body. If the Church did not restore the body to the place it occupied in Greco-Roman society, it did try to give the body back its dignity; the body is fallen nature, but in itself it is innocent. After all, Christianity, unlike Buddhism, say, is the worship of an incarnate god. The dogma of the resurrection of the dead dates from the time of primitive Christianity; the cult of the Virgin appeared later, in the Middle Ages. Both beliefs are the highest expressions of this urge for incarnation, which typifies Christian spirituality. Both came to Mesoamerica with Spanish culture, and were immediately fused, the former with the funeral worship of the Indians, the latter with the worship of the goddesses of fertility and war.

The Mexicans' vision of death, which is also the hope of resurrection, is as profoundly steeped in Catholic eschatology as in Indian naturalism. The Mexican death is of the body, exactly the opposite of the American death, which is abstract and disembodied. For Mexicans, death sees and touches itself; it is the body emptied of the soul, the pile of bones that somehow, as in the Aztec poem, must bloom again. For Americans, death is what is not seen: absence, the disappearance of the person. In the Puritan consciousness, death was always present, but as a moral entity, an idea. Later on, scientism pushed death out of the American consciousness. Death melted away and became unmentionable. Finally, in vast segments of the American population of today, progressive rationalism and idealism have been replaced by neo-hedonism. But the cult of the body and of pleasure implies the recognition and acceptance of death. The body is mortal, and the kingdom of pleasure is that of the moment, as Epicurus saw better than anyone else. American hedonism closes its eyes to death and has been incapable of exorcising the destructive power of the moment with a wisdom like that of the Epicureans of antiquity. Present-day hedonism is the last recourse of the anguished and the desperate, an expression of the nihilism that is eroding the West.

Capitalism exalts the activities and behavior patterns traditionally called virile: aggressiveness, the spirit of competition and emulation, combativeness. American society made these values its own. This perhaps explains why nothing like the Mexicans' devotion to the Virgin of Guadalupe appears in the different versions of Christianity professed by Americans, including the Catholic minority. The Virgin unites the religious sensibilities of the Mediterranean and Mesoamerica, both of them regions that fostered ancient cults of feminine divinities, Guadalupe-Tonantzin is the mother of all Mexicans—Indians, mestizos, whites—but she is also a warrior virgin whose image has often appeared on the banners of peasant uprisings. In the Virgin of Guadalupe we encounter a very ancient vision of femininity which, as was true of the pagan goddesses, is not without a heroic tint.

When I talk about the masculinity of the American capitalist society, I am not unaware that American women have gained rights and posts still denied elsewhere. But they have obtained them as "subjects under the law"; that is to say, as neuter or abstract entities, as citizens, not as women. Now, I believe that, much as our civilization needs equal rights for men and women, it also needs a feminization, like the one that courtly love brought about in the outlook of medieval Europe. Or like the feminine irradiation that the Virgin of Guadalupe casts on the imagination and sensibility of us Mexicans. Because of the Mexican woman's Hispano-Arabic and Indian heritage, her social situation is deplorable, but what I want to emphasize here is not so much the nature of the relation between men and women as the intimate relationship of woman with those elusive symbols which we call femininity and masculinity. For the reasons I noted earlier, Mexican women have a very lively awareness of the body. For them, the body, the woman's and man's, is a concrete, palpable reality. Not an abstraction or a function but an ambiguous magnetic force, in which pleasure and pain, fertility and death are inextricably intertwined.

Pre-Columbian Mexico was a mosaic of nations, tribes, and languages. For its part, Spain was also a conglomeration of nations and races, even though it had realized political unity. The heterogeneity of Mexican society was the other face of Spanish centralism. The political centralism of the Spanish monarchy had religious orthodoxy as its complement, and even as its foundation. The true, effective unity of Mexican society has been brought about slowly over several centuries, but its political and religious unity was decreed from above as the joint expression of the Spanish monarchy and the Catholic Church. Mexico had a state and a church before it was a nation. In this respect also, Mexico's evolution has been very different from that of the United States, where the small colonial communities had from their inception a clear-cut and belligerent concept of their identity as regards the state. For North Americans, the nation antedated the state.

Another difference: In those small colonial communities, a fusion had taken place among religious convictions, the embryonic national consciousness, the political institutions. So harmony, not contradiction, existed between the North Americans' religious convictions and their democratic institutions; whereas in Mexico Catholicism was identified with the viceregal regime, and was its orthodoxy. Therefore, when, after independence, the Mexican liberals tried to implant democratic institutions, they had to confront the Catholic Church. The establishment of a republican democracy in Mexico meant a radical break with the past, and led to the civil wars of the nineteenth century. These wars produced the militarism that, in turn, produced the dictatorship of Porfirio Díaz. The liberals defeated the Church, but they could not implant true democracy—only an authoritarian regime wearing democracy's mask.

A no less profound difference was the opposition between Catholic orthodoxy and Protestant reformism. In Mexico, Catholic orthodoxy had the philosophical form of Neo-Thomism, a mode of thought more apologetic than critical, and defensive in the face of the emerging modernity. Orthodoxy prevented examination and criticism. In New England, the communities were often made up of religious dissidents or, at least, of people who believed that the Scriptures should be read freely. On one side, orthodoxy, dogmatic philosophy, and the cult of authority. On the other, reading and free interpretation of the doctrine. Both societies were religious, but their religious attitudes were irreconcilable. I am not thinking only of dogmas and principles but of the very ways in which the two societies practiced and understood religion. One society fostered the complex and majestic conceptual structure of orthodoxy, an equally complex ecclesiastical hierarchy, wealthy and militant religious orders, and a ritualistic view of religion, in which the sacraments occupied a central place. The other fostered free discussion of the Scriptures, a small and often poor clergy, a tendency to eliminate the hierarchical boundaries between the simple believer and the priest, and a religious practice based not on ritual but on ethics, and not on the sacrament but on the internalizing of faith.

If one considers the historical evolution of the two societies, the main difference seems to be the following: the modern world began with the Reformation, which was the religious criticism of religion and the necessary antecedent of the Enlightenment; with the Counter-Reformation and Neo-Thomism, Spain and her possessions closed themselves to the modern world. They had no Enlightenment, because they had neither a Reformation nor an intellectual religious movement like Jansenism. And so, though Spanish-American civilization is to be admired on many counts, it reminds one of a structure of great solidity—at once convent, fortress, and palace—built to last, not to change. In the long run, that construction became a confine, a prison. The United States was born of the Reformation and the Enlightenment. It came into being under the sign of criticism and self-criticism. Now, when one talks of criticism one is talking of change. The transformation of critical philosophy into progressive ideology came about and reached its peak in the nineteenth century. The broom of rationalist criticism swept the ideological sky clean of myths and beliefs; the ideology of progress, in its turn, displaced the timeless values of Christianity and transplanted them to the earthly and linear time of history. Christian eternity became the future of liberal evolutionism.

Here is the final contradiction, and all the divergencies and differences I have mentioned culminate in it. A society is essentially defined by its position as regards time. The United States, because of its origin and its intellectual and political history, is a society oriented toward the future. The extraordinary spatial mobility of America, a nation constantly on the move, has often been pointed out. In the realm of beliefs and mental attitudes, mobility in time corresponds to physical and geographical displacement. The American lives on the very edge of the now, always ready to leap toward the future. The country's foundations are in the future, not in the past. Or, rather, its past, the act of its founding, was a promise of the future, and each time the United States returns to its source, to its past, it rediscovers the future.

Mexico's orientation, as has been seen, was just the opposite. First came the rejection of criticism, and with it rejection of the notion of change: its ideal is to conserve the image of divine immutability. Second, it has a plurality of pasts, all present and at war within every Mexican's soul. Cortes and Montezuma are still alive in Mexico. At the time of that great crisis the Mexican Revolution, the most radical faction, that of Zapata and his peasants, proposed not new forms of social organization but a return to communal ownership of land. The rebelling peasants were asking for the devolution of the land; that is, they wanted to go back to a pre-Columbian form of ownership which had been respected by the Spaniards. The image the revolutionaries instinctively made for themselves of a Golden Age lay in the remotest past. Utopia for them was not the construction of a future but a return to the source, to the beginning. The traditional Mexican attitude toward time has been expressed in this way by a Mexican poet, Ramón López Velarde: "Motherland, be still the same, faithful to each day's mirror"

In the seventeenth century, Mexican society was richer and more prosperous than American society. This situation lasted until the first half of the eighteenth century. To prove that it was so, one need only glance at the cities of those days, with their monuments and buildings—Mexico City and Boston, Puebla and Philadelphia. Then everything changed. In 1847, the United States invaded Mexico, occupied it, and imposed on it terrible and heavy conditions of peace. A century later, the United States became the dominant world power. An unusual conjunction of circumstances of a material, technological, political, ideological, and human order explains the prodigious development of the United States. But in the small religious communities of seventeenth-century New England, the future was already in bud: political democracy, capitalism, and social and economic development. In Mexico, something very different has occurred. At the end of the eighteenth century, the Mexican ruling classes—especially the intellectuals—discovered that the principles that had founded their society condemned it to immobility and backwardness. They undertook a twofold revolution: separation from Spain and modernization of the country through the adoption of new republican and democratic principles. Their examples were the American Revolution and the French Revolution. They gained independence from Spain, but the adoption of new principles was not enough: Mexico changed its laws, not its social, economic, and cultural realities.

During much of the nineteenth century, Mexico suffered an endemic civil war and three invasions by foreign powers—the United States, Spain, and France. In the latter part of the century, order was re-established, but at the expense of democracy. In the name of liberal ideology and the positivism of Comte and Spencer, a military dictatorship was imposed which lasted more than thirty years. It was a period of peace and appreciable material development—also of increasing penetration by foreign capital, especially from England and the United States. The Mexican Revolution of 1910 set itself to change direction. It succeeded only in part: Mexican democracy is not yet a reality, and the great advances achieved in certain quarters have been nullified or are in danger because of excessive political centralization, excessive population growth, social inequality, the collapse of higher education, and the actions of the economic monopolies, among them those from the United States. Like all the other states of this century, the Mexican state has had an enormous, monstrous development. A curious contradiction: The state has been the agent of modernization, but it has been unable to modernize itself entirely. It is a hybrid of the Spanish patrimonialist state of the seventeenth century and the modern bureaucracies of the West. As for its relationship with the United States, that is still the old relationship of strong and weak, oscillating between indifference and abuse, deceit and cynicism. Most Mexicans hold the justifiable conviction that the treatment received by their country is unfair.

Above and beyond success and failure, Mexico is still asking itself the question that has occurred to most clear-thinking Mexicans since the end of the eighteenth century: the question about modernization. In the nineteenth century, it was believed that to adopt the new democratic and liberal principles was enough. Today, after almost two centuries of setbacks, we have realized that countries change very slowly, and that if such changes are to be fruitful they must be in harmony with the past and the traditions of each nation. And so Mexico has to find its own road to modernity. Our past must not be an obstacle but a starting point. This is extremely difficult, given the nature of our traditions—difficult but not impossible. To avoid new disasters, we Mexicans must reconcile ourselves with our past: only in this way shall we succeed in finding a route to modernity. The search for our own model of modernization is a theme directly linked with another: today we know that modernity, both the capitalist and the pseudo-socialist versions of the totalitarian bureaucracies, is mortally wounded in its very core—the idea of continuous, unlimited progress. The nations that inspired our nineteenth-century liberals—England, France, and especially the United States—are doubting, vacillating, and cannot find their way. They have ceased to be universal examples. The Mexicans of the nineteenth century turned their eyes toward the great Western democracies; we have nowhere to turn ours.

Between 1930 and 1960, most Mexicans were sure of the path they had chosen. This certainty has vanished, and some people ask themselves if it is not necessary to begin all over again. But the question is not relevant only for Mexico; it is universal. However unsatisfactory our country's situation may seem to us, it is not desperate—especially compared with what prevails elsewhere. Latin America, with only a few exceptions, lives under military dictatorships that are pampered and often supported by the United States. Cuba escaped American domination only to become a pawn of the Soviet Union's policy in Africa. A large number of the Asian and African nations that gained their independence after the Second World War are victims of native tyrannies often more cruel and despotic than those of the old colonial powers. In the so-called Third World, with different names and attributes, a ubiquitous Caligula reigns.

In 1917, the October Revolution in Russia kindled the hopes of millions; in 1979, the world "Gulag" has become synonymous with Soviet socialism. The founders of the socialist movement firmly believed that socialism would put an end not only to the exploitation of men but to war; in the second half of the twentieth century, totalitarian "socialisms" have enslaved the working class by stripping it of its basic rights and have also covered the whole planet with the threatening uproar of their disputes and quarrels. In the name of different versions of "socialism," Vietnamese and Cambodians butcher each other. The ideological wars of the twentieth century are no less ferocious than the wars of religion of the seventeenth century. When I was young, the idea that we were witnessing the final crisis of capitalism was fashionable among intellectuals. Now we understand that the crisis is not of a socioeconomic system but of our whole civilization. It is a general, worldwide crisis, and its most extreme, acute, and dangerous expression is found in the situation of the Soviet Union and its satellites. The contradictions of totalitarian "socialism" are more profound and irreconcilable than those of the capitalist democracies.

The sickness of the West is moral rather than social and economic. It is true that the economic problems are serious and that they have not been solved. Inflation and unemployment are on the rise. Poverty has not disappeared, despite affluence. Several groups—women and racial, religious, and linguistic minorities—still are or feel excluded. But the real, most profound discord lies in the soul. The future has become the realm of horror, and the present has turned into a desert. The liberal societies spin tirelessly, not forward but round and round. If they change, they are not transfigured. The hedonism of the West is the other face of desperation; its skepticism is not wisdom but renunciation; its nihilism ends in suicide and in inferior forms of credulity, such as political fanaticisms and magical chimeras. The empty place left by Christianity in the modern soul is filled not by philosophy but by the crudest superstitions. Our eroticism is a technique, not an art or a passion.

I will not continue. The evils of the West have been described often enough, most recently by Solzhenitsyn, a man of admirable character. However, although his description seems to me accurate, his judgment of the causes of the sickness does not, nor does the remedy he proposes. We cannot renounce the critical tradition of the West; nor can we return to the medieval theocratic state. Dungeons of the Inquisition are not an answer to the Gulag camps. It is not worthwhile substituting the church-state for the party-state, one orthodoxy for another. The only effective arm against orthodoxies is criticism, and in order to defend ourselves against the vices of intolerance and fanaticism our only recourse is the exercise of the opposing virtues: tolerance and freedom of spirit. I do not disown Montesquieu, Hume, Kant.

The crisis of the United States affects the very foundation of the nation, by which I mean the principles that founded it. I have already said that there is a leitmotiv running throughout American history, from the Puritan colonies of New England to the present day; namely, the tension between freedom and equality. The struggles of the blacks, the Chicanos, and other minorities are an expression of this dualism. An external contradiction corresponds to this internal contradiction: the United States is a republic and an empire. In Rome, the first of these contradictions (the internal one between freedom and equality) was resolved by the suppression of freedom; Caesar's regime began as an egalitarian solution, but, like all solutions by force, it ended in the suppression of equality also. The second, external contradiction brought about the ruin of Athens, the first imperial republic in history.

It would be presumptuous of me to propose solutions to this

double contradiction. I think that every time a society finds itself in crisis it instinctively turns its eyes toward its origins and looks there for a sign. Colonial American society was a free, egalitarian, but exclusive society. Faithful to its origins, in its domestic and foreign policies alike, the United States has always ignored the "others." Today, the United States faces very powerful enemies, but the mortal danger comes from within: not from Moscow but from that mixture of arrogance and opportunism, blindness and short-term Machiavellianism, volubility and stubbornness which has characterized its foreign policies during recent years and which reminds us in an odd way of the Athenian state in its quarrel with Sparta. To conquer its enemies, the United States must first conquer itself—return to its origins. Not to repeat them but to rectify them: the "others"—the minorities inside as well as the marginal countries and nations outside—do exist. Not only do we "others" make up the majority of the human race, but also each marginal society, poor though it may be, represents a unique and precious version of mankind. If the United States is to recover fortitude and lucidity, it must recover itself, and to recover itself it must recover the "others"—the outcasts of the Western World.

The
Philanthropic
Ogre*

TRANSLATED BY RACHEL PHILLIPS BELASH

*First published in *Dissent* magazine (Winter 1979).

> Just look
> How big I am! Jove up there in the sky
> . . . he can't be any bigger.
> —OVID, *Metamorphoses*, 13, lines 839–42

Mexico, 1978

Liberals used to think that the "civil society" would flourish thanks to the development of free enterprise, and the function of the state would correspondingly be reduced until it was merely supervising humanity's spontaneous evolution. Marxists more optimistically thought the century that saw the rise of socialism would also see the withering-away of the state.

These hopes and prophecies have evaporated. The twentieth-century state has proved itself a force more powerful than the ancient empires and a master more terrible than the old tyrants and despots: a faceless, inhuman master who functions not like a demon but like a machine. Theologians and moralists had conceived of evil as an exception and a transgression, a blot on the universality and transparency of Being. Except for Manichaean tendencies, in the philosophic tradition of the West, evil lacked substance and could be defined only as an absence, that is to say, a lack of Being. Strictly speaking, evil did not exist, only evil men, exceptions, special cases. The twentieth-century state inverts the proposition: evil ultimately conquers universality and presents itself wearing the mask of Being. Except that, as evil grows larger, evildoers grow proportionally smaller. They are no longer exceptional beings, only mirrors of normalcy. A Hitler or a Stalin, a Himmler or a Yezhov astonish us by their mediocrity as well as by their crimes. Their intellectual insignificance confirms Hannah Arendt's verdict on "the banality of evil."

The modern state is a machine—a continually self-reproducing machine. Far from being the mere political superstructure of the capitalist system in the West, it is the model for economic organizations; large enterprises and businesses imitate it and tend to turn into states and empires more powerful than many nations. In the last fifty years we have witnessed not the expected socialization of capitalism but its gradual, irresistible bureaucratization. The great multinational companies already hint at a bureaucratic capitalism. Their counterparts are the totalitarian bureaucracies of Eastern Europe. There the process has been more rapid and more ruthless. "Civil society" has almost completely disappeared: nothing and no one exists outside the state. It is a surprising inversion of values that would have made Nietzsche himself shudder: the state is Being and exception; irregularity and even simple individualism are forms of evil, that is, of nothingness. The concentration camp, which reduces the prisoner to nonperson, is the political expression of the ontology implicit in the totalitarian ideocracies.

Despite the all-pervading presence and omnipotence of the twentieth-century state—and despite the example of the anarchist tradition, so rich in divinations and prophetic descriptions—criticism of power and of the state was reborn only a short while ago. I am thinking especially of France, Germany and the United States. In Latin America, there is much less interest in the state. Here our scholars are still obsessed by the themes of dependence and underdevelopment. It is true that our situation is different. Latin-American societies are highly peculiar: the Counter-Reformation and liberalism exist side by side as do the landed estates and industry, the illiterate and the cosmopolitan man of letters, the political boss and the banker. But the oddity of our societies should not prevent us from studying the Latin-American state, which is actually one of our greatest peculiarities. On the one hand, it is heir to the patrimonial regime of Spain; on the other, it is the lever to get modernization under way. Its nature is ambiguous, contradictory, and in a certain way fascinating. The following pages, dealing with the case best known to me—Mexico—are the result of such fascination. I need hardly warn readers that my opinions are a series of reflections, not a consistent theory.

First, the state created by the Mexican revolution is stronger than the nineteenth-century state. In this, as in so many other things, the revolutionaries have not only shown decidedly traditionalist leanings but have been unfaithful to the liberals of 1857 whom they claim as their predecessors. Except during the interregnums of anarchy and civil war, we Mexicans have lived in the shadow of governments that have been despotic or paternalistic in turn, but have always been strong: the Aztec priest-king, the viceroy, the dictator, Mr. President. The exception is the brief period that Cosio Villegas calls the Restored Republic, during which the liberals tried to blunt the claws of the state we inherited from New Spain. Those claws were (and still are) called bureaucracy and army. The liberals wanted a strong society and a weak state— an exemplary attempt that soon failed: Porfirio Díaz [who was president in 1877 and again in 1884–1911] inverted the proposition and fashioned Mexico into a weak society dominated by a strong state.

The liberals thought that modernization would be carried out by the bourgeoisie and the middle class, as it had been in other parts of the world—in England, France and the United States. This did not happen, and with Díaz the state began to turn into the agent of modernization. It is true that his regime based its economic policies on private enterprise and foreign capital. But the founding of industrial enterprises and the construction of factories and railroads was less the expression of the dynamism of a bourgeois class than the result of a deliberate government policy of stimuli and incentives. Moreover, what decided the issue was not economic policy but the goal to strengthen the state. In order for an organism to be able to complete such historic tasks as the modernization of a country, the first prerequisite is that it be strong. Under Porfirio Díaz the Mexican state recovered the power it had lost during the conflicts and wars that followed Independence.

The conservative historian Carlos Pereyra points out that the political convulsions and the chaotic state of the country right up to Díaz's dictatorship essentially resulted from the weakness of governments from Independence, in 1821, onward. The colonial state of New Spain had been a construction of extraordinary solidity, capable of withstanding both rebellious landowners and despotic bishops. When it collapsed, it left behind a rich class that was extremely powerful and divided into irreconcilable factions. The absence of a central moderating power, combined with the nonexistence of democratic traditions, explains why opposing actions quickly took to arms in order to settle their differences. And so the plague of militarism was born: the sword was a response to the weakness of the state and the power of the factions.

Why was the Mexican state weak? It was weak, says Pereyra, because it was poor. I must clarify: it was not the country but the body politic that was poor. The state was poor, compared with a church that owned half the country and a propertied and landowning class that was immensely wealthy. How could the bishops be subjugated, and how could law be made to prevail in a society where each family head considered himself a monarch? Under General Díaz's dictatorship the Mexican state began to emerge from poverty. The governments that followed Díaz, once the violent stage of the Revolution was over, went on getting richer, and soon, with Calles, another general [president 1924–28, and the power behind the presidency 1928–36], the Mexican government embarked on a career as great entrepreneur. Today it is the most powerful capitalist in the country though, as we all know, neither the most efficient nor the most honest.

The revolutionary state did more than grow and get rich. Like Japan during the Meiji period, it made use of appropriate legislation and a policy of privileges, stimuli, and credits to further and protect the development of the capitalist class. Mexican capitalism was born long before the Revolution, but it came to maturity and grew to what it is now thanks to the actions and protection of revolutionary governments. At the same time, the state stimulated and favored industrial and rural workers' organizations. These groups lived and still live in its shadow, since they form part of the PRI.*

Yet it would be wrong and simplistic to reduce our image of their relationship with public power to that of subject and ruler. This relationship is considerably more complex: for one thing, in a one-party regime like Mexico's, the popular organizations are the almost exclusive source of legitimization of the state's power; for another, the popular unions, especially the workers union, have a certain freedom of movement. The government needs the unions as much as the unions need the government. In practice, the only two forces capable of negotiating with the government are the capitalists and the leaders of the workforce. Finally, not content with stimulating and, to a certain extent, creating both the capitalist and the working-class sectors in its own image, the postrevolutionary state ended its evolution by creating two parallel bureaucracies. The first is made up of administrators and technocrats; these people are government personnel and the legitimate successors of the bureaucracies of the colony and the "Porfir-

---

*Partido Revolucionario Institucional (Institutional Revolutionary Party), which has been in power under different names since 1929.

ist" period. They are the mind and arm of modernization. The second is composed of political professionals who run the various levels and divisions of the PRI. These two bureaucracies live in a continuous osmosis, everlastingly moving from the party to the government and vice versa.

The description is hasty and schematic but not inexact. It shows that the central power in Mexico lies not in private capitalism nor in the syndicated unions nor in political parties, but in the state. The state is Capital, Work and Party—a secular Trinity. However, it is not a totalitarian state nor a dictatorship. In the Soviet Union the state owns things and human beings; I mean, it owns the means of production, products and producers. In its turn the state is owned by the Communist party and the party is owned by the Central Committee.

In Mexico, the state belongs to the double bureaucracy: the administrative technocracy and the political caste. And yet, these bureaucracies are not autonomous, and they live in a constant relationship—rivalry, complicity, alliances and ruptures—with the other two groups who dominate the country along with them: private capitalism and the working-class bureaucracies. Furthermore, these latter are not homogeneous either; they are divided by conflicts of interests, ideas and personalities.

Now, indeed, another sector is becoming more and more influential and independent: the middle class and its spokesmen, students and intellectuals. The function of the friars and clerics of New Spain now is fulfilled by university communities and writers. Ideology today occupies the place that once belonged to theology and religion. Luckily, Mexico is an increasingly diverse society, and the practice of criticism—the only antidote for ideological orthodoxies—is growing in proportion to the diversification of the country.

The interaction of all these classes, groups and individuals takes place within a framework—the international arena. Some countries indirectly influence public opinion by means of different groups—especially students, journalists and other professional sectors. As in the case of Cuba, this influence sometimes has little relation to the country's actual power and progress on the economic, social or cultural fronts. Naturally, the most substantial reality is the multiple power of the United States: a power that is economic, social, technical, scientific and military, all at one and the same time. The might of the United States becomes a fascination—that is, it inspires a contradictory feeling of attraction and revulsion. Its influence is especially profound, and frequently ominous, in the economic sphere; it also penetrates the realms of technology, science, culture, popular sensibility and, of course, politics.

The presence of the United States in Mexican life is a historical fact that needs no demonstration; it has a physical, material reality. My earlier observation about the ambiguous relationship between the unions and the Mexican state can be applied to a certain extent to the one that unites us with Washington. I mean, it is a relationship of domination that cannot be reduced purely and simply to the concept of dependence; it is a relationship that allows a certain freedom of negotiation and movement. There is a margin for action. Narrow though this margin may seem to us, it is at any rate considerably wider than that which separates Poland, Hungary, Czechoslovakia or Cuba from the Soviet Union. Of course, in moments of political crisis the influence of the American ambassador to Mexico can be—and indeed has been—as important and decisive as that of the satrap of the Great King during the Peloponnesian war.

The radical authors—Plekhanov, Lenin, Trotsky—who at the turn of the century concerned themselves with the social history of prerevolutionary Russia were at one in pointing out the weakness of the bourgeoisie when faced with the authoritarian state. One of the characteristics of Russian capitalism was its dependence on the Czarist state. The bourgeoisie never succeeded in freeing itself totally from the tutelage of the autocracy. This failing ultimately prevented it from completing the task that, according to the Marxists, was its historical mission: the modernization of Russia. All the polemics between Bolsheviks and the Mensheviks stem from the different positions that these groups adopted to deal with this situation.

Beside the weakness of the bourgeoisie, another often neglected factor must be mentioned: the Czarist state could not be an efficient agent of modernization because, in its structure, its leaders, and its animating spirit, it was still to a large extent a "patrimonialist" state, to use the term coined by Max Weber. In short, there is no doubt that the weakness of the Russian bourgeoisie, when confronted with the patrimonialist state, was the determining cause of the Revolution's final outcome. The Soviet bureaucracy, which succeeded the autocracy, took upon itself the task of modernization that, historically, according to Marxist opinion, belonged to the bourgeoisie; but the results were as contrary to the forecasts of the Mensheviks as to those of the Bolsheviks. The conjunction of political power and economic power—both of them absolute—produced neither the bourgeois democratic revolution nor socialism, but the implantation of a totalitarian ideocracy.

I have used the example of Russia, although it seems farfetched, because this sheds light, indirectly, on the peculiarities of the Mexican situation. In Mexico as in Russia at the turn of the century, the historic goals of the intellectuals and also those of many prominent groups and the enlightened bourgeoisie can be epitomized in the word "modernization" (industrial development, democracy, technology, laicity, etc.).

In Mexico as in Russia, when faced with the relative weakness of its own bourgeoisie, the central agent of modernization has been the state. Finally, as in Russia, our state inherited a patrimonial regime—that of the viceroys of New Spain.

Yet there are two basic differences. First, the brief but ineradicable democratic period of the Restored Republic (1867–76), which interposed itself between the state of New Spain and the modern state. Second, while the totalitarian state wiped out the Russian bourgeoisie, subdued the peasants and the workers, exterminated its political rivals, murdered its critics and created a new ruling class, the Mexican state has shared its power not only with the nation's bourgeoisie but also with the cadres who control the great unions. As I have pointed out, the relationship between the various Mexican governments, the leaders of Mexico's workers and peasants, and the bourgeoisie is ambiguous, a sort of unstable alliance that is not without quarrels, especially between the private and public sectors. All this can be summed up in one basic difference that contains all others and is paramount: whereas in Russia the party is the true state, in Mexico the state is the substantial element, and the party is its arm and instrument. And so, although Mexico is not really a democracy, it is not a totalitarian ideocracy either.

I still must mention mention another noteworthy characteristic of the Mexican state. Despite having been the prime agent of modernization, it has not succeeded in becoming entirely modernized itself. In many aspects, especially in its dealings with the public and its manner of conducting business, it continues to be patrimonialist. In a regime of this sort the head of government—be it prince or president—considers the state his personal patrimony. For this reason, far from constituting an impersonal bureaucracy, the body of civil servants and government employees—from the ministers to the page boys and from the magistrates and senators to the janitors—forms a huge political family bound by ties of kinship, friendship, personal obligation, similar backgrounds and other such matters.

Patrimonialism, in essence, is the incrustation of private upon public life. The ministers are the intimates and servants of the king. Therefore, although all courtiers are cut from the same cloth, patrimonialist regimes do not rigidify into orthodoxies nor turn into bureaucracies. They are the opposite of a church, and for this reason the bonds between courtiers are not ideological but personal, quite unlike the bonds formed in such bodies as the Catholic church and the Communist party. In political and ecclesiastic bureaucracies, the hierarchy is sacred and governed by such objective rules and immutable principles as initiation, novitiate or apprenticeship, length of service, competence, diligence and obedience to superiors. What counts ultimately in a patrimonial regime is the will of the prince and his relatives.

Within the Mexican state, there exists an enormous contradiction that no one has been able or even tried to resolve: the body of technocrats and administrators, the professional bureaucracy, shares the privileges and risks of public administration with the friends, intimates and favorites of the current president, and with the friends, intimates and favorites of his ministers. The Mexican bureaucracy is modern, is proposing to modernize the country and has a modern set of values. Side by side with it, sometimes as its rival and sometimes as its associate, stands a mass of friends, relations and protégés united by bonds of a personal nature. This courtly society is partially renewed every six years—that is, each time a new president comes to power. By virtue of their situation as well as their implicit ideology and method of recruitment, these bodies of courtiers are not modern; they are a remnant of patrimonialism. The contradiction between the courtly society and the technocratic bureaucracy does not immobilize the state, but it does make its progress difficult and tortuous. The state does not have two kinds of politics; it has two ways of understanding politics, two kinds of sensibilities and morals.

In England as in France the modern regimes struggled from the start to endow the new bourgeois state with an ad hoc bureaucracy, radically different from that of the seventeenth- and eighteenth-century monarchies. Or, rather, as Norbert Elias has admirably demonstrated, the nineteenth- and twentieth-century bureaucracies in the West were formed within the Third Estate, in permanent conflict with the courtly society of the absolutist regimes.

By its origin, work patterns, hierarchies and morals the new bureaucracy was the negation of patrimonialism. Its evolution was the same as that of the bourgeoisie, which moved from a world of privilege to one of economics and from judicial logic to the logic of private enterprise. So it imposed economic rationalism, which is essentially quantitative regarding the discharge of state business. An impossible requirement: the state is not an enterprise. The gains and losses of a nation are calculated differently from what the rules of accounting teach us. This is a contradiction that the liberal bourgeois state has been unable to resolve.

From the perspective of the administration of things, the bureaucracies of the democratic bourgeois societies have been incomparably superior not only to those of the old monarchies but also to those of the totalitarian states of our day. I might add that they have been more humane and more tolerant as well. But this superiority in the professional and moral spheres becomes inferiority when we turn from administration to politics. This inferiority is obvious in the realm of international relations.

Examples of the political ineptitude of the bourgeois democracies abound. Their attitude toward Hitler was an extraordinary mixture of inconsistency and blindness. At first, their intransigence and selfishness toward Germany favored the rise of Nazism; later, sometimes calculatingly and sometimes through cowardice, they became the dictator's accomplices. Their politics vis-à-vis Stalin were no more clearsighted. The same mixture of treacherous and short-term realism informs their attitude to the satraps and tyrants of the New and Old Worlds.

Opportunism does not entirely explain this shortsightedness and incoherence. The fault is congenital, and I have indicated the reason above: the state is neither a factory nor a business. The logic of history is not quantitative. Economic rationality depends on the relationship between expenditure and production, investment and earnings, work and savings. The rationale of the state is not utility nor profit but power—gaining it, conserving it and extending it. The archetype of power does not lie in economics but in war, not in the polemic relationship of capital to work but in the hierarchical relationship of commander to soldier. This is why the model of political and religious bureaucracies is a military one, the Society of Jesus, the Communist Party.

The peculiar nature of the Mexican state is shown by the presence of three different orders or formations (different, but in continuous communication and osmosis):

1. The government bureaucracy proper, more or less stable, made up of technicians and administrators, created in the image and likeness of the bureaucracies of the democratic societies of the West.

2. The heterogeneous conglomeration of friends, favorites, intimates, minions and protégés, the legacy of the courtly society of the seventeenth and eighteenth centuries.

3. The political bureaucracy of the PRI, made up of political professionals, less an ideological association than one of factional and individual interests, a broad channel for social mobility and a great fraternity open to ambitious young men, usually without means and recently graduated from the colleges and universities. The bureaucracy of the PRI is halfway between the traditional political party and the bureaucracies that operate in the name of an orthodoxy and as militias of God or history. The PRI uses no terrorist tactics; it does not want to change human beings or save the world; it wants to save itself. Therefore it wants to be reformed. But it knows that to reform itself it must reform the country. The question that history has posed in Mexico since 1968 not only consists in whether the state will be able to rule without the PRI but also in whether we Mexicans will let ourselves be ruled without a PRI.

The theme of Political Reform, as the Mexican government's recent attempts to introduce pluralism are called, merits a short digression. The PRI was born of necessity: it had to assure the continuity of the postrevolutionary regime, threatened by quarrels among the military chiefs who had outlived the wars and upsets after the overthrow of Porfirio Díaz. Its essence was compromise between a true democracy with political parties, and dictatorship of a political boss as had happened in the other Latin-American countries.

The regime born of the Mexican revolution lived on for many years before anyone called its legitimacy into question. The events of 1968, which culminated in the slaughter of several hundred students, seriously shattered this legitimacy, already worn thin by half a century of uninterrupted dominance. Since 1968, and not without contradictions, Mexican governments have been looking for a new legitimacy. The source of the former legitimacy was, on the one hand, historical or rather genealogical, since the regime has always considered itself not only the successor but the heir of the revolutionary chiefs by rights of primogeniture. On the other hand, it was constitutional, since it was the result of formal and legal elections. The new legality sought by the regime is based on the recognition that other parties and political projects exist—that is to say, it is based on pluralism. And this is one step toward democracy.

In the long run and if it does not fail, Political Reform will realize the dream of many Mexicans, a dream continuously postponed since Independence—the transformation of the country into a true, modern democracy. However, in the short run it is legitimate to doubt that a few legalistic measures will be enough to change the political structures of a society. Indeed, before all else we should ask ourselves which political parties would be able to challenge the PRI for leadership?

Leaving aside the dummy parties that have for years played the role of puppets in the electoral farce, the PRI's only serious rival has been the PAN.

The PAN is a nationalist, Catholic, conservative party, which, as its name indicates (Partido Acción Nacional, National Action Party), grew out of tendencies more or less influenced by the political thinking of Maurras and his Action Française (monarchism and anti-Semitism aside). The PAN has been the eternal loser of elections, though not always legitimately. We must not forget that the PRI is not a party that has won power: it is the political arm of power.

Up to now it has mattered only to a few people that the PRI invariably wins elections. This indifference explains why neither the PAN nor any of the other opposition groups on the right or left has been able to organize a national resistance movement. The discontent of the Mexican people has found expression in abstention and skepticism rather than in forms of political activism. Today the regime is looking for a new legality in pluralism, and herein lies the novelty of the situation. But the crisis of the Mexican political system has not favored the PAN, which has not been able to capitalize on the discontent directed at the official party. On the contrary, today the PAN is weaker than it was fifteen years ago. On top of everything else, it is torn apart by internal battles and undergoing a sort of identity crisis. Though it is trying to forget its authoritarian and "Maurrasian" leanings, it has not succeeded in becoming a Christian Democratic party.

What about the other parties?

The Mexican Communist Party is a small organization with little or no influence among the workers, even though it was founded more than fifty years ago, before the PRI. However, thanks to its control of some student groups, and especially of various unions of employees and professors, it has gained strength in the universities. The Mexican Communist Party is a university party, and this paradox (which would have scandalized Marx) indicates an appreciable strategic conquest: the universities are one of the country's sensitive spots. No doubt, inspired and encouraged by the example of the European countries (Italy, Spain and France), the Mexican Communist Party has recently declared itself a partisan of democratic pluralism, although it has not renounced Lenin's "democratic centralism." To a certain extent this change implies criticism of its own Stalinist past. Unfortunately, such criticism has not been explicit. Moreover, the Mexican CP has been too timid, and its record is riddled with silences and concealment. It is significant that in recent declarations the Mexican Communist Party has shown its affinity to the positions adopted by the French CP, the most conservative and centralist of the three great European Communist parties. (Recently, Althusser described it in *Le Monde* as a closed organization, military in nature, a "fortress.")

Another characteristic of the Mexican situation is the total lack of influence of left-wing intellectuals on the evolution of the Mexican Communist Party. The change in the European Communist parties is due in good part to the criticism of their dissident intellectuals; in Mexico—with such rare exceptions as José Revueltas, Eduardo Lizalde and a few others—Marxist intellectuals have been faithful though unimaginative apologists of "historic socialism" through all its contradictory metamorphoses from Stalin to Brezhnev.

The Mexican Democratic Party has origins similar to those of the PAN, though its supporters are not middle-class people but the poor peasants of the central region. This is an authentically plebeian party. It is the direct descendant of the National Sinarchist Union, an organization inspired by a nationalistic and religious populism recognizably based on the traditional aspirations of the revolutionary peasant movements, along with scraps of fascist ideology. Among the Sinarchists the tradition of the agrarian uprisings was still alive, as it had been in Mexican history from the seventeenth century on. A strange brew: religious brotherhood, fascism and revolutionary *Jacquerie*. The Mexican Democratic Party is suffering an identity crisis like that of the PAN, and has not yet defined its new democratic profile. However, though it is poor in material resources and in ideas, it still has an influence over some of the peasant groups in the central areas of the country. These parties have one feature in common: all three would like to forget their authoritarian past. But they have not yet exorcised the ghosts of Maurras, Mussolini and Stalin. . . .

One political organization that carries no terrible past with it and arose out of a genuine desire for social and democratic change is the Mexican Workers' Party (Partido Mexicano de Trabajadores). It was born in the 1968 crisis, and its emergence was looked upon with great sympathy by many groups of students and intellectuals, and also by those veterans of the working-class movement of the past who had survived its setbacks. Unfortunately, this party has still not been able to formulate a clear program (nor a clearly democratic one, which is no less serious) to grant it a political physiognomy and to distinguish it from the other left-wing groups. I could mention other independent parties, but they are minuscule in size and have no appreciable strength.

The most casual observer is immediately aware that there are two large gaps in this panorama. One is the lack of a conservative party like the Republican Party in the United States or the conservative parties of Great Britain, France, Germany and Spain. The other is the absence of an authentic socialist party supported by workers, intellectuals and middle class. The latter is the more lamentable and casts a harsh light on one of the most serious failings of Mexico and all Latin America: the absence of a democratic socialist tradition.

Will the Mexican pluralism for which Political Reform is preparing be composed of minority parties that barely deserve the adjective democratic? Most likely, far from alleviating the situation, this poor imitation of pluralism will aggravate the regime's identity crisis. Were this to happen the erosion of the PRI would get worse and, in order not to evaporate, the state would have to rely on other social forces: not on a political bureaucracy like the PRI but on a military bureaucracy. There is another remedy, though it is contemplated with horror by the Mexican political caste: to divide the PRI. Perhaps its left wing, united with other forces, could be the nucleus of a true socialist party.

Political Reform was thought up by one of Mexico's most intelligent men, a true intellectual who is also a shrewd politician. However, as we have seen, this project faces the same wall that has blocked the path of other initiatives by our intellectuals and men of state, from Juárez and the liberals of 1857 to our day. It is not a wall of stone or ideas or interests—it is a wall of emptiness. "Between the idea/And the reality/Between the motion/And the Act/Falls the Shadow."

Is Mexico "the dead land . . . cactus land," like the land in Eliot's poem, littered with broken idols and moth-eaten images of saints? Do we just "go round the prickly pear"? But in our mythology this prickly pear is not the plant of the kingdom of the dead; on the contrary, it is the heraldic plant chosen at the founding of Mexico Tenochtitlan, [the Aztecs' ancient name for Mexico City] and its blood-red fruit symbolizes the union of the solar element and the primordial water. Perhaps we have mistaken the path; perhaps the way out is to return to our origins.

The situation of the political parties is one of the signs of the ambiguous modernity of Mexico. Another sign is corruption. It is easier to understand this phenomenon if one looks at it from the perspective of persistent patrimonialism. In all the European courts during the seventeenth and eighteenth centuries public posts were sold and there was traffic in influences and favors. During the regency of Mariana of Austria, at a moment when the public treasury was hard pressed, her favorite, Don Fernando Valenzuela, decided to consult the theologians as to whether it was admissible to sell to the highest bidder the important positions of the kingdom, among them the viceroyalties of Aragon, New Spain, Peru and Naples. The theologians found nothing in divine or human laws that was contrary to this practice. The corruption of the Mexican public administration, a scandal at home and abroad, is basically only another manifestation of the persistence of the ways of thinking and feeling exemplified by the dictate of the Spanish theologians. People irreproachable in their private behavior, shining lights of morality on their home ground, have no scruples about disposing of public goods as if they were their own property. The issue is less one of immorality than of the unconscious operation of another set of morals: in the patrimonial regime the frontiers between public and private spheres, family and state are rather vague and fluctuating. If everyone is the king of his house, the kingdom is like a house and the nation is like a family. If the state is the king's patrimony, how can it not also be the patrimony of his relations, friends, servants and favorites? In Spain, significantly enough, the prime minister was called "Privado" (Favorite).

The presence of a courtly, patrimonialist moral code in the bosom of the Mexican state is another example of our incomplete modernity. We stumble over the disconcerting mixture of modern and archaic traits in the lowest levels of society— the peasants and their religious and moral beliefs—as well as in the middle class and the high bourgeoisie. The modernization of Mexico, begun at the close of the eighteenth century by the viceroys of Charles III, continues to be a half-completed task that affects our consciousness only superficially. Most of our profound attitudes to love, death, friendship, food and festivals are not modern. Nor are our public morality, our family life, the cult of the Virgin, or our image of the president. . . . Why not? I have tried to answer this question elsewhere. Here I will only repeat that we Mexicans have undertaken various projects of modernization since the time of the great Hispanic schism (the crisis at the end of the eighteenth century and its consequence, Independence). Not only have all these projects proved unworkable but they have disfigured us. Masks of Robespierre and Bonaparte, Jefferson and Lincoln, Comte and Marx, Lenin and Mao: if history is theater, our country's history has been a masquerade interrupted time and again by the explosions or riots and revolts.

I do not preach return to the past, imaginary as are all pasts, nor do I advocate that we go back into the clutches of a tradition that was strangling us. I believe that Mexico, like the other Latin-American countries, must find her own modernity. In a certain sense she must invent it. But she must start with the ways of living and dying, acquiring and spending, working and playing that our people has created. It is a task that demands not only favorable historic and social circumstances but an extraordinary imagination. The rebirth of imagination, in the realm of art as in that of politics, has always been prepared for and preceded by analysis and criticism. I believe that this duty has fallen to our generation and the next. But before undertaking the criticism of our societies, their history and their actuality, we Hispanic American writers must begin by criticizing ourselves. First, we must cure ourselves of the intoxication of simplistic and simplifying ideologies.

GROVE PRESS BOOKS ON LATIN AMERICA

Barnes, John / EVITA—FIRST LADY: A biography of Eva Peron / The first major biography of the beautiful and strong-willed leader of the impoverished Argentina of the 1940's. / $4.95 / 17087-3

Barry, Tom, Wood, Beth, and Preusch, Deb / DOLLARS AND DICTATORS: A Guide to Central America / "A thorough and comprehensive study of the effect the ubiquitous corporate presence in the region has had on its politics and on American foreign policy."—*The Progressive* / $6.95q62485-8

Borges, Jorge Luis / FICCIONES (ed. and intro. by Anthony Kerrigan) / A collection of short fictional pieces from the man whom *Time* has called "the greatest living writer in the Spanish language today." / $6.95 / 17244-2

Borges, Jorge Luis / A PERSONAL ANTHOLOGY (ed. and frwd. by Antony Kerrigan) / Borges' personal selections of his work, including "The Circular Ruins," "Death and the Compass," and "A New Refutation of Time." / $6.95 / 17270-1

Fried, Jonathan, et. al., eds. / GUATEMALA IN REBELLION: Unfinished History / A sourcebook on the history of Guatemala and its current crisis. / $8.95 / 62455-6

Gettleman, Marvin, et. al., eds. / EL SALVADOR: Central America in the New Cold War / A collection of essays, articles, and eye-witness reports on the conflict in El Salvador. "Highly recommended for students, scholars, and policy-makers."—*Library Journal* / $9.95 / 17956-0

Neruda, Pablo / FIVE DECADES: POEMS, 1925-1970 (Bilingual ed. tr. by Ben Belitt) / A collection of more than 200 poems by the Nobel Prize-winning Chilean poet. / $12.50 / 17869-6

Neruda, Pablo / NEW DECADE: POEMS, 1958-1967 (Bilingual ed. tr. by Ben Belitt and Alastair Reid) / $5.95 / 17275-2

Neruda, Pablo / NEW POEMS (1968-1970) (Bilingual ed. tr. and intro. by Ben Belitt) / $8.95 / 17793-2

Neruda, Pablo / SELECTED POEMS (Bilingual ed. tr. by Ben Belitt) / A selection of Neruda's finest work. Intro. by Luis Monguio. / $5.95 / 17243-4

Paz, Octavio / THE LABYRINTH OF SOLITUDE, THE OTHER MEXICO, AND OTHER ESSAYS (New preface by the author. Tr. by Lysander Kemp, Yara Milos and Rachel Phillips Belash) / A collection of Paz's best-known works and six new essays, one especially written for this volume. / $9.95 / 17992-7

Paz, Octavio / THE OTHER MEXICO: Critique of the Pyramid (tr. by Lysander Kemp) / Paz defined the character and culture of Mexico in what has now become a modern classic of critical interpretation. / $2.45 / 17773-8

Rosset, Peter and Vandermeer, John / THE NICARAGUA READER: Documents of a Revolution Under Fire / A sourcebook of articles on the Nicaraguan revolution and U.S. intervention / $8.95 / 62498-X

Rulfo, Juan / PEDRO PARAMO: A Novel of Mexico (tr. by Lysander Kemp) By the Mexican author whom the *New York Times* says will "rank among the immortals." / $3.95 / 17446-1

Thelwell, Michael / THE HARDER THEY COME / The "masterly achieved novel" (Harold Bloom) by Jamaica's finest novelist. Inspired by the now-classic film by Perry Henzell, starring Jimmy Cliff, it tells the story of a legendary gunman and folk hero who lived in Kingston in the late 1950's. / $7.95 / 17599-9

Books may be ordered directly from Grove Press. Add $1.50 per book postage and handling and send check or money order to: Order Dept., Grove Press, Inc., 920 Broadway, New York, N.Y. 10010.

Selected Grove Press Paperbacks

17411-9   CLURMAN, HAROLD (Ed.) / Nine Plays of the Modern Theater (Waiting for Godot by Samuel Beckett, The Visit by Friedrich Durrenmatt, Tango by Slawomir Mrozek, The Caucasian Chalk Circle by Bertolt Brecht, The Balcony by Jean Genet, Rhinoceros by Eugene Ionesco, American Buffalo by David Mamet, The Birthday Party by Harold Pinter, Rosencrantz and Guildenstern Are Dead by Tom Stoppard) / $14.95

17962-5   COHN, RUBY / New American Dramatists: 1960-1980 / $7.95

17971-4   COOVER, ROBERT / Spanking the Maid / $4.95

17535-2   COWARD, NOEL / Three Plays (Private Lives, Hay Fever, Blithe Spirit) / $7.95

17740-1   CRAFTS, KATHY and HAUTHER, BRENDA / How To Beat the System: The Student's Guide to Good Grades / $3.95

17219-1   CUMMINGS, E.E. / 100 Selected Poems / $3.95

17480-1   DELANEY, SHELAGH / A Taste of Honey / $6.95

17329-5   DOOLITTLE, HILDA / Selected Poems of H.D. / $8.95

17863-7   DOSS, MARGOT PATTERSON / San Francisco at Your Feet (Second Revised Edition) / $8.95

17987-0   DURAS, MARGUERITE / Four Novels: The Square; 10:30 on a Summer Night; The Afternoon of Mr. Andesmas; Moderato Cantibile / $9.95

17246-9   DURRENMATT, FRIEDRICH / The Physicists / $6.95

17239-6   DURRENMATT, FRIEDRICH / The Visit / $4.95

17990-0   FANON, FRANZ / Black Skin, White Masks / $8.95

17327-9   FANON, FRANZ / The Wretched of the Earth / $4.95

17754-1   FAWCETT, ANTHONY / John Lennon: One Day At A Time, A Personal Biography (Revised Edition) / $8.95

17483-6   FROMM, ERICH / The Forgotten Language / $6.95

62073-9   GARWOOD, DARRELL / Under Cover: Thirty-five Years of CIA Deception / $3.95

17222-1   GELBER, JACK / The Connection / $3.95

17390-2   GENET, JEAN / The Maids and Deathwatch: Two Plays / $8.95

17838-6   GENET, JEAN / Querelle / $4.95

17903-X   GENET, JEAN / Our Lady of the Flowers / $3.95

17662-6   GERVASI, TOM / Arsenal of Democracy II / $12.95

17956-0   GETTLEMAN, MARVIN, et.al. eds. / El Salvador: Central America in the New Cold War / $9.95

17994-3   GIBBS, LOIS MARIE / Love Canal: My Story / $6.95

17648-0   GIRODIAS, MAURICE, ed. / The Olympia Reader / $5.95

62150-6   GOMBROWICZ, WITOLD / Three Novels: Ferdydurke, Pornografia and Cosmos / $12.50

17764-9   GOVER, ROBERT / One Hundred Dollar Misunderstanding / $2.95

17832-7   GREENE, GERALD and CAROLINE / SM: The Last Taboo / $2.95

17869-6	NERUDA, PABLO / Five Decades: Poems 1925-1970. Bilingual ed. / $12.50
17243-4	NERUDA, PABLO / Selected Poems. Bilingual ed. / $6.95
17092-X	ODETS, CLIFFORD / Six Plays (Waiting for Lefty, Awake and Sing, Golden Boy, Rocket to the Moon, Till the Day I Die, Paradise Lost) / $7.95
17650-2	OE, KENZABURO / A Personal Matter / $6.95
17002-4	OE, KENZABURO / Teach Us To Outgrow Our Madness / $4.95
17992-7	PAZ, OCTAVIO / The Labyrinth of Solitude: Life and Thought in Mexico / $9.95
17232-9	PINTER, HAROLD / The Birthday Party & The Room / $6.95
17228-0	HAROLD PINTER / The Caretaker & The Dumb Waiter / $6.95
17938-2	PINTER, HAROLD / Family Voices: A Play for Radio / $7.95
17251-5	PINTER, HAROLD / The Homecoming / $5.95
17675-4	PINTER, HAROLD / The Hothouse / $4.95
17827-0	RAHULA, WALPOLE / What the Buddha Taught / $6.95
17658-8	REAGE, PAULINE / The Story of O, Part II; Return to the Chateau / $3.95
62169-7	RECHY, JOHN / City of Night / $4.50
62171-9	RECHY, JOHN / Numbers / $8.95
17983-8	ROBBE-GRILLET, ALAIN / Djinn / $4.95
17012-1	ROBBE-GRILLET, ALAIN / Topology of a Phantom City / $3.95
17119-5	ROBBE-GRILLET, ALAIN / The Voyeur / 4.95
62498-X	ROSSET, PETER and VANDERMEER, JOHN / The Nicaragua Reader / $9.95
17446-1	RULFO, JUAN / Pedro Paramo: A Novel of Mexico / $3.95
17119-5	SADE, MARQUIS DE / The 120 Days of Sodom and Other Writings / $12.50
17410-0	SAUNERON, SERGE / The Priests of Ancient Egypt / $3.50
62495-5	SCHEFFLER, LINDA / Help Thy Neighbor / $7.95
62009-7	SEGALL, J. PETER / Deduct This Book: How Not to Pay Taxes While Ronald Reagan is President / $6.95
17467-4	SELBY, HUBERT / Last Exit to Brooklyn / $3.95
62040-2	SETO, JUDITH ROBERTS / The Young Actor's Workbook / $8.95
17963-3	SHANK, THEODORE / American Alternative Theater / $12.50
17948-X	SHAWN, WALLACE, and GREGORY, ANDRE / My Dinner with Andre / $6.95
62496-3	SIEGAL, FREDERICK, M.D., and MARTA / Aids: The Medical Mystery / $7.95
17887-4	SINGH, KHUSHWANT / Train to Pakistan / $4.50
62446-7	SLOMAN, LARRY / Reefer Madness: Marijuana in America / $8.95
17797-5	SNOW, EDGAR / Red Star Over China / $9.95

17939-0   SRI NISARGADATA MAHARAJ / Seeds of Consciousness / $9.95
17923-4   STEINER, CLAUDE / Healing Alcoholism / $6.95
17866-1   STOPPARD, TOM / Jumpers / $4.95
17260-4   STOPPARD, TOM / Rosencrantz and Guildenstern Are Dead / $3.95
17884-X   STOPPARD, TOM / Travesties / $3.95
17474-7   SUZUKI, D.T. / Introduction to Zen Buddhism / $3.95
17224-8   SUZUKI, D.T. / Manual of Zen Buddhism / $7.95
17599-9   THELWELL, MICHAEL / The Harder They Come / $7.95
17969-2   TOOLE, JOHN KENNEDY / A Confederacy of Dunces / $4.50
17403-8   TROCCHI, ALEXANDER / Cain's Book / $3.50
62168-9   TUTUOLA, AMOS / The Palm-Wine Drinkard / $4.50
62189-1   UNGERER, TOMI / Far Out Isn't Far Enough (Illus.) / $12.95
17331-7   WALEY, ARTHUR / The Book of Songs / $9.95
17211-6   WALEY, ARTHUR / Monkey / $8.95
17207-8   WALEY, ARTHUR / The Way and Its Power: A Study of the Tao Te Ching and Its Place in Chinese Thought / $8.95
17392-9   WARNER, LANGDON / The Enduring Art of Japan / $7.95
17418-6   WATTS, ALAN W. / The Spirit of Zen / $3.95

GROVE PRESS, INC., 920 Broadway, New York, N.Y. 10010